ALL FOR THE CHILDREN

Multicultural Essentials of Literature

Denise Ann Finazzo

Delmar Publishers

an International Thomson Publishing company I(T)P®

Albany • Bonn • Boston • Cincinnati • Detroit • London • Madrid
Melbourne • Mexico City • New York • Pacific Grove • Paris • San Francisco
Singapore • Tokyo • Toronto • Washington

NOTICE TO THE READER

Cover Design: Darcie Mehall

Delmar Staff

Publisher:	William Brottmiller
Senior Editor:	Jay Whitney
Associate Editor:	Erin O'Connor Traylor
Project Editor:	Marah Bellegarde
Production Coordinator:	James Zayicek
Art and Design Coordinator:	Timothy J. Conners
Senior Editorial Assistant:	Glenna Stanfield

COPYRIGHT © 1997
By Delmar Publishers
an International Thomson Publishing company

The ITP logo is a trademark under license.
Printed in the United States of America

For more information, contact:

Delmar Publishers
3 Columbia Circle, Box 15015
Albany, New York 12212-5015

International Thomson Editores
Campos Eliseos 385, Piso 7
Col Polanco
11560 Mexico D F Mexico

International Thomson Publishing Europe
Berkshire House
168-173 High Holborn
London, WC1V 7AA
England

International Thomson Publishing GmbH
Konigswinterer Strasse 418
53227 Bonn
Germany

Thomas Nelson Australia
102 Dodds Street
South Melbourne, 3205
Victoria, Australia

International Thomson Publishing Asia
221 Henderson Road
#05-10 Henderson Building
Singapore 0315

Nelson Canada
1120 Birchmount Road
Scarborough, Ontario
Canada, M1K 5G4

International Thomson Publishing—Japan
Hirakawacho Kyowa Building, 3F
2-2-1 Hirakawacho
Chiyoda-ku, Tokyo 102
Japan

1 2 3 4 5 6 7 8 9 10 XXX 03 02 01 00 99 98 97

Library of Congress Cataloging-in-Publication Data

Finazzo, Denise Ann.
      All for the children : multicultural essentials of literature /
    Denise Ann Finazzo.
        p.   cm.
      Includes bibliographical references and index.
      ISBN 0-8273-6794-5
      1. Children's literature—History and criticism.
    2. Multiculturalism.   I. Title.
    PN1009.A1F48   1996
    809'.89282—dc20
                      96-24235
                       CIP

Brief Table of Contents

Online Services

Delmar Online
To access a wide variety of Delmar products and services on the World Wide Web, point your browser to:

http://www.delmar.com/delmar.html
or email: info@delmar.com

thomson.com
To access International Thomson Publishing's home site for information on more than 34 publishers and 20,000 products, point your browser to:

http://www.thomson.com
or email: findit@kiosk.thomson.com

A service of

Detailed Table of Contents

Preface: In Support of Today's Children and Their Time

All for the Children: Multicultural Essentials of Literature is designed as an introductory textbook for teacher training institutions that are attempting to include multicultural approaches in theory and practice. This text addresses the current issues in children's literature, particularly cultural diversity and multiculturalism. It seeks to define, compare, contrast, and apply various genres as they can be integrated within the regular curriculum in an elementary setting. The text is an introduction to children's literature for future teachers as well as a resource for teachers in service and for interested parents and community members.

Practicing teachers and those who aspire to teach are faced with a lack of knowledge of what multicultural education is and how it can be implemented in their classrooms. This text refers to recent research that defines diversity, multiculturalism, ethnicity, and pluralism. Moreover, it aims to show how multiculturalism is possible in all elementary classes if teachers are willing to explore and investigate.

In order for the reader to understand best how children's literature can serve as a vehicle for this integration of multiculturalism, it is important that the values of multicultural children's literature be explained. Conventional children's literature and that which has been categorized as multicultural are compared and contrasted. Child development theory and the influence of parents, caregivers, and the community are also addressed.

Children's literature, like all writing, has a history. Evolution from early storytelling, didacticism, childhood emergence, and the melting-pot theory are all part of the historical development of children's literature that has a culturally diverse perspective. Finally, the influence of civil rights movements and the relatively new thinking that reflects a "tossed-salad" or "patchwork-quilt" approach to teaching and learning are explained.

As a genre of its own, multicultural children's literature includes examples of picture story books, traditional literature, poetry, modern fantasy, contemporary realistic fiction, historical fiction, nonfiction and informational books, and alternative media. In this text, examples of books that fit into these categories are cited, summarized, and offered for the reader's examination.

Once educators are aware of the resources available for the teaching of multiculturalism, they need to know what multiculturalism is. The author contends that multiculturalism involves all that the student brings to the learning experience, including self-esteem, family structure, ethnicity, gender, age, exceptionality, values and ethics, socioeconomic status, and communication systems. Throughout the text, wherever possible, the linking of theory and practice are made evident. In other words, examples of children's literature that support theory are shared, along with strategies for their most effective use.

Educators are becoming empowered with the selection and evaluation of curricula and texts. One chapter in this text distinguishes between the story elements and the visual elements that are integral parts of children's literature. Moreover, the author challenges the readers to engage themselves in critical thinking and then become role models for their students. Evaluation tools and survey instruments that can be readily used in classrooms are also shared.

At the end of each chapter is a summary as well as reflective questions that could be used for writing, dialogue, and active learning by college students and professors. Lists of children's books as well as theoretical references are also offered at the ends of the chapters.

The unique portion of this children's literature textbook is its final part. Here practicing teachers, teachers in training, and parents can access real lessons that have been developed, researched, tested, and evaluated with real elementary students in rural, suburban, and urban settings. In this part of the book, theory is again linked to practice. Detailed, structured lessons, designed for the beginning teacher or the college student, are included under specific topical headings: promoting self-esteem, recognizing similarities and differences, accepting cultural pluralism, seeing diversity in families, developing values, communicating and problem solving, and determining group and set membership. Truly these lessons could function as the practicum of a course that teaches multiculturalism as it relates to children's books.

The writing of such a textbook did not come without struggles and dilemmas. Many children's literature textbooks briefly address this controversial issue. None are as dedicated to the inclusion of all of the groups mentioned as this text is.

Multiculturalism has become a passion with this author. Knowing when to complete the research as well as continually exploring more and more new children's books was the hardest job of all. Struggling with the need to include all groups while maintaining the original framework and purpose was an ongoing challenge.

The book is the result of much research and a great deal of reading and writing, but most of all, it is a result of the children and the students. The title, *All for the Children,* says it best. The children's books that are referenced are wonderful examples of writing for our children. The activities serve our children well. But primarily the book is dedicated to the children, for those who voice clearly their need to be part of today's classrooms and for those who cannot or choose not to speak for whatever reason. The book is a testimony to the children who have little or no self-esteem, those whose ethnicity has been a stumbling block for learning, and those whose family or socioeconomic status tends to stereotype them in our classrooms. This book is written for all the college students who have spent time in our offices asking for explanations, definitions, and understanding of this complex issue. *All for the Children* includes books that are about children, for children, with children, and to children. It challenges the educators of today to remember the children of yesterday, serve the children of today, and create excitement and life for the children of tomorrow.

Acknowledgments

My appreciation is extended to the reviewers enlisted through Delmar for their constructive criticism and helpful suggestions.

Charles J. Blume, MEd
Towson State University
Towson, MD

Susanne P. Kirk, PhD
Xavier University
Cincinnati, OH

Dolores P. Dickerson, PhD
Howard University
Washington, DC

Ana L. McCall, PhD
University of Wisconsin
Oshkosh, WI

Colin DuColon, MEd
Champlain College
Burlington, VT

Margaret E. McIntosh, PhD
University of Nevada
Reno, NV

Arlene Hambrick, PhD
Bluefield College
Bluefield, VA

Sandra M. Stokes, PhD
University of Wisconsin
Green Bay, WI

Rosemary Oliphant Ingham, EdD
Belmont University
Nashville, TN

It is very important that I acknowledge the many people who have given me support and assistance in the writing of this book:

To Edinboro University of Pennsylvania Presidents Foster Diebold and Frank Pogue for their encouragement and review of my text drafts;

To my fellow members of the Elementary Education Department who have given me new insights about curriculum development and the integration of children's literature in elementary and early childhood settings;

To the many students who have been a part of my Children's Literature classes who have contributed to the book and have tested the many activities and lessons;

To the following students who have helped in my office: Marie Brown Forst, William Cross, Erika Cinti, Allison Barkley, Linda Sekeres, and Susan Galle;

To Michael Figurski for his wonderful artistic renditions;

To all the children of Carolyn Pakiela of Sacred Heart School, Ernest Dettore of Miller School, and Janet Plavcan at Emerson-Gridley School who have tried the lessons and contributed artwork and photography;

To Jay Whitney and Erin O'Conner for their patience in the editing department;

To Impressions Book and Journal Services, Inc. for the wonderful copyediting;

To Fr. Michael Gaines for his constant encouragement and his work in transcribing bibliography;

To my parents, Dr. and Mrs. Ray Dombrowski, for their undying love and modeling of what tolerance and acceptance is all about;

And finally, this book is dedicated to my sons, Damon Ray and Devin Joseph, who have sacrificed time with their mom so that I could write and research, and who represent all the children who have been a part of my life.

PART I

Children's Literature: A History and Definition

College students, practicing teachers, and parents have many questions as they begin to explore and investigate children's literature. Adults who use children's literature with young people need to know what constitutes "good" and "appropriate" selections. Moreover, there are many categories of children's literature that are comparable to genres within traditional adult literature. Some children's books can be classified as multicultural. The characteristics of children's books that are multicultural connect to developmental theory and curriculum content. Part I of this text offers a brief historical perspective of multicultural children's literature and definitions of various genres of multicultural children's literature. Beyond definition, each genre will be discussed in terms of its particular characteristics and value for contemporary classrooms. In essence, this portion of the text will answer the following questions: what constitutes children's literature? how did multicultural children's literature evolve? and what are the various types of multicultural children's literature?

CHAPTER 1

And those of us who write for children need to be sure we are opening the doors to full human potential, not closing them.

Mem Fox

Why Is Children's Literature Important?

▌ Comparing conventional literature and children's literature that is multicultural
▌ Recognizing theories of child development: multiculturalism in children
▌ Reading for pleasure: feeling good about oneself
▌ Reading to increase academic achievement in culturally diverse settings
▌ Reading aloud and the influence of family
▌ Fusing the cultural gaps

❖ Introduction

It is important to treat *literature, children's literature,* and *children's literature that is multicultural* as separate terms when dealing with the education of children using books. This chapter will define children's literature that is in fact multicultural by nature (as compared to conventional literature and other children's literature). It will also show how literature that is specifically multicultural and for children supports child development theory and confirms the importance of parental involvement. Beyond their ties with developmental theory and family support of literacy, children's books that take a multicultural approach also offer individual pleasure, academic support, and cultural understanding.

❖ How Does the Educator Compare Conventional Literature and Children's Literature That Is Multicultural?

Children and books, reading and learning, language and print have all been commonly linked by teachers and parents in the education of young people. However, these relationships are unique ones that give young (and older) learners opportunity to explore, relate, recall, question, and better understand themselves and others.

Literature as we know it encompasses the various forms of writing that reflect times, cultures, and people with special beauty and style. It includes story, song, poetry, and drama, realistic and imaginative, factual and fantastic. It can be short or long in format, with or without words, with or without illustrations, happy or sad, comical or realistic. Children's literature, and in particular that which is multicultural, likewise encompasses various forms of writing, but in its specific style it possesses its own unique qualities.

Children's literature that is multicultural is written for the child's eyes, and thus it sends a simple and straightforward message. It reflects the childhood of a culture or a group and expresses a child's viewpoint with a sense of optimism, hope, and excitement. Cox and Galda refer to books of this kind as "mirrors" for minority and immigrant children as they reflect and accept their experiences and cultures and as "windows" for those in the mainstream who seek a better understanding of people who are like or unlike themselves (Cox & Galda, 1990). In essence, the books that we feel are truly children's books with a multicultural flavor are those that we read and continue to cherish for their richness of information both about ourselves as a people and its children and about others who share our world. The appearance of these books is essential in the elementary classroom, according to Tway (1989); they are a valuable means for young people to grow in the understanding of themselves and others.

These books of "mirror and window images," when shared with children and adults, offer the following:

1. An opportunity for all individuals to view realistically the diversity of the American population and the world through the power of words; for example, Hamilton's *In the beginning: Creation Stories from Around the World* (1988).

2. Enjoyment and discovery of the poetic, rhythmic language of various cultures as shared through very old stories and new renditions and retellings; for example, Tomie dePaola's *The Legend of Bluebonnet* (1983).

3. A recognition of differences and likenesses of various groups of people; for example, Peter Spier's *People* (1980).

4. A study of the contributions of particular members of various groups, historically and in the present, in the academic, political, religious, and scientific realms; for example, *Sojourner Truth: Ain't I a Woman?* by Patricia and Fredrick McKissack (1992).

5. An understanding of oneself and a sense of pride as a member of a family, a group, a community, a country, and the world; for example, Greenfeld's *The Hidden Children* (1993).

6. A movement to a greater understanding of others as reflected in story, poetry, and song; for example, Gaige's *We Are a Thunderstorm* (1990).

7. Expansion to a concern for larger problems and issues outside the learner's immediate environment—a sense of social discovery, caring, and action; for example, Pfister's *The Rainbow Fish* (1992).

8. Integrated child development—social, emotional, cognitive, and language—that occurs when students, teachers, and parents discuss, observe, reflect, apply, criticize, question, characterize, summarize, and create using high-quality children's literature; for example, Paulsen's *Hatchet* (1987).

Like other types of literature and children's literature in general, children's books that are specifically multicultural can be read for pure enjoyment as well as for learning. As we compare various types of literature, then, we recognize that works of literature—for children and for adults—are similar in purpose while perhaps being different in approach. Primarily, children seek to read books from which they derive information and joy, according to their personal interests. Authors of such books write to encourage student readers to discover more about themselves and others. As author and teacher Mem Fox affirms,

> Those of us who teach need to be aware of this so we remember to provide affirming literature for all children in our care, not just for those who belong to the prevailing, dominant ruling classes or genders. And those of us who write for children need to be sure we are opening doors to full human potential, not closing them. (1993, p. 657).

The books that will be highlighted in this text are ones that specifically meet those needs while focusing on the individual, his or her relationship with others, and group memberships and the effects on society as a whole.

FIGURE 1–1 "Playing ball with my Dad" by Anthony

❖ How Does Multiculturalism in Children Connect with Child Development Theory?

In order to understand better the value of children's literature that is multicultural, the educator needs to recognize the implications of developmental theory for children's learning. Theories of development include *language, cognitive, social-emotional,* and *artistic* (creative and imaginative). In a culturally pluralistic society—one that recognizes and celebrates the similarities and differences of its peoples—it is critical to eliminate ethnic and cultural illiteracy, make students comfortable and capable of functioning well in diverse settings, and encourage students to become politically aware as well as socially active (Gay, 1975). Recognizing and linking child development theory with children's literature is the key to accomplishing those objectives.

Language Development

The common joys of language are found in all cultures. Young children play with sound in many languages and can be taught and teased in various ways through culturally rich children's books. As children learn more about how sounds create meaning, they enjoy the discovery of poetry and song from many different groups of people. *Pass It On: African-American Poetry for Children,* selected by Hudson (1993), and Wyndham's *Chinese Mother Goose Rhymes* (1982) are examples of how the history and traditions of family and culture can be passed from generation to generation at early ages through the oral tradition of poetry. These books and others like them can serve as examples for children's own attempts at poetry writing and cooperative learning strategies for teachers, such as choral readings and readers theater.

Conversations and questions about others are an important part of the language development of very young children. Children's books that describe settings, action, and characters for the primary-level reader and listener (ages 3–5) should reflect the diverse family structures, experiences, and environments of all children. Bradman's *Wait and See* (1987) and Joyce Durham Barrett's *Willie's Not the Hugging Kind* (1989) offer preschoolers and kindergartners experiences with urban settings and family situations. The repetition found in folklore and the retelling possibilities in language development make works of multicultural children's literature excellent sources. Examples are *Bringing the Rain to Kapiti Plain: A Nandi Tale* by Aardema (1981) and the old favorite *Tikki Tikki Tembo* by Mosel (1968), where language is consistent and playful, and primary children are able to recall and retell the stories easily.

Vocabulary development is an important facet of learning in the elementary years. Legends and folktales of many cultures and groups aid children in this area. Some quality multicultural tales include Johnson's *Tell Me a Story, Mama* (1989), Aardema's *Why Mosquitoes Buzz in People's Ears* (1975), and Hamilton's *The People Could Fly: American Black Folktales* (1985). These books serve as excellent sources of shared reading and reading aloud by adults and peers for vocabulary exposure and extension.

Finally, storytelling, the greatest example of the sharing of the oral tradition in its purest sense, can be enhanced by the use of multicultural selections. The passing down of story from group to group and age to age encourages discussion by children and their teachers or parents, entailing questioning and restating. Haley's *A Story, a Story* (1970) is a prime example as it explains how storytelling and the oral tradition first came to be.

Cognitive Development

As important as language development in its relationship to literature is cognitive development. Cognitive development theories address memory, classification, seriation, concept development, relationships within time and space, and higher-level thinking skills such as comparing, contrasting, organizing, hypothesizing, criticizing, applying, and evaluating.

The most-noted theory of cognitive development is that of Piaget (1972). His developmental steps, which build on one another in sequence, coincide with children's literature that is multicultural. In the sensorimotor period (birth to 2 years), children are very egocentric. Their world is that which they can see, and they are incapable of establishing what is known as *object permanence*—in other words, they do not understand that certain objects (or people) exist even if they are not seen. Multicultural books that contain rich, colorful pictures help in cognitive development at this stage. Tactile books like Amy and Henry Schwartz's *Make a Face: A Book with a Mirror* (1994) allow very young children to see themselves and express their emotions.

Within the preoperational period (ages 2 to 7), Piaget (1972) identifies two stages: a preconceptual stage (2 to 3 years) and an intuitive stage (4 to 7 years). During the preconceptual stage, the child can classify things according to changing criteria and uses very subjective logic—a single point of view. At this stage, folktales, stories that involve animals, fantasies, and inanimate objects taking on human characteristics, are most enjoyed. *Lon Po Po: A Red-Riding Hood Story from China* by Ed Young (1989) involves all of these areas as children read a different version of the adventures of Chinese girls and a wolf. The intuitive stage includes that period when elementary children develop their language skills and become more aware of the world around them. Being less egocentric, they are interested in others and their languages and customs. Multicultural author Musgrove and the illustrators, the Dillons, work together in *Ashanti to Zulu* (1976) to let children discover the customs of twenty-six African peoples in an alphabetical concept book. Swahili words and customs can be found in the books *Moja Means One* (Feelings, 1971) and *Jambo Means Hello* (Feelings, 1974).

In what Piaget (1972) calls the period of concrete operations (ages 7 to 11), the child's life becomes more concerned with logic, problem solving, and the understanding of time and spatial relationships. Multicultural books that include everyday problems confronting the family, historical fiction, and stories about other lands are the most popular with youngsters at this stage of cognitive development. Here students begin to employ the higher-level thinking strategies of comparing, contrasting, questioning, applying, and evaluating. *Whale Brother* by Barbara Steiner (1988) features an Inuit boy and his relationship with a dying killer whale. Deborah Davis's *The Secret of the Seal* (1989) gives youngsters the opportunity to discuss the conflict between modern and traditional values when a young boy must decide if he really wants to kill a beautiful female seal. Stories about others in family situations, like Laura Ingalls Wilder's *Little House in the Big Woods* (1932) series, fit in this category as well.

In the latter part of the elementary and middle-school years (ages 11 to 15), the period of formal operations is most evident. Full cognitive maturity is seen, and students can effectively use formal logic, engage in a true exchange of ideas and thoughts, and begin to comprehend the viewpoints of others. Ultimately they seek to understand better the world around them as a place where human beings and the environment interact. At this stage students enjoy hearing and reading about real-life situations—realistic and contemporary fiction. It is appropriate to ask students to read, debate, and apply what they have read in books such as Jane Yolen's *The Devil's Arithmetic* (1988), concerning a young Jewish girl in the time of World War II, and Judy Blume's *Blubber* (1974), involving peer conflict.

❖ Social-Emotional Development

Social-emotional development closely parallels the cognitive developmental stages previously discussed. Two experts in these fields are Erikson, known for his psychosocial development theory, and Kohlberg, who outlined the stages of moral development.

Erikson's (1963) theory is that a series of psychosocial conflicts occurs in the space of a young person's lifetime, conflicts that help to create maturity. These five stages of development are sequential, and the conflict in one stage must be resolved before the child can successfully move on to the next stage. The movement from stage to stage can be enhanced through the use of children's books. The first stage is that of *trust versus mistrust* (birth to 18 months), when babies most require security, comfort, and affection. Predictable stories and nursery rhymes help to reassure the very young child at this stage. Nursery rhymes from other lands and in other languages are appropriate—for example, the Chinese rhymes in *Dragon Kites and Dragonflies* (Demi, 1986) and the Griego, Bucks, Gilbert, and Kimball collection of Spanish and English nursery rhymes in *Tortillitas para Mama and Other Spanish Nursery Rhymes* (1981).

In stage two, *autonomy versus doubt* (18 months to 3 years), children become more aware of others around them, begin exploring, and try to establish their own identities. Books that offer moral dilemmas to confront are enjoyable at this stage. Potter's *The Tale of Peter Rabbit* (1900) helps little ones to understand bad and good choices in life. Pili Mandelbaum, in the book *You Be Me, I'll Be You* (1990), helps biracial children achieve a better sense of identity.

Children aged 3 to 6 begin to realize their own responsibilities and understand interpersonal conflicts during stage 3, *initiative versus guilt*. René Escudie's *Paul and Sebastian* (1994), a story from France, deals with mothers' prejudices and the problems their sons must deal with in the process.

Stage 4, *industry versus inferiority* (ages 7 to 11), sees young elementary children beginning to work cooperatively and worrying about peer acceptance. Sometimes they feel left out and wanting, unable to measure up to others. Cleary's *Ramona Quimby, Age 8* (1981) and other books in that series are popular at this stage. They deal with friendships among peers and the related difficulties.

The final stage is that of *identity versus role confusion*, most commonly seen in adolescence and beyond. The discovery of identity that occurs in this stage encompasses personal (self) identity and cultural and social identity. Culturally diverse books that are realistic and fictional help students realize their roles at home and in the world. An example is *Maniac Magee* by Jerry Spinelli (1990), which concerns an adolescent's struggle with family, peers, prejudice, and poverty.

Lawrence Kohlberg's stages of moral development (Kohlberg & Turiel, 1971) relate to decision making by children. Studies of children's literature using Kohlberg's stages involve three levels, each comprising two stages, that are consecutive and irreversible (Hoskisson & Biskin, 1979). The *pre-moral level* includes *Stage I: Punishment and obedience orientation*, where the child must obey rules in order to avoid punishment. In this stage the child does not really understand rules or authority, but he or she begins to see that good is pleasant and bad can be painful or fearful. Beatrix Potter's books work well at this stage, helping children see the consequences of disobedience. In *Stage II: Naive instrumental hedonism*, rules are obeyed because rewards are often the result. *Me First* by Helen Lester (1992) uses humor to educate children about selfishness and the power that can be wielded if rules are broken.

The second level is the *morality of conventional role conformity*. In *Stage III: "Good boy" or "good girl" orientation*, the child understands the "good-boy morality" of maintaining good relations and tries very hard to avoid disapproval from others (Gosa, 1977). A fine example of how a picture book can nudge young children toward appropriate behavior is *Send Wendell* by Genevieve Gray (1974). Wendell is the very cooperative son who is a "good boy" in the eyes of the other characters and the reader because he is always willing to be a helper. The story shows him progressing into *Stage IV: Authority maintaining morality* in a way that proves he can conform to avoid guilt and ostracism by authority figures.

Kohlberg's third level, *morality of self-accepted principles*, begins with *Stage V: Morality of contract*. The rights of others are very critical at this stage, and young people will avoid violating those rights as they believe in the greatest good for the greatest number. Appropriate reading at this stage includes historical fiction and biographies of famous, culturally diverse contributors to society—for example, *Malcolm X* by Walter Dean Myers (1993). In *Stage VI: Morality of individual principles of conscience*, the individual worries less about the law and more about what is right for the welfare of the world and people at large. Paula Fox's *Slave Dancer* (1973) addresses history in all its violence but delivers a powerful message to young adolescents as they relate to the injustices of history and peoples.

Lisa Paul (1988) sums up the importance of the role of children's literature to social-emotional development:

> What we, as teachers, have to remember is that stories create a space where moral and social issues can be explored safely—without threat. And therein lies their value. . . . Injustices of society can be tempered through the sustenance of imaginative art. (p. 4)

Artistic Development

Like the other aspects of children's development, artistic development is enriched by children's literature that is multicultural. As children step outside of themselves into the experiences and lives of others in different circumstances and similar situations, they are challenged to use their imaginations and build on what we refer to as *schema*—the scaffold, the understandings and previous life experiences that help a person relate effectively to learning and to others. Using quality children's books, young learners can role-play characters, think critically and creatively to change story endings, and write stories and poems that reflect their own lives. Communication, song, and language play into the imaginations of

FIGURE 1–2 Communication, song, and language play into children's imaginations.

FIGURE 1–3 Chart of developmental theory and children's literature

Area of development	Theory	Uses of children's literature
Linguistic	Sound, song Vocabulary Models of language	• Encourages passing on of cultures and stories • Can be used as readers theater experiences
Cognitive	Piaget: stages of development—preoperational, concrete, formal	• Provides hands-on experiences with text/words • Stimulates higher-level thinking processes • Encourages children's understanding of the world around them
Social-emotional	Erikson: social development Kohlberg: moral development	• Explores moral issues • Introduces contemporary issues that affect decision making • Allows for expression of emotions after reading and/or listening to a book
Artistic	Development of critical and creative thinking; Use of imagination	• Encourages imagination, thinking • Introduces creative dramatics and movement • Provides study of illustrators' styles • Motivates children to make their own books • Encourages playing with song, story, words

children when they look at others from different perspectives. Books like *Arroz Con Leche: Popular Songs and Rhymes from Latin America* by Lulu Delacre (1989) and *The First Thousand Words in Russian* by Amery and Kirilenko (1989) encourage children to play with language, song, and games of other peoples.

Certainly all of the areas of child development can be addressed within the realm of children's literature that is multicultural. Educators and parents can select books that will make transitions within each developmental level easier and more enjoyable.

❖ How Can Reading Books Make Children Feel Better about Themselves?

The element of schema, mentioned previously, is the level of personal experience that the learner brings to the learning situation—the back-

FIGURE 1–4 Children's books that are multicultural best explain who children are.

ground of life situations that allows one to understand what is new and adventurous. How does the child know what family is? How does the child know what loving and fear are? The level of experience, the schema or scaffold that children build in relationships with others and with *books*, becomes the basis for children's knowledge of who they are; where they fit in the family, the community, and the world; and how they ultimately affect the society of which they are valuable members.

Children's books that are multicultural best explain who children are, why they are here or there, and how they deal with life situations and the environment. Reading for the simple pleasure of communicating with others through words is important for the self-esteem of all children, regardless of background.

We are again reminded of the analogy of mirrors and windows. Children and adult readers see themselves mirrored in books about fictional characters like Brian in Gary Paulsen's *Hatchet* (1987) as they deal with divorce, fear, and loneliness. They can step outside of themselves to look through the windows of others like Cammy and her extended family in the rural midwest, characters in Virginia Hamilton's *Cousins* (1993).

❖ How Is Reading an Effective Method for Increasing Academic Achievement in Culturally Diverse Settings?

Christine Bennett, in *Comprehensive Multicultural Education: Theory and Practice* (1990), addresses the levels of achievement of children. She defines academic achievement level as "the knowledge a student has previously acquired that relates to what is being taught" (p. 177). As academic achievement relates directly to the use of children's literature in culturally diverse settings, it is important to note that educators have been closely regarding the content of the material they deliver and thus consider their students' recall of that content as achievement.

The use of children's literature that relates directly to children's experiences, featuring characters like themselves and situations much like their own, helps to empower students of all groups. It also helps to educate those who are not members of minority or disadvantaged groups. This empowerment of young children helps in the building of positive self-esteem and thus increases children's confidence in their ability to succeed academically (Banks & Banks, 1989).

FIGURE 1–5 Multicultural literature expands knowledge.

Prior research in this area by Coleman (1966) found that academic success is directly related to one's control over one's environment. The selection of books that relate well and directly to students' culture can only enhance the achievement of all students.

Finally, Tiedt and Tiedt (1990) report that studies in language arts curriculum and instruction show that "literature must be an integral part of instruction across the curriculum at all levels . . . that the work of both the reader and writer are influenced by prior knowledge . . . which includes cultural backgrounds" (p. 186). Allowing for individual interests and prior knowledge enables learners to succeed academically. Multicultural literature expands individuals' knowledge about themselves and others, geography and natural history, and environmental, social, and historical changes. It gives children an opportunity to think, read, and write critically and systematically.

❖   What Are the Effects of Reading Aloud and Family Involvement on Children's Learning?

One of the most effective methods of increasing academic achievement in our students is to read aloud to them. Reading aloud and children's books are a natural match. Children's books are meant to be heard—words trip off the reader's tongue, and expression can be added to develop and visualize characters, set the scene, and establish the theme of the book. Reading aloud to a child makes both the reader and the listener better aware of the pictures and the words that convey the story line. It enables all to recognize the patterns of the text, to observe what is construed as good writing and storytelling.

A leading authority on reading aloud to children is Jim Trelease, author of *The New Read-Aloud Handbook* (1989). He agrees with the National Institute of Education Commission on Reading, whose 1985 report *Becoming a Nation of Readers* states, "The single most important activity building the knowledge required for eventual success in reading is *reading aloud* to children" (Trelease, 1989, p. 2).

Trelease encourages teachers, parents, and caregivers to share books with children orally and often. As children's literature that is multicultural is the focus of this text, the advantages of reading aloud to children hold particularly true when culturally diverse selections are shared. The following is an adaptation of Trelease's (1989) reasons for encouraging reading aloud:

- ▌ Reading aloud provides a positive reading role model.
- ▌ Reading aloud exposes students to new information—about themselves, others, and the world around them.
- ▌ Reading aloud gives pleasure to the reader and the listener.

FIGURE 1-6 Paula and her book

- Reading aloud offers exposure to rich and diverse vocabulary.
- Reading aloud offers a broad variety of books that the child might not necessarily choose.
- Reading aloud exposes the listener to richly textured lives outside his or her own experiences.
- Reading aloud exposes the listener to the English language as well as to many others.

Reading aloud has proven to be successful for several reasons: It is an enjoyable activity that does not require training and much more than time on the part of the participants; it is simple and can be done by various groups—parents, peers, and educators; it is inexpensive because readers can borrow books from libraries or even from friends; it is an effective way to model reading behavior for children. Moreover, reading aloud to children books that deal with their interests and with the lives and cultures of others similar to and different from them enhances cognitive knowledge base, vocabulary, writing ability, and level of experience—schema and scaffolding.

Parents are encouraged to take a very active role as models of reading behavior in this reading-aloud partnership. Bernice Cullinan (1992) states that "reading is for all people, all times, and all places . . . because no matter what the language, we *must* read to our children" (p. 13). In *Read to Me: Raising Kids Who Love to Read,* Cullinan explains to parents and caregivers that the stories they tell children become part of the children's long-term memories, building upon the lifetime of experiences and helping explain the new experiences that lie ahead for them. She lists advantages of active parent involvement in the reading-aloud process that particularly apply to culturally diverse books: reading aloud

- is fun
- opens doors
- builds the desire to read
- gives educational advantage
- becomes part of the family heritage
- establishes bonds of love
- develops ability to read alone (pp. 22–23)

Both Cullinan (1992) and Trelease (1989) have determined that read-aloud times with children are most effective in the learning process. Using children's literature that is multicultural as the resource for this reading can only increase the impact of the experience on our children's learning.

❖ How Can Cultural Gaps Be Fused in the Education of Young People?

The education of today's young people will cease to be effective if it does not recognize that diversity exists within its walls and address that diversity. School curriculum reform movements currently under way will help our students understand and accept cultural pluralism and ethnic diversity in American life. New curriculum includes the celebration of diversity and reflects the coexistence of many cultures and groups.

Children's books that are multicultural serve as vehicles for this celebration and the reeducation of students and faculty. Literature is the means for understanding others and fusing gaps between cultures and groups. As Gordon Wells (1986) states in *The Meaning Makers,* stories can be the basis for grasping information in a painless fashion:

> What I want to suggest is that stories have a role in education that goes far beyond their contribution to the acquisition of literacy. Constructing stories in the mind—or storying, as it has been called—is one of the most fundamental means of making meaning; as such, it is an activity that pervades all aspects of learning. Through the exchange of stories teachers and students can share their understandings of a topic and bring their mental models of the world into closer alignment. In this sense, stories and storying are relevant in all areas of the curriculum. (p. 194)

Stories about and for children that reflect cultural diversity become bridges between personal experiences and the relationships with others' experiences. Stories and books create a kaleidoscope of excitement about life as children see it and dare to explore it. Fused together, multicultural tales and books become a magical patchwork quilt of sorts, with individual colors and patterns sewn together to make the world take on a warm and comforting tone.

❖ Summary

Children's literature that is multicultural is written for the child and reflects the childhood of a culture or a group by expressing the viewpoint of the child with a sense of optimism, hope, and excitement. Its enjoyment can be characterized as looking into a mirror or through a window as different groups of children see themselves and others in books. The views of various developmental theorists—Piaget, Kohlberg, Erikson—can be connected to children's literature. Families, caregivers, and teachers will discover the power of reading aloud culturally diverse books to children. Reading about ourselves and others helps us to build tolerance and acceptance.

❖ Reflections and Questions to Consider

1. Select from one of the following age groupings:
    Preschool: ages 2–3
    Preschool: ages 3–4
    Preschool: ages 4–5
    Preschool kindergarten: ages 5–6

Early elementary: ages 6-8

Middle elementary: ages 8-10

Upper elementary: ages 10-12

Then determine a list of five to ten books you would recommend to parents for reading aloud to children in that age group. Include the following:

A. A letter (one page) to parents explaining the importance of reading aloud to their children (refer to class notes and your text).

B. An explanation of how each title selected meets the growth and developmental needs of children in that age group (these are pages that are added to the letter and serve as additional information and support for the parents).

C. Typed pages that include the following heading:

Letter: Children's Literature   Section _____

Name_____   Date _____

Letter Format (page 1)

Dear Parents of (age grouping chosen):

[Include information about reading aloud here.]

Your signature

Growth and developmental needs of (age of group chosen) (page 2+)

Book Title, Author   Main idea of the book

How this book meets growth and developmental needs of these children

2. Explain why children's literature that is multicultural impacts our schools today.

3. What are the differences between conventional literature, children's literature, and children's literature that is multicultural?

❖ Children's Literature Cited

Aardema, V. (1975). *Why mosquitoes buzz in people's ears.* New York: Dial.
Aardema, V. (1981). *Bringing the rain to Kapiti Plain: a Nandi tale.* New York: Dial.
Amery, H., & Kirilenko, K. (1989). *The first thousand words in Russian.* London: Usborne House.

Barrett, J. D. (1989). *Willie's not the hugging kind.* New York: Harper & Row.

Blume, J. (1974). *Blubber.* Scarsdale, NY: Bradbury.

Bradman, T. (1987). *Wait and see.* New York: Oxford.

Cleary, B. (1981). *Ramona Quimby, age 8.* New York: Morrow.

Davis, D. (1989). *The secret of the seal.* New York: Crown

Delacre, L. (1989). *Arroz con leche: Popular songs and rhymes from Latin America.* New York: Scholastic.

Demi (1986). *Dragon kites and dragonflies.* Orlando, FL: Harcourt Brace Jovanovich.

dePaola, T. (1983). *The legend of bluebonnet.* New York: Putnam.

Escudie, R. (1994). *Paul and Sebastian.* New York: Kane/Miller.

Feelings, M. (1971). *Moja means one: Swahili counting book.* New York: Dial.

Feelings, M. (1974). *Jambo means hello: Swahili alphabet book.* New York: Dial.

Fox, P. (1973). *Slave dancer.* New York: Dell.

Gaige, A. (1990). *We are a thunderstorm.* Kansas City: Landmark Editions.

Gray, G. (1974). *Send Wendell.* New York: McGraw-Hill.

Greenfield, H. (1993). *The hidden children.* New York: Ticknor & Fields.

Griego, M., Bucks, B., Gilbert, S., & Kimball, L. (1981). *Tortillitas para Mama and other Spanish nursery rhymes.* Austin, TX: Holt, Rinehart & Winston.

Haley, G. (1970). *A story, a story.* New York: Atheneum.

Hamilton, V. (1985). *The people could fly: American black folktales.* New York: Knopf.

Hamilton, V. (1988). *In the beginning: Creation stories from around the world.* San Diego: Harcourt Brace Jovanovich.

Hamilton, V. (1993). *Cousins.* New York: Scholastic.

Hudson, W. (1993). *Pass it on: African-American poetry for children.* New York: Scholastic.

Johnson, A. (1989). *Tell me a story, Mama.* New York: Orchard.

Lester, H. (1992). *Me first.* Boston: Houghton Mifflin.

Mandelbaum, P. (1990). *You be me, I'll be you.* New York: Kane/Miller.

McKissack, P., & McKissack, F. (1992). *Sojourner Truth: Ain't I a woman?* New York: Scholastic.

Mosel, A. (1968). *Tikki tikki tembo.* New York: Holt, Rinehart & Winston.

Musgrove, M. (1976). *Ashanti to Zulu.* New York: Dial.

Myers, W. D. (1993). *Malcoln X: By any means necessary.* New York: Scholastic.

Paulsen, G. (1987). *Hatchet.* New York: Puffin.

Pfister, M. (1992). *The rainbow fish.* New York: Scholastic.

Potter, B. (1900). *The Tale of Peter Rabbit.* New York: F. Warne.

Schwartz, A., & Schwartz, H. (1994). *Make a face: A book with a mirror.* New York: Scholastic.

Spier, P. (1980). *People.* New York: Doubleday.

Spinelli, J. (1990). *Maniac Magee.* New York: Little, Brown.

Steiner, B. (1988). *Whale brother.* New York: Walker.

Wilder, L. (1932). *Little house in the big woods.* New York: Harper & Row.

Wyndham, R. (1982). *Chinese Mother Goose Rhymes.* New York: Philomel.

Yolen, J. (1988). *The devil's arithmetic.* New York: Viking Kestrel.

Young, E. (1989). *Lon Po Po: A Red-Riding Hood story from China.* New York: Philomel.

❖ References

Banks, J., & Banks, C. (1989). *Multicultural education: Issues and perspectives.* Boston: Allyn & Bacon.

Bennett, C. (1990). *Comprehensive multicultural education: Theory and practice.* Boston: Allyn & Bacon.

Biskin, D., & Hoskisson, K. (1977). The experimental test of the effects of structured discussions of moral dilemmas found in children's literature on moral reasoning. *The Elementary School Journal, 77*(5), 407–415.

Coleman, J. (1966). *Equality of educational opportunity.* Washington, DC: U.S. Government Printing Office.

Cox, S., & Galda, L. (1990). Multicultural literature: Mirrors and windows on a global community. *The Reading Teacher,* 582–89.

Cullinan, B. (1992). *Read to me: Raising kids who love to read.* New York: Scholastic.

Diakiw, J. (1990). Children's literature and global education: Understanding the developing world. *The Reading Teacher, 33*(4), 296–300.

Erikson, E. H. (1963). Theories of human development. In D. R. Shaffer (Ed.), *Developmental psychology: Childhood and adolescence* (3rd ed., 52–56). Pacific Grove, CA: Brooks/Cole.

Fox, M. (1993). Politics and literature: Chasing the "isms" from children's books. *The Reading Teacher, 46*(8), 654–58.

Gay, G. (1975). Organizing and designing culturally pluralistic curriculum. *Educational Leadership, 33*(3), 176–183.

Gosa, C. (1977). Moral development in current fiction for children and young adults. *Language Arts, 54*(5), 529–536.

Hoskisson, K., & Biskin, D. (1979). Analyzing and discussing children's literature using Kohlberg's stages of moral development. *The Reading Teacher, 33*(2), 141–151.

Kohlberg, L., & Turiel, E. (1971). *Moral development and moral education. Psychology and educational practice.* Chicago: Scott, Foresman.

Norton, D. (1985). Language and cognitive development through multicultural literature. *Childhood Education, 62*(2), 103–108.

Paul, L. (1988). *What stories have to do with life. Growing with books.* Toronto, Ontario: Provincial Ministry of Education.

Piaget, J. (1972). Cognition and cognitive development: A Piagetian perspective. In D. R. Shaffer, (Ed.), *Developmental psychology: Childhood and adolescence* (3rd ed., 235–271). Pacific Grove, CA: Brooks/Cole.

Tiedt, P., & Tiedt, I. (1990). *Multicultural teaching: A handbook of activities, information, and resources.* Boston: Allyn & Bacon.

Trelease, J. (1989). *The new read-aloud handbook.* New York: Penguin.

Tway, E. (1989). Dimensions of multicultural literature for children. In M. K. Rudman (Ed.), *Children's literature: Resource for the classroom* (109–138). Needham Heights, MA: Christopher-Gordon.

Wells, G. (1986). *The meaning makers.* Portsmouth, NH: Heinemann.

CHAPTER 2

Understanding our roots and beginnings will help each of us to become more tolerant and accepting of others.

What Is the History behind Multicultural Children's Literature?

❚ Storytelling and the passing on of culture
❚ The emergence of childhood and books for children
❚ The melting-pot theory
❚ Movement to a "tossed salad" or "patchwork quilt": new thinking in literature for children

❖ How Has Culture Been Passed on to Our Children through Storytelling?

As long as we know of our existence on earth, we know of stories—the sharing of language, events, characters, and experiences with one another in some form. Referred to as "love gifts" by Lewis Carroll, stories have been the basis for understanding phenomena, life, and spirituality for adults and children alike. As stories about humans and nature have been passed on from generation to generation through oral language and finally in written form, the cultural gifts of our peoples have been propagated.

Baker and Greene (1987) state that

> curiosity about the past, the search for an understanding of beginnings, the need for entertainment, and the desire to keep alive a heroic past established the early storyteller as the bringer of news, historian, disperser of culture, upholder of religion and morals, as well as entertainer. (p. 1)

Certainly children accompanied parents and adults in the storytelling events, and though the stories were not originally designed for children's ears and interpretation, the role of the storyteller and the stories shared have become the beginnings of multicultural enlightenment. The stories that reflected the times became the legends and folklore that we cherish and continue to pass on today.

Within different cultures, the role of the storyteller varied. Resident storytellers were evident in the early African cultures. The storyteller lived within a particular household and had the job of passing on the stories that related to the chief of that household—one way to keep the memory of this leader prominent and alive for the people of the region. Another type of African storyteller was the traveling storyteller who moved throughout the land, sharing many stories in legendary and folklore format with those who would listen. In the Asian cultures, one would recognize the storyteller as a member of the religious community (a priest), a teacher or noted scholar, or sometimes a very common peasant (Baker & Greene, 1987).

Both the Egyptians and the Sumerians engaged in storytelling in times recorded as 2000 B.C. Those who engaged in pyramid building and those who recorded the first written text listened avidly to stories that told how the world was created and how creatures and nature interacted.

As storytellers in Europe moved from place to place, they often sang their stories. They were the Anglo-Saxon gleemen, Norman minstrels, German minnesingers, and Irish ollams and shanachies. When printing came into use around 1450, the stories purveyed by many of these singers, dancers, and storytellers took on a more formal form of retelling by individuals we readily recall, such as the Brothers Grimm, Hans Christian Andersen, and Jeremiah Curtin (Baker & Greene, 1987).

In our own country, the storytelling tradition was enriched by oral storytelling among the early African-American slaves. Animals often had symbolic significance in such tales as Brer Rabbit's adventures with the other more powerful animals in the forest. These stories were retold by the storyteller Uncle Remus. Humor and craftiness on the part of Brer Rabbit established this small creature as a leader and a clever individual. The role of the rabbit was well understood by the slaves: They could identify with his stature but recognized the power of higher-level thinking, communication, and adaptation to the environment (Harris, 1986a, 1986b, 1987a, 1987b).

Other heroic characters whose stories were passed on through early African-American storytellers were John Henry and High John. Determination, power in spite of adversity, and wit were characteristics of these individuals, whose stories can be read in Keats's *John Henry: An American Legend* (1987) and Sanfield's *The Adventures of High John the Conquerer* (1989).

Early Native North Americans told stories to explain their close relationship with nature. As Caduto and Bruchac share in *Keepers of the Animals* (1991), "Native North Americans see themselves as *part* of nature, not apart from it" (p. xviii). Therefore, members of this culture believe that acts of care or neglect toward animals, birds, trees, flowers, and wildlife apply to nature the same as they do to people. Because this culture believes in a specific order of life, with humans being the last of the order, stories passed on through Native American storytellers reflect a deep respect for all living things as they relate to one another. Native American stories and tales have also passed on ceremonies and rituals. Vine Deloria Jr. states that folktales "present some of the basic perspectives that Native North American parents, aunts and uncles use to teach the young . . . and if these stories can help develop in young people a strong sense of the wonder of other forms of life, this sharing of Native North American knowledge will certainly have been worth the effort" (Caduto & Bruchac, 1991, p. xi). Thus the passing on of story was very prevalent in the early years of our country, through legends and oral transmission by elder tribal leaders who sought to explain to younger members the importance of respect for all living things and their significance to the world at large.

Reflection upon the history of storytelling and the transmission of cultural heritage is significant in the context of children's literature that is multicultural. What better way is there than the sharing of tales by parents, grandparents, and teachers to inform children about who they are and how they came to be? As Ann Nolan Clark (1969) states,

> Children need to know of other nationalities and races so that, inheriting an adult world, they find a free and joyous interchange for awareness that each group of people has its own special traditions and customs. . . . There is need that respectful recognition be given these special traditions and customs. There is need for acceptance of these differences. There is tragic need for loving communication between children and children, children and adults, adults and adults—between group and group. (p. 89).

Children's literature that can be categorized as multicultural often takes the form of story, fable, legend, or folklore retold and thus has emerged from what we as educators know as the storytelling of long ago.

❖ How Did Books Emerge for Children?

In addition to storytelling, children through the ages have been exposed to the written word in ever-evolving forms.

In the 1400s, literature for children existed as didactic text—words in print that were meant to teach skills and concepts. The materials were in the form of hornbooks made of wood and covered with animal skin to help them endure weather and wear. Hornbooks often included alphabets, numbers, and prayers that adults deemed most appropriate for children to remember. Thus, early on, the primary purpose for written words for children was for teaching in a controlled environment.

Chapbooks followed in the 1500s. These were very cheaply constructed paper books that peddlers sold from their wagons and at fairs, markets, and festivals. Chapbook stories were written forms of legends, ballads, and brief histories of the times. They remained popular in America through the 1700s.

The influence of religion was evident in Puritan primers, prevalent through the 1800s and designed to teach children religious beliefs and morals. In 1693, the English philosopher John Locke wrote in *Some Thoughts Concerning Education* (1910) of more appropriate methods for teaching the young using gentler approaches. As a result of Locke's influence and with a growing regard for childhood and its recognition, parents and teachers began to realize that children were different from adults and could learn from other types of books written particularly for them.

Retold versions of folktales, legends, and fairy tales were the work of the familiar writers Charles Perrault, John Newbery, Jacob and Wilhelm Grimm, and Hans Christian Andersen. However, the stories from non-European cultures tended not to be shared formally within this country. Instead, they remained in the oral traditions of legend and folklore of Asians, Native Americans, Latinos, and Africans.

❖ What Is the Melting-Pot Theory and How Does It Relate to Children's Literature?

Throughout the early history of children's literature, the emphasis was on the teaching of the young and the passing on of particular beliefs and values. This trend continued as the United States developed as a nation and as representatives from various countries and cultures settled here. The stories and legends of those cultures were preserved and transmitted within families and homes but not necessarily in formal educational settings. Although immigrants' reasons for settling in the United States commonly centered on freedom of self-expression, religious belief, and political affiliation, their individual cultures were often not openly acknowledged in the school environment or in the selection of reading materials.

During this time of development of the United States, the "melting-pot" theory was most evident. Differences were in fact discouraged; commonalities and the effacement of individual identities based on culture were stressed. According to the theory of the melting pot, people of different cultures blended, as do the ingredients of a pot of stew, to make a new and tasty "dish" that reflected its own identity instead of separate ones. This theory emerged from a play written in 1908 by the English-Jewish author Israel Zangwill and entitled *The Melting Pot*. In the play, the idea of creating a new and superior group of people became the passion of the main character, David Quixano. [However, rather than only occurring within the play itself, what Americans saw was the elimination of contributions by most ethnic groups, thus creating an Anglo-American dominated culture.] The play thus became a model for the American education community—instead of promoting cultural differences & identity, contributions from ethnic populations would feed into one major culture and create the greatest culture. Schools and educational approaches adapted this philosophy by encouraging various cultural groups to become members of the larger group of Americans, releasing themselves from the linkages to family traditions, neighborhood groupings, and customs that they had retained for many years (Banks, 1987, pp. 19–36).

As noted by Ramirez and Ramirez in *Multiethnic Children's Literature* (1994), children's books in the 1940s era of American development reflected the melting-pot theory. They may have represented minority group members in a superficial way, but with no real regard for issues or concerns based on cultural diversity, race, and ethnicity. Groups of people were not heterogeneous but took on the identity of one another with different ethnic physical characteristics and names. Chu and Schuler (1992) believe that this process was valuable in that members of diverse cultures found their primary identities in the American macroculture rather than in the African-American, Latino, Asian, or other microculture. The understanding was that individuals were to be regarded as Americans, with little or no recognition or mention of personal heritage.

❖ What Is the Current Thinking in Children's Literature?

The civil rights movement of the 1960s and the influence of the federal government in policy making set the stage for recognition of multicultural education, acceptance of diversity in our nation's schools, and changes in curricular approaches. The turmoil of the 1960s greatly influenced the evolution of the multicultural education movement. During the

1960s and 1970s, there was federal funding for ethnic studies programs, integration in schools gained a certain momentum, and the concerns of black Americans regarding inequities began to have an effect on curriculum and how it was delivered. The feeling of unrest among blacks in the 1960s was not unlike the unrest after the last great wave of immigration in the 1940s. According to Nathan Glazer (1981a), the period between the 1940s and 1960s saw a general decline of confidence in the virtues of American society, government, and culture; a loss of prestige of public schools as they failed to deal effectively with diverse cultures; and a resultant increase in the federal government's role in educational policy making. The latter development became most evident with the enactment of the Ethnic Heritage Studies Act of 1965 (Ramsey, Vold, & Williams, 1989). Carl A. Grant (1988) has noted that reform reports issued from the 1960s through the 1980s, some of which were mandated by the government, demanded that changes take place in educational policy but then failed properly to address equity and excellence in regard to diversity of students.

However, developments in the 1960s and 1970s surrounding blacks and their striving for equity in education had impact on other minority groups as well. "What began in the late 1960s with the political demand of racial minority groups—that their heritages and experiences be reflected accurately in school curricula—has now extended to other ethnic groups and to all aspects of the education enterprise" (Gay, 1983, p. 560). Some believe that from a historical perspective, blacks during the 1970s were guided by "ethnocentric liberal ideology which denied cultural differences and thus acted against the best interests of the people it wished to understand and eventually help" (Corder & Quisenberry, 1987, p. 156).

Ramsey, Vold, and Williams (1989) have reviewed the historical development of multiculturalism in an overlapping time frame that lets one see the historical development of multicultural education as it was prompted and influenced by social events in our history. The first progress toward multicultural education came with the promotion of intergroup education and the movement toward desegregation in the 1950s, when the focus was on racial balance and institutional change rather than on curriculum development. The recognition of inequities in work, housing, and education gave impetus in the 1960s to the ethnic studies movement and the revitalization of ethnic content in curriculum. Differences in group membership and the acknowledgment of minority and ethnic experience, history, and traditions became the basis for additions to existing curricula. The multicultural education approach originated in the mid-1970s, when the country was becoming aware of cultural pluralism as opposed to the melting-pot theory. Sensitization of all individuals toward ethnic and racial differences and increased awareness of the traditions and sociological experiences of various cultures were encouraged in order to foster more peaceful coexistence and understanding. The 1980s and 1990s have brought a social reconstructionist approach to education as more and more minority groups have begun to question inequities and the lack of social justice.

The reactions to these events within the school setting, and particularly in regard to the selection and development of children's literature that is multicultural, encouraged more social consciousness (Sims, 1983). Children's books that addressed diversity issues dealt with the need to understand others better in order to coexist in society and the world. These books were fairly predictable in that their plots showed difficulties of minority group members in everyday life, situations that encouraged cooperation between groups, and resolutions of the difficulties (Ramirez & Ramirez, 1994). Stories and depictions of activity by minority groups were predominantly stereotypical. Thus, although cultural diversity was shown, accuracy was questionable.

In a September 1965 *Saturday Review* article entitled "The All-White World of Children's Books," Nancy Larrick shocked American families and educators with her assessment of the status of children's literature. Larrick revealed that although the American education system was open to all types of learners and people, the white population filled children's books, to the near-exclusion of other groups and cultures. Sims contends that, since 1970, the theme has moved from social consciousness to "cultural consciousness," a concerted effort to show true-to-life experiences of members of diverse cultural groups in a way that helps children of today's society accept and identify with those experiences (Sims, 1983).

Children's books now are reflections of the mirrors and windows of children's minds—who they are and whom they come to see and know through literature. Replacing the melting pot are metaphors of salad bowl, patchwork quilt, mosaic, and tapestry, where individual ingredients, fabrics, and threads take on dimensions that add to the richness of the whole while retaining their individuality. Stories of the times are contemporary realistic fiction with rich experiences often drawn from the authors' lives. Nonfiction stories include accounts of significant contributions of minority peoples. In historical fiction, characters are often of color and of diverse cultures. Whereas illustrations in earlier children's books were limited and showed stereotypical characters and settings, contemporary illustrations are vivid and realistic. Often, photographs and audio supplements enhance the text.

The implications are clear. We are moving toward an era of broadening awareness, acceptance, cooperation, and collaboration where diverse cultures are concerned. However, as Rudman (1995) aptly states,

> The United States is not yet a utopia: People are still ignorant of others' cultures and beliefs, certain that their own heritages are superior or so insecure about their own identities that they act negatively and demean others because of religion, color of skin, or national origin. (p. 219)

FIGURE 2–1 Educational progression

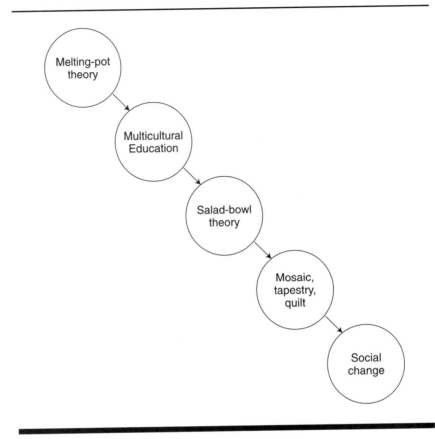

Educational progress in the direction of multicultural education is still rather limited. We remain at the awareness stage (see chapter 4). At this level we are concerned and hope to gain insight into others' cultures as we read more and more truth about one another, as adult teachers as well as young learners.

Margaret Mead, noted anthropologist and futurist, has developed a theory regarding the passing on of culture through learning. In *Culture and Commitment* (1970), Mead has described her "goal to explore living people, all existing at the present time but exhibiting essential differences and discontinuities . . . and identified three major types of cultures: cultures of the Historical Past; cultures of the Present; and cultures of the Future" (King, Chipman, & Cruz-Janzen, 1994, p. 207). Mead's research relates directly to the emergence of thinking and learning within early childhood and elementary education, literature, and culture.

In the "cultures of the Historical Past," the relationships between the elders and the young are very strong. In fact, the bonding is such that little change occurs, and the culture is passed on as it was shared with the elders and their predecessors. Examples of such cultures are the Samoans, the Venezuelan Indians, and the New Guinea Arapesh peoples. To preserve their cultures, these groups isolate themselves from others so that new knowledge of a different world cannot change their lifestyles and security.

Margaret Mead defines "cultures of the Present" "as ones in which the prevailing model for members of the society is the behavior of their contemporaries" (King, Chipman, & Cruz-Janzen, 1994, p. 208). Children of these cultures seem to experience more new skills and methods of learning than did their parents and grandparents. They in fact become the knowledge bearers, and the elders and parents seem to lose power, as Mead (1970) explains: "Young people everywhere share a kind of experience that none of the elders ever have had or will have. Conversely the older generation will never see repeated in the lives of young people their own unprecedented experience of sequentially emerging change" (p. 64). Examples of such changes in cultural and educational growth are evident in areas of India, Pakistan, and Africa.

Finally, with the emergence of the "cultures of the Future," parents learn from their children. The not-so-gradual movement from the oral transmission of culture through storytelling to the use of high-speed technology for sharing of information has brought educators to the realization that we are rapidly approaching many more cultures of the Future in our schools and our world.

What are the implications for our teaching of Mead's research and the influence of past dynamics on children's literature and learning? What value does storytelling have in the child's recognition of self, in the child's cognitive development, in the continuation of his or her cultural history?

Literacy studies by many, including Baghban (1984), Cochran-Smith (1984), Crago and Crago (1983), Morrow (1984), and Wells (1986), support a view of early literacy development that is attained through listening, telling, reading, and retelling in the storytelling act. Children follow the modeling of adults, caregivers, teachers, and peers who show them methods of oral and dramatic response to dialogue, action, character, and scene. With the linkage of oral language skills and listening, children explore new realms of imagination in attempting their own storytelling, retelling, and developing of piggy-back storylines. Ultimately they respond to the passing on of their very own cultures and those of others in a traditional sense. Powerful stories shared in both formal and informal situations (at school and at home) become deep-seated memories that "excite our imaginations, remain with us for the rest of our lives" (Fleischman, 1988, p. 83).

Through continued exposure to others via high-quality curricular texts and children's literature reflecting cultural diversity, we can immerse our young learners in their own cultures and those of others close by or very, very distant. We must recognize that acceptance and understanding of others comes from increased knowledge and the removal of fear. Our knowledge bases have foundation in the history of ourselves as thinking beings. Our histories are our stories; our stories are the answers. The circle of knowledge, while complete, continues as generations of people share through story.

People can share storytelling with or without props, books, and materials. Often the act of storytelling is enhanced by the creativity of the

FIGURE 2-2 Felt board and story apron

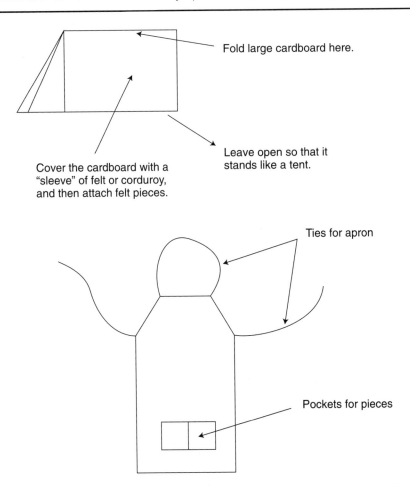

Fold large cardboard here.

Leave open so that it stands like a tent.

Cover the cardboard with a "sleeve" of felt or corduroy, and then attach felt pieces.

Ties for apron

Pockets for pieces

teller. Aids such as story aprons or felt boards can provide vehicles for this creativity. One can easily construct such devices with or without patterns, using felt or corduroy (see Figure 2-2). Pictures representing characters, setting, and action can be attached to the apron or board with velcro or constructed from durable felt pieces.

Following is a lesson plan/activity for sharing with young children that utilizes the storytelling technique. It is based on a folktale, "The Man Who Couldn't Read Chinese."

FOCUS

Reading—cloze procedure; retelling in Big Book creation

Rationale

The purpose of this lesson is to demonstrate to students that the Chinese writing system, though different from the English alphabet system with which they are most familiar, represents a historically derived, valid, and intriguing system of communication. Through active participation in the discovery of the Chinese language and calligraphy, students will remove the mystery of this method of communication.

SUBJECT/CONTENT AREA

Reading

Goals

To introduce a contrasting method of communication through the use of Chinese language and calligraphy and to encourage new inquiry approaches in reading: forming hypotheses and generalizations from clues in the story.

Objectives

The students will recognize characteristics of the Chinese writing system.

The students will understand Chinese characters in the context of a story to gain meaning.

The students will develop a positive attitude toward pictographic and ideographic writing forms.

The students will develop and refine group skills.

The students will gain some competence with new linguistic terms and language forms.

The students will discover new ideas through inquiry approaches; they will make hypotheses and generalizations from a story.

The students will work with abstract meaning and inferences.

The students will practice iconic (pictorial/symbolic) learning skills.

The students will view Chinese written characters in the context of a story.

The students will use clues to understand a story.

The students will understand how the Chinese writing system communicates ideas.

The students will construct a Big Book retelling the story of "The Man Who Couldn't Read Chinese."

Terms/Vocabulary

Calligraphy

Glossary

Characters

Cloze procedure

Materials

Demystifying the Chinese Language (1988)—The China Project/SPICE— "The Man Who Couldn't Read Chinese"

Experience paper

Markers

Construction paper for Big Book

Readiness/Motivation

Review with the students the term *calligraphy,* noted previously, as the method of Chinese writing. Ask students to tell you what they do when they are unsure of a word in a book or story in English. How do they arrive at the meaning? Set the stage by telling the students that there is a mystery about this story—that part of it is written in Chinese and that they need to be detectives and use all types of methods to come up with the story's meaning. In the end they will have an opportunity to illustrate parts of the story and practice writing some of the Chinese characters.

Procedures/Instructions

1. Gather students in a group in a comfortable sitting area (on the carpet, on the floor, or in chairs in a circle). Tell the students that a folktale will be shared with them today but that it is written with some Chinese characters. Ask these questions:

   What is this kind of writing called? (calligraphy)

   When you read a story and you are unsure of a word, what might you do?

2. Instruct the students that they will be playing a game of detective with one another to figure out the story that will be read to them.

3. Remind them of what "brainstorming" technique is, and encourage them to use it in this activity.

4. Present the first page of the story—the title page (see p. i)—to the students. When the students come to the Chinese symbol, they are to read "blank"

The 来 who couldn't read 字

Once upon a time in 中国 , there was a 老 who lived by

a 林 . In the 林 was a mean-spirited 老虎 who came in

and killed the 老 's 马 . The 老 decided to try to catch

the 老虎 by setting a 阱 for him. He made the 阱 by

the 川 where the water was flowing and the tiger would come for a

drink. The 老 wanted other 人 and 老 's to know about

the 阱 so he made a sign that said:

"To all 人 who come for water at the 川 , there is

a 阱 for a 老虎 here. Be very 小心 ."

Now many 人 came by to gather water at the 川 . One day,

a 来 who planned on stealing the 马 came by the 川 for a

drink. This nasty 来 could not read 字 and so he stepped in

the 阱 and was captured. The 老 heard his 囚 's cries

and came running to the 阱 to help him out. The 来 in his

gratitude became a good 工 and helped the 老 finally capture

the 老虎 . And he learned to read 字 .

(continued)

man	人	farmer	尤
Chinese	字	stream	巛
horses	馬	gentleman	士
trap	阱	careful	心
China	中国	forest	林
thief	來	prisoner	囚
tiger	老虎		

Adapted from a story prepared by Caryn White for the University of Arizona East Asia Study Center.

aloud or guess its meaning. (Note: The story may be presented on an overhead transparency or on large chart paper so all can see.)

5. As the story progresses, encourage students to work on their memory skills and recall if the same character appeared earlier in the story. All students are to pay close attention to the story content in order to figure out the meaning of each character or combination of characters. Warn students that sometimes *two* Chinese characters are the equivalent of *one* word in English.

6. As students give meaning to the characters, write these meanings on the chart paper or transparency as record.

7. Upon completion of the story, have the group reread it without the Chinese characters. Then send them off in pairs to illustrate different pages of the story for creation of the Big Book.

8. Encourage students to practice the new characters in their journals. Tell students that they will also get copies of the story to take home, with copies of the glossary. (Ask them to define that term and tell where they would find a glossary in a book.)

Student Evaluation

Students will be evaluated on the successful completion of a retold version of a Big Book. Their illustrations will indicate comprehension as they explain their pictures to the teacher individually. Active participation in the cloze procedure will be noted for individuals. Continued and extended cooperation in small groups and pairs will be checked by the teacher.

FIGURE 2–3 Book talk on *House for Hermit Crab*

❖ Summary

Storytelling in its earliest forms was the basis for the sharing of language, events, characters, and experiences within cultures. Stories explained phenomena, life, and spirituality for adults and children alike. Children often listened to these stories, and eventually the stories became teaching tools, didactic in nature. The early books shared with children reflected the thinking of the time—the melting-pot theory, a view in which separate cultures were not recognized nor encouraged. As situations within our country changed—thanks to the civil rights movement and other movements for equity—so did the approach. The notion of the salad bowl came into play. Children and teachers will now see different cultures and groups reflected in stories and retellings.

❖ Reflections and Questions to Consider

1. How has the change from the melting-pot theory to the salad bowl affected the teaching of children and, particularly, the use of children's literature in elementary classrooms?

FIGURE 2-4 Book talk on *Swimmy*

2. Create a mosaic, quilt, or collage of children's literature that is multi-cultural as it reflects current philosophy.

3. Recall or research an old story that has been passed on through your family or other group. Share that story with the group through visuals.

❖ Children's Literature Cited

Caduto, M., & Bruchac, J. (1991). *Keepers of the animals: Native American stories and wildlife activities for young children.* Golden, CO: Fulcrum.

Harris, J. C. (1986a). *Jump! The adventures of Brer Rabbit.* Orlando, FL: Harcourt Brace Jovanovich.

Harris, J. C. (1986b). *More tales of Uncle Remus: Further adventures of Brer Rabbit, his friends, enemies, and others.* New York: Dial.

Harris, J. C. (1987a). *Jump! again! More adventures of Brer Rabbit.* Orlando, FL: Harcourt Brace Jovanovich.

Harris, J. C. (1987b). *The tales of Uncle Remus: Further adventures of Brer Rabbit.* New York: Dial.

Keats, E. J. (1987). *John Henry: An American legend.* New York: Knopf.

Sanfield, S. (1989). *The adventures of High John the Conquerer.* New York: Watts.

❖ References

Baghban, M. (1984). *Our daughter learns to read and write.* Newark, DE: International Reading Association.

Baker, A., & Greene, E. (1987). *Storytelling art and technique.* New York: R. R. Bowker.

Banks, J. A. (1987). *Multiethnic education: Theory and practice.* Boston: Allyn & Bacon.

Burke, E. M. (1990). *Literature for the young child.* Boston: Allyn and Bacon.

Chu, E., & Schuler, C. V. (1992). United States: Asian American. In L. Miller-Lachmann (Ed.), *Our family, our friends, our world: An annotated guide to significant multicultural books for children and teenagers.* New York: R. R. Bowker.

Clark, A. N. (1969). *Journey to the people.* New York: Viking.

Cochran-Smith, M. (1984). *The making of a reader.* Norwood, NJ: Ablex.

Corder, L. J., & Quisenberry, N. (1987). *Early education and Afro-Americans. Childhood Education, 63*(3), 154–158.

Crago, M., & Crago, H. (1983). *Prelude to literacy.* Carbondale: Southern Illinois University Press.

Fleischman, S. (1988). The magic story. *The Five Owls, 11*(6), 83.

Gay, G. (1983). Multiethnic education: Historical developments and future prospects. *Phi Delta Kappan, 64*(8), 560–563.

Glazer, N. (1981a). Ethnicity and education: Some hard questions. *Phi Delta Kappan, 62*(5), 386–389.

Glazer, N. (1981b). Pluralism and the new immigrants. *Society,* pp. 31–36.

Grant, C. A. (1988). The persistent significance of race in schooling. *The Elementary School Journal, 88*(5), 561–569.

King, E. W., Chipman, M., & Cruz-Janzen, M. (1994). *Educating young children in a diverse society.* Boston: Allyn & Bacon.

Larrick, N. (1965, September 11). The all-white world of children's books. *Saturday Review,* pp. 63–65, 84, 85.

Locke, J. (1910). Some thoughts concerning education. In C. W. Eliot (Ed.), *English Philosophers. Harvard Classics, Vol. 37.* New York: Viller.

Mead, M. (1970). *Culture and commitment.* Garden City, NY: Doubleday.

Morrow, L. M. (1984). Effects of story retelling on young children's comprehension and sense of story structure. In *Thirty-Third Yearbook of the National Reading Conference* (95–100). Rochester, NY: National Reading Conference.

Pelkowski, A. (1984). *The story vine.* New York: Macmillan Publishing Company.

Ramirez, G. Jr., & Ramirez, J. L. (1994). *Multiethnic children's literature.* Albany, NY: Delmar.

Ramsey, P. (1987). *Teaching and learning in a diverse world.* New York: Teacher's College Press.

Ramsey, P. G., Vold, E. B., & Williams, L. R. (1989). *Multicultural education: A source book.* New York: Garland.

Rudman, M. K. (1995). *Children's literature: An issues approach.* White Plains, NY: Longman.

Sims, R. (1983). What has happened to the "all-white" world of children's books? *Phi Delta Kappan, 64*(9), 650–653.

Stanford Program on International and Cross-Cultural Educating (SPICE)/The China Project. (1988). *Demystifying the Chinese language.* Stanford, CA: Stanford University.

Wells, G. (1986). *The meaning makers.* Portsmouth, NH: Heinemann.

Zangwill, I. (1975). *The melting pot.* North Strafford, NH: Ayer.

CHAPTER 3

Tell me a story, sing me a song. Let me see myself in books, in print, in real life.

Children's Literature:
A Genre of Its Own

▊ Picture books
▊ Traditional literature
▊ Poetry
▊ Modern fantasy
▊ Contemporary realistic fiction
▊ Historical fiction
▊ Nonfiction, informational books
▊ Alternative media

❖ What Do We Mean When We Say That Children's Literature May Be a Genre of Its Own?

Before we attempt to define children's literature as a genre of its own, it is important first to define *genre* itself. When reading specialists, educators, librarians, and writers look at books in print, they tend to categorize them according to particular characteristics and styles. These categories in regard to literature are termed *genres*. Sometimes these genres are considered story patterns by readers and authors (Nodelman, 1992).

Perry Nodelman, in *The Pleasures of Children's Literature* (1992), states that children's literature has its own unique pattern and therefore can be considered a genre of its own. He identifies the following common traits of works for children:

1. Children's literature contains simple and straightforward language that is directed toward children and their needs and interests.
2. Children's literature contains much action within the stories.
3. Children's literature is intended for a childhood audience and embodies youthful themes and ideas. Often these themes relate to current issues that trouble both youth and adults and help explain situations and alternative solutions to problems.
4. Children's literature appears to be seen through the eyes of children and expresses their points of view.
5. Children's literature is hopeful and optimistic in its approach.
6. Children's literature often uses fantasy and imaginative themes to explain reality.
7. Children's literature expresses innocence as it views the world and circumstances around it.
8. Children's literature may be used to teach children about the world of adults.
9. Children's literature reflects a closeness to nature, friends, and rural life—such as in a pastoral idyll.
10. Children's literature uses repetition and predictability to tell its stories.
11. Children's literature can effectively combine the best from what is a teaching tool and what is idyllic (happiness and joyfulness). (Nodelman, 1992, pp. 79–88)

With these common characteristics in mind, one can easily see why children's literature can be viewed as a genre. The rest of this chapter will look at the more common categories of literature, define them as genres, explain their characteristics and purposes, and provide examples of children's literature that fit the genres. In all cases, the works cited as examples will be ones that are multicultural because it is very important in this text not to separate multicultural books as a solitary genre. Instead, there are overarching themes or standards that have guided the selections of genre examples.

❖ What Are Multicultural Picture Books?

Picture books are books for children that use both illustrations and words to tell their stories. Sometimes the pictures, drawings, photographs, renditions, or prints are more prominent than the words themselves. The author and illustrator work together (in some cases, they are one and the same person) to identify both the literary elements and the artistic elements (see chapter 5). Together they make it possible for the very young child and the adolescent to identify with the story through imaginative pictures and visual cues.

Picture books that embody multicultural themes feature children, people, places, events, and circumstances that reflect cultural diversity. They lend themselves to personal awareness and self-esteem building. They use accurate yet imaginative pictures that reflect diverse people and their worlds.

Alphabet Books

An *alphabet book* is a didactic book that teaches children the letters of the alphabet with pictures and letters. There are several books for children, both very young and older, that introduce and reinforce the alphabet, using diversity as the theme. Leo and Diane Dillon illustrated Margaret Musgrove's *Ashanti to Zulu: African Traditions* (1976). The book includes detailed color pictures of the life of twenty-six different African peoples. In keeping with the African theme, the Swahili alphabet is shared in *Jambo Means Hello: Swahili Alphabet Book* by Muriel Feelings (1985).

Learning others' cultures through the alphabet is made possible by Ruth Brown's *Alphabet Times Four: An International ABC* (1991) and Anita Lobel's *Away from Home* (1994). Brown's artistic rendition of the alphabet focuses on the English, Spanish, French, German languages; Lobel takes children around the world alphabetically through their names and the names of places that they visit. In our own country, children learn about the Louisiana Cajuns with James Rice in *Cajun Alphabet* (1991), featuring an alligator named Gaston. Native American culture is taught through the alphabet in R. Red Hawk's *ABC's The American Indian Way* (1988). *Hieroglyphs from A to Z* by Peter Der Manuelian (1993) is an interactive book that introduces the ancient Egyptian communication system to youngsters. It is rhyming and patterned so that students will find it easy and enjoyable to recreate their own hieroglyphics.

Shape Books

A *shape book* or *toy book* is one that is manipulative and allows very young children to interact in some fashion with the book itself. With toy books the child interacts by moving objects, pieces, figures, tabs, characters, puppets, and the like. A shape book usually is cut in the shape of the object or subject that is portrayed. Other durable books for the very young are called board books because they are made of heavy-duty cardboard and covered with washable material that can be handled easily by toddlers. Fiona Pragoff's *Baby Days* (1995), *Baby Plays* (1995), *Baby Says*

(1995), and *Baby Ways* (1995), are a unique series of board books designed to show babies of diverse cultures engaged in real activity, simply presented but beautifully photographed. Jan Pienkowski helps babies to identify with their surroundings and become more accepting of themselves as they play with the cloth interactive books entitled *Bronto's Brunch* (1994) and *Good Night, Moo!* (1995). Amy Schwartz and illustrator Henry Schwartz use a mirror and cutouts of children's faces showing various emotions in *Make a Face: A Book with a Mirror* (1994). All of these books are designed to help children of all cultural groups become more acquainted with themselves and one another.

Concept Books

Concept books are picture books that are instructional. They tend to teach things like shapes, textures, sounds, time, and various other "how to's." Alphabet books and *counting books* are considered concept books. As an alphabet book exposes children to the alphabet through pictures and words, *counting books* do the same in regard to numbers, numerals, and objects. *One Sun Rises: An African Wildlife Counting Book* by Wendy Hartmann (1994), illustrated by Nicolaas Maritz, provides a visit to the African continent through the animals that are counted and then described in detail at the end of the text. For children who are not feeling well and are in need of humor, Christine Loomis offers *One Cow Coughs: A Counting Book for the Sick and Miserable* (1994). The simple message and the comical pictures are sure to cheer any child or adult. Focusing on the Swahili number words is Feelings' book entitled *Moja Means One: Swahili Counting Book* (1994). Familiarizing readers with the land down under of Australia is the goal of *One Woolly Wombat* by Kerry Argent, (1987), which introduces Australian animals, numbers, and rhyme in a single picture book.

One of the finest authors of concept books is Tana Hoban. Photographs of everyday objects help children to learn more about themselves, their environments, and their families in such books as *Circles, Triangles, and Squares* (1974); *Under, Over, and Through* (1987); *Of Colors and Things* (1989); and *All about Where* (1991). Emberley (1989) takes children into an urban area to learn sounds in *City Sounds*. These concept books help inner-city children become more comfortable with their own settings and let children from suburban and rural environments view this country from a very different perspective.

Wordless Books

Wordless books are those whose stories are told through pictures alone. Children can make up their own stories for these books. Some are renditions of old tales and are easy to tell; others require the imagination of the reader or viewer. These books allow for much student interaction and are meant to prompt creative, independent, open-ended endeavors on the part of teacher and students.

One wordless book that deals with friendship is Eric Carle's *Do You Want to Be My Friend?* (1987). Family structure and the appearance of a new sibling are depicted in *Changes, Changes* by Pat Hutchins (1987). *Sing, Pierrot, Sing* by Tomie de Paola (1987) features a mime who realizes the importance of friendship with young children when he fails in his love for Columbine. With each of these books, children can create their own language to make the stories work, and teachers can encourage them to write and express themselves freely in the telling of the tales.

Nursery Rhymes

The very popular *Mother Goose rhymes* and *nursery rhymes* as we remember them are purveyed in picture books. These books are generally collections of traditional rhymes that children and adults can easily recall and recite. They are useful to teachers in that they begin to develop language and vocabulary in early readers. Because their stories are short and retellable, they are of high interest to young children.

Marguerite DeAngeli's *Book of Nursery and Mother Goose Rhymes* (1954) is an appropriate book for educators to use in classrooms, but Griego, Bucks, Gilbert, and Kimball offer a multiculticultural point of view with Spanish nursery rhymes in both Spanish and English in *Tortillitas Para Mama: And Other Nursery Rhymes*, Spanish and English (1988). Asian rhymes are found in Demi's *Dragon Kites and Dragonflies,* (1986), about the Chinese and Wyndham's *Chinese Mother Goose Rhymes* (1989), illustrated by Ed Young and featuring authentic Chinese calligraphy in a vertical column on each page.

Picture Storybooks

Thousands of books fall within the *picture storybook* category. These are books that utilize quality pictures to enhance the story line, with author and illustrator taking care to include the literary elements of character, setting, plot, theme, style, and point of view. The illustrations contribute to the development of each element.

Some picture storybooks are also *predictable stories,* meaning that the story progresses using certain language that is predictable and repetitive, easy for young children to follow and remember. It has a definite rhythm, and it moves the literary elements through the story with very particular language and illustration. One such book is *Here Comes the Cat!* by Frank Asch and Vladimir Vagin (1991). Using both Russian and English languages, the reader follows pictures of mice preparing for a visit by the cat. After the second page, children of all ages will be saying "Here comes the cat!" with enthusiasm.

Picture storybooks may follow themes and issues. Ageism and the family are themes in the well-illustrated books *Song and Dance Man* by Karen Ackerman (1988) and *Wilfred Gordon McDonald Partridge* by Mem Fox (1989). Both stories give children the opportunity to understand better an older generation and its contributions to their lives by seeing vibrantly colored pictures of elderly people. Treating the theme of ageism is *Nana Upstairs & Nana Downstairs* by Tomie de Paola (1978), which also addresses the issue of a loved one's death as a very young boy (and later a young adult) copes with the loss of a grandparent.

Animals, fish, and insects often are the main characters in picture books. Leo Lionni's *Swimmy* (1987) shows the importance of cooperation and creative problem solving. The illustrations are crucial to the story as they show the reader how important cooperation can be for survival. Sometimes things are not clear to us, and the story *Seven Blind Mice* by Ed Young (1992) helps children see and understand that "knowing in part may make a fine tale, but wisdom comes from seeing the whole" (p. 36). (There is some controversy about this picture book; further discussion can be found in chapter 5 of this text.) Other illustrations by Ed Young in *I Wish I Were a Butterfly* by James Howe (1987) convey the idea that it is all right to be dissatisfied with oneself but that if one confides in friends about those feelings, they will give reassurance. The book uses large drawings in bold splashes of color to portray the insects and other creatures encountered by a cricket.

Some picturebooks depict specific ethnic groups, communities, or countries. The Latino population is seen in *Hill of Fire* by Thomas P. Lewis (1987). The effects of a volcano on the Mexican people is depicted factually in this story of Pablo and his family. The simple text is coupled with pen-and-ink drawings with an addition of a sierra color that brings out the characters in the story. A current piece of literature is Soto's *Too Many Tamales* (1993). Readers follow the expressions of worry, fear, and relief in the faces of children who must find a missing ring in twenty-four tamales.

The Egyptian culture is represented in *The Day of Ahmed's Secret* (1995), written by Heide and Gilliland and illustrated by Lewin. Ahmed carries a secret around with him as he travels through the city doing work for his family. Watercolor scenery rich with details of people, their habits, and their lives assist children in understanding that Ahmed's pride is much like their own. *Tigress* by Helen Cowcher (1993) is another boldly illustrated story of the animals of Asian lands. The eye on the book's cover captures the attention of the reader and becomes the focal point for the entire story.

Coping with changes and cultural assimilation are the themes of *The Bracelet*, written by Uchida and illustrated by Yardley (1993). When two young girls, one Japanese and the other American, separate, the American gives a bracelet to her friend. During the sorrowful journey to an internment camp, Emi loses the bracelet. With the guidance of her

FIGURE 3–1 Cover illustration by Joanna Yardley

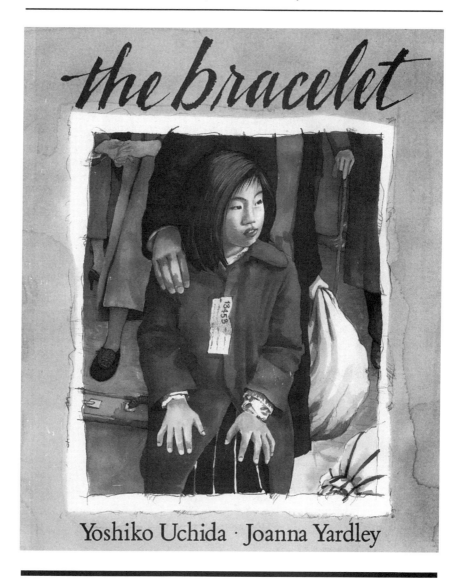

mother, she comes to realize that friendships and memories stay in the heart and do not need to be left with tangibles for endurance. The watercolor pictures show the pain in the faces of the Japanese, and the reader steps back in time with the aid of the illustrations. Yashima's *Crow Boy* (1955) is a very old book that expresses the isolation of a new, shy child in a Japanese school. Students will easily identify with Chibi's feelings as they look at the many pictures of the other children and the school setting. Children can compare and contrast what they see in the book with what they commonly see in their own schools. Ina Friedman's narrative and Allen Say's drawings explain the difficulty of adapting to another culture's eating habits in *How My Parents Learned to Eat* (1984). Pictures on alternate pages tell the story as an American sailor and a Japanese schoolgirl meet, fall in love, marry, and share each other's customs. Allen Say has written and illustrated two other beautiful Japanese stories entitled *Tree of Cranes* (1991) and *Grandfather's Journey* (1993). The extra large and very poignant watercolors make the stories come alive. Say's tremendous warmth and love for his art come through in both the illustrations and the rich language. Vietnamese life and struggle are portrayed in the picture tale called *The Lotus Seed* by Sherry Garland (1993). The last remnant of a young girl's Vietnamese culture is the treasured lotus seed taken from her homeland by her grandmother. Terror and hope are evoked in oil paintings by Tatsuro Kiuchi.

Many picture storybooks are inspired by African-American culture. James Ransome illustrated Mitchell's *Uncle Jed's Barbershop* (1993). Children of all cultures can identify with the extended family caring that is so apparent in this story. The oil and acrylic paintings make the characters come alive. The classic story of Ezra Jack Keat's *The Snowy Day* (1976) features Peter and his fun in the snow. Shapes and shadows carry the reader through the winter wonderland, and even the very young can readily retell this story by referring to the pictures. The history of slavery is retold in Faith Ringgold's *Aunt Harriet's Underground in the Sky* (1993). Great movement and use of line and color drive the reader through the book and across each page. Another aunt is the main character in *Aunt Flossie's Hats (and Crab Cakes Later)* by Elizabeth Fitzgerald Howard (1991), another book illustrated by James Ransome. The oil paintings depict the lives of an extended family and the joy they have in sharing. The reader can nearly feel the texture of the cotton fibers in Carole Byard's illustrations in *Working Cotton* by Sherley Anne Williams (1992). The acrylic paintings on Stonehenge-white paper enhance the African-American dialect of the young slave girl who tells her story. Some of the pictures are nearly life-size, and the artist virtually challenges the reader to reach out and "feel" the characters on the page.

Vera B. Williams, in *Cherry and Cherry Pits* (1986), remembers the pictures her father saved and the stories he told. Watercolors and marker dots fill pages with the lives of African-American children, families, and friends in the city. A similar setting is that of *Not So Fast, Songololo* by Niki Daly (1987), another tale that reinforces the richness of child-grandparent relationships. If features a young boy's adventure with his granny, Gogo, on a shopping spree. Shadows and line movement on the page entertain the reader in Mildred Pitts Walter's *Ty's One-Man Band* (1987), illustrated by Margot Tomes. Bored and alone, Ty meets a traveler who plays a spoon and dances with a peg leg. Enjoying the talents the man has been given, Ty shares them with his friends. This book is a favorite for children as the author uses combinations of letters to convey the sounds of rhythm and dance.

Patricia Polacco is a well-known author and illustrator who often combines cultures in her picture books. *Chicken Sunday* (1992) and *Mrs. Katz and Tush* (1994) are excellent examples. In *Chicken Sunday,* children of all ethnic groups learn how to make pysanky, Ukranian eggs, and share their Baptist beliefs with a Russian merchant. In *Mrs. Katz and Tush,* celebrating the Passover seder with a Polish immigrant marks the beginning of a close relationship between Larnel, a black boy, and Mrs. Katz. As in all of Polacco's stories, the dialogue and story line are enhanced by the exquisite pictures that somehow manage to detail every hair on each character's head and yet are not so overwhelming as to distract the reader from the story but instead just whet the appetite for more.

Another picture storybook relating to ethnicity is *Sacajawea: The Journey West.* This Native American history by Raphael and Bolognese (1994) is presented uniquely as readers are encouraged to "draw" their own characters toward the end of the book. Patterns and instructions are included for those who aspire to be future illustrators.

Pieces of culture are often passed on from generation to generation through material and story—rags and quilts. Significant pieces of the lives of children from different backgrounds are the focus in two picture storybooks entitled *The Quilt Story* by Tony Johnston and Tomie de Paola (1992) and *The Rag Coat* by Lauren Mills (1991). The pioneer days are seen in de Paola's rounded and warm country illustrations. Soft watercolor sensations are evoked by Mills's drawings as readers learn about life in the Appalachian mountains.

Finally, Jane Cowen-Fletcher expands on the theme of this text as she explains that *It Takes a Village* (1994) to raise a child. Set in the African country of Benin, the story follows the adventures of a young girl and her toddler brother who slips from her care in the village. The colors of the vendors and the earth make the story believable and enchanting.

Surely it is easy to see the purposes and value of picture books. As teachers select these books for their classrooms, they are challenged to ask themselves if they can identify these purposes:

❚ A sharing of story through oral reading of simple language, often repetitive and predictable
❚ An effective blending of illustration and written text to aid the visual learner as well as the auditory learner
❚ An honest depiction of various cultures, groups of people, and characters

■ Presentation of simple, yet rich language in interesting ways
■ Modeling of both writing and illustration that children may explore on their own for retelling or self-expression

The books mentioned are but a few of the hundreds that fulfill these purposes. The goal throughout this text is to share as many different children's books that are multicultural as possible. Certainly not all that meet these criteria have been cited, nor have they been purposely ignored.

❖ What Is Traditional Literature That Is Multicultural?

Traditional literature encompasses the stories for children that have been passed on from generation to generation as explanations of the phenomena of nature and spirituality. These are the fairy tales, folktales, and legends that early on were shared orally by storytellers with people young and old and then became more easily shared with children in the written storybook form that we know. Originally, these stories sought to answer the following questions:

■ Who are we?
■ Why are we here?
■ How did we get to be here?
■ How do we continue to exist?
■ How are the mysteries of nature, creatures, and the environment to be understood?

Now, as diverse cultural groups endeavor to discover their own identities and people try to acknowledge, understand, and accept cultural differences and similarities, these traditional tales have become the basis of global knowledge and growth. It is very important that teachers who wish to use children's books that are multicultural in their classrooms become very familiar with the traditional literature of the various cultural groups before exploring other genres. The traditional tales that reflect the basis of cultural development and the extension of a culture through its people are the starting point for any program that deals with cultural diversity. When teachers explore the ancient stories and retellings, they can be more critical when evaluating the authenticity of more current genres.

Within traditional stories, many common characteristics can be noted. The literary elements of character, setting, theme, style, and plot are evident, but the emphasis on these areas is significant in traditional literature.

Characters are generally one-dimensional—usually recognized as "good" or "evil." Settings are not definitive because most tales begin with familiar phrases such as "once upon a time" or "in a faraway land a very long time ago." The most common themes show the struggle of good versus evil or the main character's journey or quest. The good characters are often the princess, the prince, and the small and helpless children. The evil ones are the witch, the giant, and the wicked old woman.

The style of traditional stories is characterized by patterns and predictability. Readers will notice objects, people, and action in sets of three, five, and seven—for example, three wishes, three brothers, three sisters, five brothers, and three bears. Repetitive verses and chants embellish the text. Witches chant and ask, "Who is the fairest one of all?" while bears repeat, "Who's been sleeping in *my* bed?" Prevalence of magic and potions may also be seen as part of the style as magicians, fairies, spirits, gods and goddesses, and other creatures help the main characters overcome obstacles and vanquish evil.

The action of the story features the main character dealing with a specific problem and, more than likely, an evil being. Through many trials and some type of confrontation, resolution is attained, and there is a happy ending to the story. However, the plot may include violence and gruesome episodes, such as the swallowing of children and the killing of mean, evil characters. Often the stories conclude on the ever-popular refrain, "And they lived happily ever after."

This chapter will survey many categories within traditional literature: folklore and folktales, fables, myths, legends and tall tales, and retellings. As each category is explained in brief terms, there will be mention of some good children's books that are multicultural that exemplify the category.

Folklore and Folktales

Folklore has been defined by Judith Hillman (1995) as "the traditional beliefs, legends, customs, etc., of a community or a society" (p. 258). Under the umbrella of this definition, then, are the traditional stories as teachers and children recognize them. *Folktales* are the stories shared through oral narrative. Lynch-Brown and Tomlinson (1996) remind us that folktales have always been the favorites of children and that regardless of the culture portrayed or represented, they are universal—they are very similar in style, structure, story line, and outcome.

Whereas American children are familiar with the tale of Cinderella, *Yeh-Shen* (1990) is a Chinese version of the same tale retold by Ai-Ling Louie and illustrated by Ed Young. Framed panels of muted-color pictures carry the reader through the story of an orphan girl who is guided by an old man and the spirit of the bones of fish eventually to leave her stepmother and become the bride of the king. *Ma Ling and His Magic Brush*, a Chinese tale adapted by Han Xing (1985), is shared with youngsters in a cartoon style that resembles Walt Disney illustrations. Vivid cartoon designs catch the attention of readers who meet a devil that changes form, a dragon king, and a tiny boy born in a lotus bud. Catherine Edwards Sadler (1985) has accumulated a collection of fairy tales from China in her book entitled *Heaven's Reward*. The stories are very old, the title story dating from the days of Confucius. Contrasting with this story are the Taoist tales of Pu Sung-Ling, in which the reader hears of the desire for inner peace expressed by the people. Other more modern fairy tales like "The Greedy Brother" are included. Ed Young continues to share colored-pencil drawings in the Chinese tale *White Wave* by Diane Wolkstein (1979). Another Taoist tale, it features magic and hope. *The Weaving of a Dream* by Marilee Heyer (1989) has all the common elements of traditional folktales—good versus evil, three sons/brothers, fairies, and an old crone. The repetitive or cumulative story is brought to full life through exquisite illustrations that include great detail and use bold Chinese reds and golds. Woodcuts appear on each page as well. An appreciation of the Chinese language and its written characters is fostered by the stories in *The Chinese Word for Horse and Other Stories* by John Lewis (1980). Children can explore the stories behind the written characters and can easily duplicate them after following the text.

Like the Chinese, the Japanese have many popular folktales. In *Journey to the Bright Kingdom*, Elizabeth Winthrop (1979) shares the story of a blind woman and her relationship with a kingdom of mice who help her to "see" her daughter and the world around her through her fingers and her determination. It is a touching tale that involves trust, love, and special needs. Morimoto's *The Inch Boy* (1988) is a humorous tale of a very little boy who, through bravery in overcoming the Red Demon, becomes General Horikawa, a Samurai warrior. The illustrations use great texture and line with extremes, showing direction and definition. A more current version of the same tale, retold by Ralph McCarthy and illustrated by Shiro Kasamatsu, is *The Inch-High Samurai* (1993). This tale and two others are available in a three-book set. The accompanying folktales are *The Moon Princess*, illustrated by Kancho Oda (1993), which is about the discovery of a beautiful female child and her growth into womanhood, and *Grandfather Cherry Blossom* (1993), which deals with the results of good and bad deeds. Illustrations by Leo and Diane Dillon in Katherine Paterson's *The Tale of the Mandarin Ducks* (1990) utilize vertical and horizontal lines in the fashion of Japanese woodcuts. In this predictable tale, poor beasts or woodland creatures take on human form to return kindnesses shown them. Receiving a Caldecott Honor Award was *The Boy of the Three-Year Nap*, retold by Dianne Snyder (1988), illustrated by Allen Say. The framed fine brush drawings depict the story of a lazy poor boy who wants to gain a fortune in the simplest fashion. I. G. Edmonds (1994) collected seventeen Japanese folktales with a favorite character, the legendary judge Ooka Tadasuke, for whom the book *Ooka the Wise: Tales of Old Japan* was named. Each tale includes a problem that the main character(s) must solve and reaches resolution in the end.

FIGURE 3–2 *The Tale of the Mandarin Ducks* student artwork by Michael Figurski, age 13

African cultures have many folktales that explain their beliefs and feelings about the world. *Bringing the Rain to Kapiti Plain* by Verna Aardema (1981) is cumulative, repetitive, and rhythmic as it explains the Kenyan story of how Ki-pat causes the rain to fall. It is best read aloud, with students eventually encouraged to join in. A story that uses talking animals and humor to compare and contrast two individuals seeking the favor of Miss Louise is *Anancy and Mr. Dry Bones* by Fiona French (1991). Black and white figures and scenes playing with rainbows of color enhance the story. Using human dialect and talking animals, Patricia C. McKissack tells the story her grandfather used to tell her in *Flossie & the Fox* (1986). Greed and its effect on people driven by it are the theme of *Mufaro's Beautiful Daughters* by John Steptoe (1987). The message of serving even the most lowly creatures is conveyed through the language and the realistic illustrations of this Caldecott Honor Award–winning story. Lloyd Alexander, well known for his fantasies, wrote the tale *The Fortune Tellers* (1992), set in Cameroon. The magic of the people and the humor of the culture are evident in the tale's brightly garbed characters.

FIGURE 3–3 *The Fortune Teller* student artwork by Michael Figurski, age 13

Mayan peoples are the subject of *Rain Player* (1991), written and illustrated by David Wisniewski with a unique use of paper cuttings. These cuttings nearly jump off the page as their shadows and images are so strong in texture. *The Boy Who Could Do Anything and Other Mexican Folktales* by Anita Brenner (1992) is a collection of twenty-six stories that explain the phenomena of life of the pre-Columbian Indian culture.

Sometimes folktales explain why and how things occur in nature. Some examples are collected in *How Many Spots Does a Leopard Have and Other Tales* by Julius Lester (1994). These tales are *pourquoi* tales, from the French word meaning "why." Animals, brothers, princesses, magic, and courage are prominent in this collection of African and Jewish folktales. Phoebe Gilman adapted a Jewish folktale to write *Something from Nothing* (1993). This cumulative tale that follows the fate of a handcrafted blanket is funny yet thought provoking for the young reader. It is also a great story to share aloud.

Three folktales that deal with Christmas are *Star Mother's Youngest Child* by Louise Moeri (1980), *Baboushka and the Three Kings* by Ruth Robbins (1960), and *The Fir Tree* by Hans Christian Andersen (1990). Compassion, love, and understanding are common elements in these renditions of stories from European traditions. *Baboushka and the Three Kings* won the Caldecott Medal for Nicolas Sidjakov's illustrations using basic shapes and lines to depict the relationship of an old Russian woman with the Three Kings in the Christmas story. Another relationship, is the one between an ugly child and an unhappy old woman who both want to celebrate Christmas and do so together in *Star Mother's Youngest Child*, illustrated by Trina Hyman. Andersen's classic about the tree that wanted more in life offers the message, "Watch what you ask for, because you just might get it."

For very authentic Russian stories, the collections of Aleksandr Afanasev feature *Russian Fairy Tales* (1976) that are sometimes very gruesome and violent. Popular tales such as "Baba Yaga" and "The Turnip" are included in this book. Jan Brett takes the reader to the Ukraine in the folktale entitled *The Mitten* (1990), where all the animals in the woods find Nicki's lost mitten and snuggle into it to stay warm until. . . . Brett's illustrations draw the reader's attention to the eyes of each animal as well as to Nicki and the folk-art framing on each page.

The Glass Mountain: Twenty-Six Ancient Polish Folktales and Fables by W. S. Kuniczak (1992) is the author's way of sharing the many stories he heard from his nurse when he was a child. He states that "the purpose is to stir the imagination and arouse curiosity about this enchanted and enchanting world of simple moral lessons, broad wit, sly allegory, and an abiding faith in the betterment of our lot" (p. 9). Readers visit the mossy hills of Scotland in Sorche NicLeodhas's *Always Room for One More* (1965), where they meet the man who continues to invite people into his home even though he has a houseful of ten already. Uri Shulevitz, in *The Treasure* (1978), a tale of a very poor man who travels, shares the message that "sometimes one must travel far to discover what is near" (p. 29). Another Russian folktale is the retold version of *The Snow Child* by Freya Littledale (1978). Generations together will appreciate the sadness of the old man and old woman who could not have children and the joy they experienced when they created a pretty child out of snow and she came alive before their eyes. Magic misused is the underlying theme of *The Sorcerer's Apprentice* (1993), written by Nancy Willard and illustrated by Leo and Diane Dillon. Based on the poem entitled "The Magician's Assistant" by Johann Wolfgang von Goethe, this tale exhibits a great of deal of innovation and imagination in both word and illustration.

Tales that feature talking animals and that involve honesty, exaggeration, and real-life situations include Beatrix Potter's *Tales of Peter Rabbit and His Friends* (1988) and *The Little Red Hen* (1985), by Patricia and Frederick McKissack with pictures by Dennis Hockerman. As children determine good decision-making options, both of these sources are appropriate for sharing.

To teach children about cooperation, compassion, and understanding, Margaret Read MacDonald collected thirty-four tales and proverbs related to peace in the world. The selections in *Peace Tales: World Folktales to Talk About* (1992) teach about conflict and its resolution in a childlike fashion acceptable to all.

Australian folklore is represented in *Rainbow Bird: An Aboriginal Folktale* (1993) by Eric Maddern. Bright yellow, orange, and green artwork helps the reader discover how the Crocodile Man kept fire to himself and did not share it with the other creatures in the land.

Native American folktales are many. Rafe Martin wrote and David Shannon illustrated the Algonquin Indian version of Cinderella in *The Rough-Face Girl* (1992). In this story, which takes place on the shores of Lake Ontario, we meet three sisters who desire to marry the Invisible Being. The touching words that describe the sister of the Invisible Being should be read aloud to children: "When she looked at you she would look you right in the eyes and she could see all the way down to your heart" (p. 20). *The Girl Who Loved Wild Horses* (1993), a Caldecott Medal winner by Paul Goble, recounts a young girl's longing to be free to become one of the wild horses that she cared for so very much and her release from her people to be with them. Goble incorporates Navaho and Sioux songs that speak of the love of horses, and his pictures draw the reader's eyes quickly from page to page through brilliant Native American color: reds, yellows, blacks, and oranges. Another folktale in which humans are changed to animals is *Antelope Woman: An Apache Folktale* (1992) by Michael Lacapa. In this tale a beautiful young woman follows a young man whose message of compassion for all things and people leads her to change into an antelope as he does. A revised edition of the *Cherokee Animal Tales* (Scheer, 1991) shows animals and humans on equal terms, even able to communicate in a common language. Jane

Louise Curry has developed a collection of twenty-two stories that explain the world's beginnings and its creatures in *Back in the Beforetime: Tales of the California Indians* (1987). The origin of fire is explained by Jonathan London and Lanny Pinola in *Fire Race: A Karuk Coyote Tale about How Fire Came to the People* (1993).

These tales of diverse cultures and peoples are just a small sampling of the many available for children as they connect to life's explanations and the stories of our pasts.

Fables

A *fable* can be defined as a short tale or story that features as the main characters animals acting like humans with their good traits and their bad ones. Ultimately, a fable leaves a moral or a passing thought that should be learned as the result of the actions of the characters. The most famous fables are those of the Greek teacher Aesop. His stories and morals have been retold by many authors and illustrators. One version is Charles Santore's *Aesop's Fables* (1988), in which twenty-six full-page watercolors bring the stories alive for the reader. The expressions on the animals' faces are dramatic and bold. In contrast, *Aesop & Company: With Scenes from His Legendary Life* (1991), prepared by Barbara Bader and illustrated by Arthur Geisert, is a retelling of nineteen fables with black-on-beige pen-and-ink drawings that are extremely intricate in cross-hatch design. This book includes an account of the origins of Aesop's storytelling and the transmission of the fables from generation to generation across continents and oceans. Arnold Lobel's *Fables* (1980) won the Caldecott Medal for the comical scenes of beasts dealing with life's dilemmas.

Once a Mouse . . . (1961) is a fable from ancient India by Marcia Brown. With illustrations cut in wood prints, the author tells the story of a hermit who rescues a mouse by turning him into ever larger and stronger creatures until he is a "proud and handsome" tiger. As a tiger, however, he forgets how he got to be so strong and who was responsible. When this happens, the hermit orders him back to being a lowly mouse. The moral is unspoken but is apparent as the hermit and the reader think about what it means to be big, small, powerful, and thankful.

Myths

Myths are generally stories that explain the origins of various peoples and that feature the gods, goddesses, and heroes of particular cultures. These stories connect with the spirituality of a culture, and they seek to explain how many of its beliefs and traditions originated.

The best-known myths are those of the Greeks and Romans. Mary Pope Osborne has retold *Favorite Greek Myths* (1989) with the help of illustrator Troy Howell. Her introduction states that "the ancient Greeks invented stories to help explain nature and to free them from their fears of the unknown." Vibrant, realistic paintings by Howell give this book a special character.

Legends and Tall Tales

Legends are a facet of folklore relating the life stories of famous people in a particular culture or land. Those life stories are often inspirational to those who read them. Usually the central characters are depicted as heros or heroines. When their feats are quite exaggerated, the legends become what we know as *tall tales*. *Epics* are poetic versions of stories that are long and full of adventure. When these stories are sung, they are known as *ballads*.

The paintings of Susan Jeffers accompany the epic legend of *Hiawatha* by Henry Wadsworth Longfellow (1983). Jeffers' introduction tells of her deep interest in the epic as a child and her longtime desire to illustrate it for readers. The child Hiawatha is portrayed as wide-eyed and curious, in a style typical of Jeffers' work.

Sleeping Bear: Its Lore, Legends, and First People by George Weeks (1991) is both an educational resource for teachers and a storybook for children about the Michigan Indians. Black-and-white sketches and photographs of landscapes and artifacts enhance this book.

A collection of Native American Legends published by Watermill Press includes the following titles by Terri Cohlene (1990): *Turquoise Boy: A Navajo Legend*; *Quillworker: A Cheyenne Legend*; *Little Firefly: An Algonquian Legend*; *Ka-ha-si and the Loon: An Eskimo Legend*; *Dancing Drum: A Cherokee Legend*; and *Clamshell Boy: A Makah Legend*. In each book, a wonderful story is first told through a traditional format with illustrations, then followed by photographs, maps, and a history of the particular Native American tribe or group. Artifacts, timelines, and glossaries of appropriate terms are included as well. These legends are very suitable introductory texts for elementary-level children becoming familiar with diverse cultures and their contributions to their world.

Tomie de Paola has retold and illustrated Native American legends in his renditions of *The Legend of the Indian Paintbrush* (1991) and *The Legend of the Bluebonnet* (1983). These stories explain the origins of wildflowers that the American people enjoy. De Paola's art captures the Native American way of life.

The Mohawk (Kanienkehaka) legend *Owl Eyes* by Frieda Gates (1994) describes the trouble that Raweno, the Master of All Spirits, has with the creature named Owl. Yoshi Miyake's framed illustrations on each page depict the People of the Flint and their maker's work in creating the animals of the forest. The nosy, interfering owl offers suggestions for the appearance of each creature, suggestions that Raweno tends to ignore. Finally Raweno determines the owl's own appearance in a very special way as the bird takes flight into the woodlands.

FIGURE 3–4 From *The Legend of the Bluebonnet*

"Great Spirits,
the land is dying. Your People are dying, too,"
the long line of dancers sang.
"Tell us what we have done to anger you.
End this drought. Save your People.
Tell us what we must do so you will send the rain
that will bring back life."

Copyright © 1983 by Tomie dePaola. Reprinted by permission of G.P. Putnam's Sons

Hispanic-American culture is represented in legendary form in Randall Reinstedt's *Tales and Treasures of California's Missions* (1992). The characters play an important part in this collection of stories, set in seven missions that are described with the Hispanic population in mind.

A Chinese legend that recalls the American tales of Paul Bunyan and John Henry is *Pie-Biter* by Ruthanne Lum McCunn (1983). You-shan Tang's illustrations take the reader through the physical changes experienced by a very skinny Chinese boy named Hoi, a worker on the American railroad. Hoi's love for American pies helps him develop into a very strong man who eventually joins up with a Spaniard named Louie to create a pack train. After years of this work and great success, Hoi is not yet satisfied and decides to return to China to establish his own family. It is said that his story is still told today. Tang's illustrations convey characterization and setting through bold brush strokes and detailed drawings.

Retellings

Retellings are present-day renditions of traditional folktales. Many of the stories previously mentioned are retellings. Though the stories are not original, the interest lies in the particular approaches of the retelling authors.

Anansi and the Moss-Covered Rock (1988), retold by Eric A. Kimmel with illustrations by Janet Stevens, is a comical African tale about the trickster spider Anansi and his discovery of a magic rock that knocks over all the creatures when they say a repetitive, predictable phrase. In the end, Anansi is himself tricked when the animals discover his techniques.

Ananse, better known as the "spider man" in African lands, has a very important role in *A Story, a Story*, retold by Gail E. Haley (1988). In the introduction to the tale, the author/illustrator explains that the name "Ananse" was the original name of the spider, evolving to "Anancy" in the Caribbean and "Aunt Nancy" in the American South.

The traditional tale of Cinderella and the Grimms' "Many Furs" are combined in the retelling of *Princess Furball* by Charlotte Huck (1994), with rounded, bright, and colorful drawings by Anita Lobel. A princess destined to marry an ogre runs away, carrying a walnut shell packed with her dresses, a gold ring, a gold thimble, a little gold spinning wheel, and her coat made of many animal furs. In the process of her escape, she meets the king of the woods into which she has vanished. Later, at a ball, the king becomes attracted to the princess and seeks her out. Through her wonderful cooking, the princess meets three times with the king but keeps her silence. In the end, the two come together and marry at last. This book is a perfect vehicle to discuss different renditions of the same or a similar tale.

Italy's favorite character, named *Strega Nona,* is the subject of the book by the same name. Tomie de Paola (1992) both wrote and illustrated this funny tale of a little old Italian woman who is generous and fair to her neighbors. With her magic touch, repetition, and chants, the main character Strega Nona is refreshing and comical. The reader learns about the value of honesty and the problem of greed.

FIGURE 3–5 *Strega Nona's Neighbor* student artwork by Michael Figurski, age 13

Traditional literature has long been the foundation of what we know as children's literature that is multicultural. It embodies the truths of the cultures it represents while capturing dreams of the future and explanations of the past. Following are the benefits and purposes of the presentation of traditional literature:

- Seeing and hearing how various cultures have explained natural phenomena
- Hearing the colorful language of old, typical stories that were part of the oral tradition
- Telling and retelling known tales to pass on from generation to generation
- Recognizing values and morals that have been shared through stories
- Viewing the commonalities of cultures and peoples as depicted and shared in story form
- Following predictable story lines that can serve as foundations or models for children's own sharing or writing
- Enjoying the humor, simplicity, brevity, and predictability of stories for children

Children's literature that is multicultural and traditional is rich, full of possibilities for learning (about values, morals, and understandings), and direct in approach. Its strength is its ability to be shared over and over, retold from generation to generation by different storytellers and new illustrators. Surely it is a form of lifelong learning extending beyond all expectations of the original writers and storytellers.

❖ What Is Poetry That Is Multicultural and Appropriate for Children?

Poetry is a rhythmic sharing of colorful language that expresses the feelings, beliefs, and/or thoughts of the poet. In the history of children's literature that is multicultural, the first stories passed on to children came from the oral storytellers of various cultures. These stories were often poetic or songlike. Like traditional tales, they reflected various peoples' explanations of life.

Each poetic writing includes certain elements:

- Rhythm—the beat within the poem itself
- Purpose—the reason for sharing words through poetry; the feelings, beliefs, and thoughts of the poet; the underlying theme
- Language that is colorful and figurative—the use of such figures of speech as simile, metaphor, personification, and hyperbole; reference to the senses through narrative and descriptive language

▌ Pattern—words, phrases, and groupings that create repetition or combination (These arrangements may be reflected in sound patterns (rhyme, assonance, alliteration, consonance, and onomatopoeia) and patterns of design.)

Literature in the poetic genre is found in anthologies, collections, and storybooks. There are narrative and lyrical poems. Other poems reflect specific forms or styles, such as haiku, cinquain, and concrete poetry. Some poems are humorous (e.g., limericks); some, as free verse, have their own unique features.

Collections

Each of these categories includes examples of multicultural poems written with children in mind. *All the Colors of the Race* is a collection of poems by Arnold Adoff (1982). (In a *collection,* the poems are related in some fashion, by theme or authorship.) Adoff, the husband of well-known author Virginia Hamilton, states that "writing a poem is making music with words and space. . . . A fine poem combines the elements of meaning, music, and a form like a living frame that holds it together" (p. 60). Adoff's collection received the NCTE Award for Poetry for Children; its expressive writing attempts to explain to children the combinations of color, religion, heritage, and family. *Nathaniel Talking* by Eloise Greenfield (1988) is another collection of African-American poetry. Strong pencil-and-ink sketches surround contemporary poems featuring the raps of a young African-American boy. *Pass It On: African-American Poetry for Children* was selected by Wade Hudson (1993) to depict the joys, sorrows, fears, worries, and courage of people from the African-American culture.

Families are the focus in *Fathers, Mothers, Sisters, Brothers: A Collection of Family Poems* by Mary Ann Hoberman, (1993). Although ethnicity is not the primary concern of this collection, various groups are represented, as are adopted family members, relatives, stepfamilies, and grandparents. The collection of humorous poems by Ruth Krauss entitled *I'll Be You and You Be Me* (1973) lends itself to building self-esteem through poetry. This book is a dated piece of work with early illustrations by Maurice Sendak, but the message of self-acceptance is timeless.

Other collections of poems related to particular ethnic groups are *In the Eyes of the Cat: Japanese Poetry for All Seasons* by Demi (1994) and *The Animals: Selected Poems* by Michio Mado (1992), which represent Asian-American culture; *Dancing Teepees: Poems of American Indian Youth* by Virginia Driving Hawk Sneve (1991) and *Rising Voices: Writings of Young Native Americans* by Hirschfelder and Singer (1992), about Native Americans; and *A Fire in My Hands: A Book of Poems* by Gary Soto (1992) and *Sing to the Sun* by Ashley Bryan (1992), which reflect Hispanic and Caribbean cultures.

FIGURE 3–6 Cover illustration from *Pass It On.*

Anthologies are collections as well, but they are not always limited as to authorship or theme. Instead the poems are grouped around ideas, themes, or poets within the book. A general anthology of multicultural poems is Naomi Nye's *This Same Sky: A Collection of Poems from around the World* (1992). Another is *And the Green Grass Grew All Around: Folk Poetry from Everyone,* collected by Alvin Schwartz (1992).

Teenager Amity Gaige used her own photographs to illustrate the ways she lives through poetry and sees the world in other's faces in her collection entitled *We Are a Thunderstorm* (1990). Gaige challenges readers to become more socially conscious and active in a rapidly changing world. This work won the 1989 National Written and Illustrated by. . . . Awards Contest for Students in the 14-to-19 age category.

Another poetry book that utilizes photography to show children, families, and friends is a collaborative effort of photography by Norma Jean Hiller and the poetry of Diane Christin Zenchenko Esser. *Look to the Light: A Celebration of Children and Friendship* (1995) was written to benefit the needs of special children, with the book's proceeds going toward the creation of an organization called Butterflies for Kids. The poems in this collection, which reflect the feelings of both writer and photographer, are appropriate for older students as well as for parents or caregivers who would like a timeless keepsake.

Relating to the humor of growing up and becoming more self-aware and accepting are two collections of poetry: Iona and Peter Opie's *I Saw Esau* (1992), with Maurice Sendak illustrations that children understand so well, and Jack Prelutsky's *Something Big Has Been Here* (1990), with drawings by James Stevenson. Children reading these fast-paced and humorous rhymes will identify with the fears and energy they express.

Directly related to repetitive storytelling, poetry, and rhyme are the songs and story-songs that have been written for sharing with young children. Many of these are also culturally diverse. *Follow the Drinking Gourd,* with story and pictures by Jeanette Winter (1988), concerns the secret network of the underground railroad through which slaves traveled to freedom. It features the song with the same title as the book's. *Lift Every Voice and Sing* by James Weldon Johnson (1993) highlights the song that is widely known as the African-American national anthem. The illustrations are bold linocut prints by Elizabeth Catlett.

Abiyoyo by Pete Seeger (1994) is his adaptation of an old South African folktale that he told and retold. The end of the story includes the song Abiyoyo, which consists of only that one word. Lulu Declare has selected songs and poems from the Latino culture in *Arroz Con Leche: Popular Songs and Rhymes from Latin America* (1989). Words, music, and colorful paintings show Latin American ways; footnotes and explanations describe the actions portrayed. Paul Fralick (1989) has created an

FIGURE 3–7 Cover illustration from *We Are a Thunderstorm.*

From the published book, *We Are a Thunderstorm.* Written and photographed by Amity Gaige. Copyright 1990 by Amity Gaige. Reproduced by special permission of Landmark Editions, Inc., Kansas City, Missouri.

activity book for teachers that utilizes a multicultural approach. Entitled *Make It Multicultural—Musical Activities for Early Childhood Education*, it establishes connections with children's books as it explains the need for music in early elementary settings.

The influence of more traditional American folklore as found in song cannot be overlooked. An excellent collection of American folk songs has been collected and arranged by Kathleen Krull in *Gonna Sing My Head Off!* (1992). Preceding each song is an explanation or history. Illustrations by Allen Garns add richness and understanding.

Poetry and song have been the impetus for cultural sharing with children for many generations. They are valuable in the elementary curriculum for many reasons:

- They provide vivid images through words that describe people and their ways of thinking, believing, and acting.
- They render short versions of cultural thought.
- They expose children to patterns in language and writing not found in other genres.
- They share visions of the past, present, and future of peoples and groups from many different backgrounds.
- They explain natural phenomena in an oral fashion.
- They are meant to be shared orally and expressively in rhythm, harmony, and cadence.

Poems and songs, like works of traditional literature, transcend time and space and are meant to be shared from generation to generation, with interpretations well into the future.

❖ How Are Fantasies Used to Promote Multiculturalism?

After having had the opportunity to experience stories that come from the tradition, the reader can progress to the discovery and exploration of fantasies. A *fantasy* is a story written to excite the imaginations of children. Fantasies include situations in which there is great exaggeration, themes of good versus evil, exploits and quests, characters of great courage portrayed in multidimensional fashion, and believable yet imaginative settings.

Fantasies can promote the standards of multiculturalism when the characters represent ethnic diversity and the courage to be self-aware, when the themes and quests relate to cultural adventures, and when the settings reflect concern for equity.

Jerry Spinelli's *Maniac Magee* (1990) could be considered a fantasy for young readers in that the character's physical abilities are quite exaggerated and not exactly probable. This story includes many references to

FIGURE 3–8 From *Look to the Light* (pp. 90–91) by N. J. Hiller and D. Esser, 1995, Erie, PA: Fireside Gallerie, Inc.

Our Children –

Don't forget to walk with them
Don't forget to talk with them
Don't forget to pray with them
Don't forget to play with them,
and, most of all –
Don't forget – to listen to them.

cultural differences and the struggle that young people face in regard to these differences.

Animal fantasies are those in which the animals have human characteristics in combination with the ordinary animal qualities—better known as *personification*. Many popular animal fantasies embody the characteristics of children's literature that is multicultural. One is E. B. White's *Charlotte's Web* (1974), in which friendship, loyalty, values, differences, and acceptance are addressed. Mem Fox's *Possum Magic* (1991) is a picture book that is an animal fantasy from the "land down under". The theme of friendship is prominent in this book as well.

Understanding the religious customs of others and the impact of the Holocaust on the present lives of Jewish people are the underlying themes of Jane Yolen's fantasy *The Devil's Arithmetic* (1990). This book is considered a time fantasy because the main character, Hannah, travels out of the contemporary era to the past life of Chaya, who lived during World War II in Poland.

Another book that deals with contemporary issues and fantasy is *Things in Corners* by Ruth Park (1993). Dealing with his desire to explore why his mother gave him up for adoption as well as coping with mononucleosis, Theo, the main character, confronts a crying figure who is the projection of his mother. The incidents in the story are so realistic that fantasy is often combined with reality.

Other fantasies that deal with culturally diverse groups are Virginia Hamilton's *Sweet Whispers, Brother Rush* (1982) and Mary James's *Shoebag* (1992). Another book, *The Indian in the Cupboard* by Banks (1985), is thought by some to portray a member of a minority group in a stereotypical fashion. It is this author's opinion, however, that although the character of the Native American is treated with language that is somewhat derogatory, the plot and action are well accepted and enjoyed by children. Moreover, it is appropriate for children to discover for themselves the problems of stereotyping.

Fantasies that have a multicultural basis are valuable to young readers for several reasons:

- They promote the use of imagination while exposing the reader to different cultures and peoples.
- They encourage children to become critical, evaluative thinkers.
- They utilize humor, exaggeration, and extremes to allow students to step out of reality and have fun in the reading process.
- They seek to expose children to ideas and themes that are difficult and controversial in a nonthreatening fashion.

The use of fantasies in the multicultural classroom is certainly appropriate after students have shared picture books, traditional literature, and poetry. This order is a natural progression from the known to unknown.

❖ What Is Contemporary Realistic Fiction?

Contemporary realistic fiction includes stories that take place in the time in which the child lives and that involve characters, actions, themes, and settings that appear to be real. These elements need not be literally real, but they must be portrayed as such. In other words, although the characters, setting, and plot may not correspond to actual people, places, and events, they could be found in real life.

In order for stories, both picture books and chapter books, to qualify as contemporary realistic fiction, they must meet the following criteria:

- Characters must be believable and current.
- Settings must appear real.
- Current issues, trends, problems, and conditions should be addressed.
- Actions should appear capable of being replicated by children and their families, friends, and acquaintances.
- Conflicts that are evident should be solved in natural ways in which young and old people cope with everyday or extraordinary situations.
- Animals and creatures act naturalistically and do not take on human characteristics.

When the category of contemporary realistic fiction is expanded to include children's books that are multicultural, other criteria are added:

- Characters from different cultures are depicted honestly and without stereotyping.
- Events and actions represent contributions from all types of people and groups.
- Controversial issues such as divorce, homelessness, death, mental illness, and abuse are often presented, but the book itself is not the cure-all or panacea for problems or situations; it instead becomes the vehicle for discussion and dialogue.

Many excellent books fit this latter category. Some are picture storybooks that deal with contemporary issues and problems. When these problems are introduced through children's literature, the practice is often referred to as "bibliotherapy." As children question their own values, self-worth, and social circumstances, books are an appropriate starting point for dialogue and subsequent action. Teachers should feel free to use some of these carefully selected books to initiate discussion about current issues in a very controlled, sensitive way. Again, educators should remember that although the themes selected by authors of contemporary realistic fiction are often chosen to raise controversial issues, the books themselves should not be interpreted as answers to the problems, nor should they supersede recommendations by teachers, family members, physicians, or school administrators concerning professional help for our children.

Sometimes children are faced with the fact that members of their families are too busy to listen to them. A book that deals with this theme is Martha Alexander's *Even That Moose Won't Listen to Me* (1991). Having observed a moose in the garden, Rebecca approaches many members of her family for help in removing it, but no one is really paying attention to her. Eventually, when the moose has eaten the garden, the family members seek out Rebecca, who is then too busy for them. The humor in this story is contagious and illustrates the importance of communication difficulties and needs even in the best of situations.

The theme of self-esteem emerges in the enjoyable picture book by ALIKI entitled *Feelings* (1986). Using simple illustrations that children will love, Aliki encourages youngsters to get in touch with their feelings of happiness, anger, illness, and boredom, to name a few.

Unconditional love that transcends the aging process is portrayed in the book *Love You Forever* by Robert Munsch (1986). Following the growth of a boy from babyhood to adulthood, children and parents will be able to identify with the caring and nurturing that accompany parenting and childhood. The line "I'll love you forever" reappears as part of a song, predictable and repetitive, encouraging children to participate when the story is read aloud.

The Inuit culture is represented in a similar story about a mother and her daughter in *Mama, Do You Love Me?* by Barbara M. Joosse (1991). Illustrations by Barbara Lavallee capture the heart of the Inuit people with shadowing and rounded forms. An extra feature is a glossary that describes animals mentioned in the story as they relate to the Inuit people.

An older book for young readers is *The Important Book* by Margaret Wise Brown (1949). Although the illustrations are somewhat dated, the message of self-acceptance is very clear. The relationship between the human condition and the importance of nature is drawn in a subtle, intriguing way.

Using one word per page, Chris Raschka, in *Yo! Yes?* (1993), shows how two boys of different backgrounds become instant friends. The close-up illustrations of the two characters allow the reader to see reluctance, fear, joy, and love in the faces of children who have feelings much like their own.

Often feelings are unpleasant ones. Dealing with the issue of death, authors Sanford, Mellonie, Ingpen, Buscaglia, and de Paola write about children's views of dying. Sanford addresses the anger and hurt felt by a child whose pet is killed in an accident in *It Must Hurt a Lot: A Child's Book about Death* (1985). Explaining the mysteries of the life, growth, and death of plants, birds, fish, animals, and people is Mellonie and Ingpen's *Lifetimes: The Beautiful Way to Explain Death to Children* (1983). In *The Fall of Freddie the Leaf* by Buscaglia (1982), children learn about the seasons and how life passes through to death. Told through the eyes of Freddie and his friend Daniel (both leaves), children and adults are offered a very sensitive presentation of life and death. In de Paola's *Nana Upstairs & Nana Downstairs* (1978), Tommy knew two special women in his life—his grandmother and his great-grandmother, the one called Nana Downstairs and the other Nana Upstairs. The great-grandmother was always found upstairs in bed. When this special lady died, Tommy had only one Nana. After many years passed and this Nana too died, Tommy came to regard both of his grandmothers as "Nana Upstairs."

Family structure is the theme of *Adoption is for Always* (1986) and *We Adopted You, Benjamin Koo* (1989) by Linda Walvoord Girard. Children who wonder what it means or how it feels to be brought into a family by choice will identify well with these books. Kathy Stinson (1984) and Christine Tangrald (1988), in their books both entitled *Mom and Dad Don't Live Together Any More,* explain that some children will deal with separation and divorce in their families.

The issues of homelessness and poverty receive powerful treatment in books written by Eve Bunting and illustrated by Ronald Himler. The young reader of *Fly Away Home* (1991), following a young boy and his father in a large city airport, will hear the boy's feelings as he expresses his anger and concern about being homeless and his desire to be free of the worry. Another Bunting and Himler book that deals with a controversial issue is *The Wall* (1990), which tells of a father and son who visit the Vietnam veterans' memorial to see the grandfather's name, the only way that the grandson can recall the grandfather he has never met. This is a very touching, sensitive story about a powerful place and people who are somewhat powerless.

Many novels, sometimes called "chapter books" by children, are classified as contemporary realistic fiction. Gary Paulsen has written a number of books based on his personal experiences and dealing with the conflicts and adventures of young men. Some of the most popular titles are *Hatchet,* (1988) *The River* (1993), *The Monument* (1992), and *The Haymeadow* (1992). *My Side of the Mountain* by Jean Craighead George (1991) resembles the survival story of Paulsen's *Hatchet* in that George's character Sam Gribley survives the adventures in the Catskill Mountains on his own.

Shiloh by Phyllis Reynolds Naylor (1991) deals with the abuse of an animal and its subsequent rescue by Marty Preston. Through this story set in the hills of West Virginia, the reader begins to identify with various types of people who live in the United States.

Patricia MacLachlan's *Journey* (1993) is the story of an 11-year-old boy who searches for the mother who abandoned him and his sister. This book leads readers to discover values, loyalty, differences in family structure, and love for one another.

Another book that deals with family loyalty in the context of African-American culture is *The Hundred Penny Box* by Sharon Bell Mathis (1986). Great-great-aunt Dew cherishes an old box that contains a penny for every one of her birthdays, with a story for every penny. Her nephew Michael becomes her best advocate and grows very attached to the pennies as well as to his aunt, finally inheriting her treasure as his own.

June Rae Wood tells a story based on her own brother's life as a person with Down's syndrome in *The Man Who Loved Clowns* (1992). Innocence and love prevail as the character of Punky Holloway is developed.

Asian culture is reflected in *Shizuko's Daughter* by Kyoko Mori (1993) and *Dragonwings* by Laurence Yep (1975). Mori's book relates the tragedy of suicide in a family as it concerns the rite of passage into adulthood of a teenage Japanese girl. *Dragonwings* deals with the movement from China to America of an 8-year-old boy and his newfound father. The story progresses with the development of each of the characters, in particular of Moon Shadow and his father.

Works of contemporary realistic fiction have specific value when they represent multiculturalism and are used in the elementary classroom:

- They serve as mirrors or windows, allowing children of various cultures to see themselves reflected or see into others' worlds; in either case, they help readers better understand the conditions and issues of daily life.
- They encourage discussion and dialogue about current issues that have social implications and that could be affected in some way by the contributions of young people today.
- They become vehicles for self-acceptance and self-awareness for members of all groups and cultures.
- They become models for the future writings of young people as they relate their own stories imaginatively.

After young people have read traditional literature and come to understand the backgrounds of their own and others' cultures, they can naturally identify, finally, with imaginative stories related to their own time. These stories become the most popular way for young people to identify their own needs, growth processes, and emotions as well as their peers'.

❖ What Is Multicultural Historical Fiction?

When multicultural children's literature is integrated within the regular elementary curriculum, the suggested progression is (1) to begin with a discovery of the original folklore of a particular culture or group, (2) to explore the nonfiction related to that culture (e.g., autobiographies, biographies, and historical nonfiction), (3) to read the historical fiction based on the nonfiction that preceded it, and finally, (4) to share the contemporary realistic fiction that is true to the culture and its members. This teaching progression is sequential in that it tests the authenticity of each genre as it is related to multiculturalism. Although this text does not necessarily present the genres in this sequence, it supports the theory suggested by such experts in children's literature as Donna E. Norton (1987).

Historical fiction conveys the history of a culture and its people in a way that is consistent with real characters and settings but introduces a new, imaginative story twist with fictitious characters and events. Like contemporary realistic fiction, historical fiction is also realistic, but it is based on settings and characters from the past rather than from current times.

The use of historical fiction in the classroom enriches young children's learning by

- giving them the opportunity to evaluate fiction with a historical perspective for its authenticity and relative accuracy,
- creating realistic characters of various ages with whom children of any era can identify, and
- providing a bridge between fictional stories from the past and from the present.

A beautiful picture storybook in the historical fiction genre is *Brother Eagle, Sister Sky: A Message from Chief Seattle* by Susan Jeffers (1991). The writer has adapted the words of one of the leaders of the northwest Indian nations in this powerful message of peace and preservation to the people of his nation and ultimately to our entire country. As usual, the characters are best known through their expressions, their vibrant eyes, and the intricate settings in which they are found.

Patricia MacLachlan's *Sarah, Plain and Tall* (1985) tells the story of a family in need of a mother and wife. When Sarah answers the family's newspaper ad by traveling from Maine to their prairie home, she surprises them with her warmth, adaptability, and ability to become a member of their existing family. The book deals with alternative family structures, love, and comparisons and contrasts of geographic areas.

Another story of a farm family, this one Georgina Caroline Lott's family of Ohio, is the *The Borning Room* by Paul Fleischman (1991). Memories of births, conflicts, historical events such as slavery and battles, inventions, and deaths were stored in this special room that changed the lives of young and old.

Works of historical fiction that deal with the plight of African-Americans in a developing country are *Toning the Sweep* by Angela Johnson (1993), the story of the lives of three generations of African-American women; *The Slave Dancer* by Paula Fox (1973), Jessie's story of growing up on a ship with young slaves for whom he played his fife as they danced for their survival; *Nettie's Trip South* by Ann Turner (1987), based on the diary of a young girl and relating the feelings of a white girl who has viewed a slave auction and become an abolitionist as a result; and *Pink and Say* by Patricia Polacco (1994), which deals with the relationship between young black and white men who faced the Civil War and its losses.

The lives of young people and their struggles to protect and provide for their families are portrayed in *Peppe the Lamplighter* by Elisa Bartone (1993), a story of a young boy who came to American from Italy and provided for his family by lighting the evening lamps on the streets of a big American city; *The Trumpeter of Krakow* by Eric P. Kelly (1956), which tells of Joseph Charnetski's role in the saving of the great Tarnov crystal in the royal castle in Krakow, Poland; and Lois Lowry's *Number the Stars* (1989), which reveals the trauma and horror of the Nazi invasion as seen through the eyes of Annemarie Johansen and Ellen Rosen in Copenhagen in 1943.

Sweetgrass by Jan Hudson (1984), a work of historical fiction based on Native American culture, very adequately includes the language of the times of the Blackfoot people. Other effective stories based on Native American history are *Sing Down the Moon* by O'Dell (1992), representing the Navaho, and *The Sign of the Beaver* by Speare (1993), depicting the Penobscot people.

Historical fiction with an Asian flavor includes Linda Crew's *Children of the River* (1991), the story of a young girl's flight from Cambodia and her adaptation to American life in Oregon, and Sook Nyul Choi's *Year of Impossible Goodbyes* (1991), which shows the courage of a 10-year-old girl in the midst of the 1945 invasions of Korea. Both stories exemplify the power of authenticity in fictional stories with a historical perspective.

Children's literature that is multicultural and that qualifies as historical fiction adds a further dimension to learning in the elementary classroom. Selections from this literature enable children to

- identify better with real characters in historical settings and situations,
- discover the authenticity of written works that reflect different cultures with historical perspectives, and
- compare these selections with nonfiction that treats similar situations and circumstances.

❖ What Nonfiction Selections That Lend a Multicultural Flavor Can Be Shared with Children?

Nonfiction writings include books and stories that tell the truth about people, the environments in which they live, and the circumstances in which

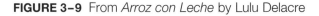

FIGURE 3–9 From *Arroz con Leche* by Lulu Delacre

Copyright © 1989 by Lulu Delacre. Reprinted by permission of Scholastic Inc.

they find themselves. Nonfiction commonly takes the form of biographies, informational texts, and reference books.

Nonfiction books that take a multicultural approach have great impact:

- They offer children models of individuals who are successful leaders of particular cultural groups.
- They tell children the truth about the history of ethnic, religious, and cultural heritage.
- They allow children to get in touch with their own true heritage.
- They become the basis for research and study of many peoples of the world.
- They reflect similarities and differences among people in regard to religion, language, education, customs, values, interests, food, and shelter.

Two picture books that are wonderful for introducing cultural pluralism to children are Peter Spier's *People* (1980) and *We Are All Alike . . . We Are All Different,* written and illustrated by the Cheltenham Elementary School Kindergartners (1991). Both books use drawings of faces of many different people to show young children and their teachers that although each of us is unique, we all desire the same things in life and often enjoy the same activities regardless of our origins, our lifestyles, or our environmental conditions.

Biographies narrate the lives of people and tell of their accomplishments, contributions, backgrounds, and relationships. There are many multicultural biographies. African-American biographies include *Sojourner Truth: Ain't I a Woman?* by Patricia C. and Fredrick McKissack (1992), the story of a slave named Isabella who, when freed, took the name Sojourner Truth; *Malcolm X: By Any Means Necessary* by Walter Dean Myers (1993), about the rebel who led youth gangs, served time in prison, and left a legacy of beliefs about his people to be followed for many generations; *Martin Luther King, Jr.* by Kathie Billingslea Smith (1987), the history of life and death contributions of the civil rights leader; *Nelson Mandela: "No Easy Walk to Freedom"* by Barry Denenberg (1991), about the South African crusader for black rights who spent twenty-six years in jail before being released to lead his people again in freedom; and *Daddy and Me: A Photo Story of Arthur Ashe and His Daughter Camera* (1993), written and photographed by Ashe's wife Jeanne Moutoussamy-Ashe and with the words of little Camera describing the effect of the AIDS virus on her father and her realization of his impending death. *Book of Black Heroes from A to Z* by Wade Hudson and Valerie Wilson Wesley (1988) offers one-page summaries of the lives of fifty significant African-Americans, ranging from Ira Aldridge, Duke Ellington, and Jesse Jackson to Jesse Owens and Bessie Smith. Peter Golenbock and Paul Bacon describe the unique friendship between Jackie Robinson and Pee Wee Reese in *Teammates* (1990), the story of the first black man to be a part of a major league. The words of men and women who endured the torture of slavery are heard in *To Be a Slave* by Julius Lester (1968).

Some Asian biographies take the form of picture books. Allen Say recounts the life of the first Chinese bullfighter, Bong Way "Billy" Wong. Say's watercolors capture the essence of the bull and the fight in *El Chino* (1990). *The Little Lama of Tibet* by Lois Raimondo (1994) is the true story of Ling Rinpoche, a 6-year-old Tibetan Buddhist monk, and his life in Dharamsala, India. The inside covers of the book display the Tibetan alphabet. Photographs portray the youth and tenacity of Ling.

Native Americans are also represented in biographies. Candice F. Ransom wrote *Between Two Worlds* (1994), based on the life story of Sarah Winnemucca, the daughter of a Paiute Indian chief, and her struggle to make peace with the white people. The life of Pocahontas is portrayed in

FIGURE 3–10 From *The Little Lama of Tibet* by Lois Raimondo

The Double Life of Pocahontas by Jean Fritz (1983) and *Pocahontas: Girl of Jamestown* by Kate Jassem (1979).

The adventures of the French man Louis Bleriot are presented in *The Glorious Flight* by Alice and Martin Provensen (1983). Bleriot's heroic flight across the English Channel in 1909 provides a model for children who want to strive for higher achievement and greater possibilities.

The contributions of many notable women are memorialized in biographies. *They Led the Way: 14 American Women* by Johanna Johnston (1973) includes the lives of Abigail Adams, Elizabeth Blackwell, and Nellie Bly, among others. The role of women in war is addressed in *A Separate Battle: Women and The Civil War* by Ina Chang (1991). This photobiographical essay also includes reproductions of some very old paintings of the Civil War and of women in battle zones. *Invincible Louisa* by Cornelia Meigs (1933) is a biography of Louisa May Alcott, the author of *Little Women. Helen Keller* by Margaret Davidson (1969) is the story of the woman who created awareness of and generated support for the handicaps of blindness and hearing loss. A picture storybook that narrates the life of a princess is *The Last Princess: The Story of Princess Ka'iulani of Hawaii* by Fay Stanley (1991). Diane Stanley's portraits enhance her mother's text, which describes the courage and disappointment of this princess.

The Holocaust is remembered in *A Place to Hide: True Stories of Holocaust Rescues* by Jayne Pettit (1993) and *The Big Lie: A True Story* by Isabella Leitner (1992). Like Leitner, who recalls her own experiences of captivity in a war-torn country, Zlata Filipovic shares her story of war and fear in *Zlata's Diary: A Child's Life in Sarajevo* (1994). Photos accompany Zlata's daily words and reflections. The story of the woman who in 1955 refused to sit in the back of a segregated bus and thus changed the direction of history is *Rosa Parks: My Story* as told by Rosa Parks to Jim Haskins (1992).

Photo histories reflect on the contributions of culturally diverse groups. Jim Haskins wrote and prepared *The Day Martin Luther King, Jr., Was Shot: A Photo History of the Civil Rights Movement* (1992). *Now Is Your Time: The African-American Struggle for Freedom* by Walter Dean Myers (1991) takes the reader from the early times of slavery on the plantation to the last days of Martin Luther King Jr. Russell Freedman developed three books based on Native American culture: *An Indian Winter* (1992), *Buffalo Hunt* (1988), and *Indian Chiefs* (1987). *Children of the Wild West* by Freedman (1983), *Pioneer Children of Appalachia* by Joan Anderson (1986), and Jim Murphy's *The Boy's War: Confederate and Union Soldiers Talk about the Civil War* (1990) focus on the contributions of children to events and to their cultural groups. In each book, illustrations and photographs provide powerful visual representation to accompany the text.

Other *informational books* are those that offer facts and figures about people, their environments, and their lifestyles. They are primarily reference works. *People of the Three Fires: The Ottawa, Potawatomi, and Ojibway of Michigan* by Clifton, Cornell, and McClurken (1986) includes maps of Michigan, photographs, stories, and descriptions of artifacts of these Native American peoples. *Walk in Peace: Legends and Stories of the Michigan Indians,* written by Simon Otto (1990), accompanies this book. Otto has also retold legends in *Aube Na Bing: A Pictorial History of Michigan Indians* (1990). *The Native Americans: The Indigenous People of North America,* edited by Colin F. Taylor (1995), serves as a very comprehensive reference book. It includes photographs, descriptions of artifacts, and artwork depicting various tribes and peoples. Michael Caduto and Joseph Bruchac prepared *Keepers of the Animals: Native American Stories and Wildlife Activities for Children* (1991), which connects folklore with classroom delivery and includes suggestions for practical application at all levels in the elementary classroom. Aliki's picture book *Corn Is Maize: The Gift of the Indians* (1976) can be used in both reading and science instruction to explain the process of growing and using corn.

Informational books often focus on language and on the traditions of various cultures. *Ashanti to Zulu: African Traditions* by Margaret Musgrove (1976), with illustrations by Leo and Dianne Dillon, takes the reader through the African continent as particular groups of people are described and presented visually. Harry McNaught has developed a picture dictionary for Spanish-speaking children in *500 Palabras nuevas para ti* (1982); a similar book is *The First Thousand Words in Russian* by Amery, Kirilenko, and Cartwright (1983). Both books feature labeled illustrations. Sign language is introduced in *A Show of Hands: Say It in Sign Language* by Mary Beth Sullivan (1980) and Linda Bourke and William Tomkins' *Indian Sign Language* (1969).

Exposure to quality literature can help children understand differences and similarities in religious beliefs. Written from a child's perspective, *I Wanted to Know All about God* by Virginia L. Kroll (1994) emphasizes nature, sharing, and love of one's neighbor. Jewish traditions are shared in *Light Another Candle: The Story and Meaning of Hanukkah* by Miriam Chaikin (1981), Groner and Wikler's *All about Hanukkah* (1988), *Succoth: A Joyous Holiday* by Barbara Soloff-Levy (1991), and the comical version of *Hershel and the Hanukkah Goblins* by Eric Kimmel (1985). June Behrens explains the Chinese New Year in *Gung Hay Fat Choy: Happy New Year* (1982), and Deborah M. Newton Chocolate describes the African celebration in *My First Kwanzaa Book* (1992). *The Big Book for Peace* (1990), edited by Ann Durell and Marilyn Sachs, is a collection of readings from well-known writers, with supportive illustrations by Maurice Sendak. Tomie de Paola tells the story of *Our Lady of Guadalupe* (1980) and the miracles she performed in response to prayer.

Certain books, considered specialty books, may be narrated from the author's point of view. Examples are Nila K. Leigh's *Learning to Swim in Swaziland: A Child's-Eye View of a Southern African Country* (1993), Maya

Angelou's *My Painted House, My Friendly Chicken, and Me* (1994), and Ann Morris's *Bread, Bread, Bread* (1989).

Some issue-focused texts that are picture books featuring animals in imaginative settings are also worth noting. Jan Brett addresses the issue of belonging and acceptance in *Fritz and the Beautiful Horses* (1981). *Imogene's Antlers* by David Small (1985) also deals with acceptance as well as humor and adaptability. Books taking a direct approach are Nancy Carlson's *I Like Me!* (1990) and Dr. Seuss's *Oh, the Places You'll Go!* (1993). Cooperation and group membership and participation are key issues in Marcus Pfister's *The Rainbow Fish* (1992) and Helen Lester's *Me First* (1992). In *The Lovables in the Kingdom of Self-Esteem*, a vibrantly illustrated book by Diane Loomans with drawings by Kim Howard, animals tell readers how to feel good about themselves.

Nonfiction selections that reflect cultural diversity can only enrich the informational base of any elementary classroom. These works seek to

▮ serve as models for children who are looking for contributions from various cultural groups,
▮ become reference tools for children who will be researching and reporting information, and
▮ act as sources of fact against which to evaluate books in other genres.

❖ How Can Alternative Media Be Used to Teach Multiculturalism?

Alternative media refers to innovative methods for sharing stories and texts with children. Advancements in technology have made it possible for young children to interact with text and pictures through interactive video and CD ROMs. Some very popular resources are Mercer Mayer's *Just Grandma and Me* (1994), where children can travel with grandma and watch the story come to life; Marc Brown's *Arthur's Birthday* (1993); *Thumbelina,* the traditional tale by Hans Christian Andersen (1994); Mercer Mayer's *Little Monster at School* (1994), which deals with making new friends; and Get-Away stories, such as *Whale of a Tale*, which follows a whale as he learns about friendship and *Annabel's Dream of Ancient Egypt,* which concerns sibling rivalry and teasing. *How the Leopard Got His Spots* (1991) by Rudyard Kipling is a video production that features the traditional tales so important to children. Other well-known stories are available in video- and audiocassette format for students who have difficulty attending to the written word. They include the ever-popular *Hatchet* by Gary Paulsen (1988) and E. B. White's classic fantasy, *Charlotte's Web* (1990).

Alternative media allow children to

■ explore books and stories in an interactive fashion,
■ use all their senses and their diverse learning styles to the fullest extent,
■ relate directly and one-on-one with narrative and visual elements, and
■ access the most current and accurate information for reference and research.

Use of alternative media is one of many approaches for exposing children to quality children's literature that is multicultural. Teachers and parents should be selective and critical in its application with children in the classroom and at home.

❖ Summary

Many different genres are represented in children's literature: picture books, traditional literature, modern fantasy, poetry, contemporary realistic fiction, historical fiction, nonfiction/informational books, and alternative media. Each genre has specific characteristics, values, and applications. All in all, however, children's literature constitutes a genre of its own because it has its own set of unique characteristics, values, and application.

❖ Reflections and Questions to Consider

1. Select a particular author and prepare an author/book talk for your class. Tell your colleagues about your book in a creative, interactive way and encourage them to read your selection. Have your colleagues evaluate your talk using the form on page 90.

2. Read and react to several Caldecott and Newbery award–winning books and selected chapter books by using the evaluation forms on pages 91–95.

3. Read a book aloud in a primary classroom, a preschool/nursery setting, or a senior citizens' center. Practice reading so that you will appear confident and competent.

❖ Children's Literature Cited and References

Aardema, V. (1981). *Bringing the rain to Kapiti Plain.* New York: Dial Books for Young Readers.

Ackerman, K. (1988). *Song and dance man.* New York: Knopf Books for Young Readers.

Adoff, A. (1982). *All the colors of the race.* New York: Beech Tree Paperback Books.

Afanasev, A. (1976). *Russian fairy tales.* New York: Pantheon.

Alexander, L. (1992). *The fortune tellers.* New York: Dutton Children's Books.

Alexander, M. (1991). *Even that moose won't listen to me.* New York: Puffin.

Aliki. (1976). *Corn is maize: The gift of the indians.* New York: HarperCollins.

Aliki. (1986). *Feelings.* New York: Morrow, William.

Amery, H., Kirilenko, K., & Cartwright, S. (1983). *The first thousand words in Russian.* Tulsa, OK: Educational Development.

Andersen, H. C. (1990). *The fir tree.* New York: North-South Books.

Anderson, J. (1986). *Pioneer children of appalachia.* New York: Clarion.

Angelou, M. (1994). *My painted house, my friendly chicken, and me.* New York: Crown.

Argent, K. (1987). *One wooly wombat.* Brooklyn, NY: Kane-Miller.

Asch, F., & Vagin, V. (1991). *Here comes the cat!* New York: Scholastic.

Bader, B. (1991). *Aesop & company: With scenes from his legendary life.* Boston, MA: Houghton Mifflin.

Banks, L. R. (1985). *The Indian in the cupboard.* New York: Doubleday.

Bartone, E. (1993). *Peppe the lamplighter.* New York: Scholastic.

Behrens, J. (1982). *Gung hay fat choy: Happy New Year.* Chicago: Children's Press.

Brenner, A. (1992). *The boy who could do anything and other Mexican folktales.* Seattle: ShoeString.

Brett, J. (1981). *Fritz and the beautiful horses.* Boston: Houghton Mifflin.

Brett, J. (1990). *The mitten.* New York: Putnam.

Brown, M. (1961). *Once a mouse . . .* New York: Charles Scribner's Sons.

Brown, M. W. (1949). *The important book.* New York: HarperCollins.

Brown, R. (1991). *Alphabet times four: An international ABC.* New York: Dutton Child Books.

Bryan, A. (1992). *Sing to the sun.* New York: HarperCollins Children's Books.

Bunting, E. (1990). *The wall.* New York: Clarion.

Bunting, E. (1991). *Fly away home.* New York: Clarion.

Buscaglia, L. (1982). *The fall of Freddie the leaf.* Thorofare, NJ: Slack.

Bussey, M. T. (1988). *Aube na bing.* Grand Rapids: Michigan Indian Press.

Caduto, M. J. & Bruchac, J. (1991). *Keepers of the animals.* Golden, CO: Fulcrum.

Carle, E. (1987). *Do you want to be my friend?* New York: HarperCollins Children's Books.

Carlson, N. (1990). *I like me!* New York: Puffin.

Chaikin, M. (1981). *Light another candle: The story and meaning of Hanukkah.* New York: Clarion.

Chang, I. (1991). *A separate battle: Women and the Civil War.* New York: Scholastic.

Cheltenham Elementary School Kindergartners. (1991). *We are all alike . . . we are all different.* New York: Scholastic.

Chocolate, D. M. (1992). *My first Kwanzaa book.* New York: Scholastic.

Choi, S. N. (1991). *Year of impossible goodbyes.* New York: Dell.

Clifton, J. A., Cornell, G. L., & McClurken, J. M. (1986). *People of the three fires: The Ottawa, Potawatomi, and Ojibway of Michigan.* Grand Rapids: Michigan Indian Press.

Cohlene, T. (1990). *Clamshell Boy: A Makah legend.* Mahwah, NJ: Watermill Press.

Cohlene, T. (1990). *Dancing drum: A Cherokee legend.* Mahwah, NJ: Watermill Press.

Cohlene, T. (1990). *Ka-ha-si and the loon: An Eskimo legend.* Mahwah, NJ: Watermill Press.

Cohlene, T. (1990). *Little Firefly: An Algonquian legend.* Mahwah, NJ: Watermill Press.

Cohlene, T. (1990). *Quillworker: A Cheyenne legend.* Mahwah, NJ: Watermill Press.

Cohlene, T. (1990). *Turquois Boy: A Navajo legend.* Mahwah, NJ: Watermill Press.

Cowcher, H. (1993). *Tigress.* New York: Farrar, Straus, & Giroux.

Cowen-Fletcher, J. (1994). *It takes a village.* New York: Scholastic.

Crew, L. (1991). *Children of the river.* New York: Dell.

Cullinan, B. E., & Galda, L. (1994). *Literature and the child.* Fort Worth, TX: Harcourt Brace College.

Curry, J. L. (1987). *Back in the beforetime: Tales of the California Indians.* New York: Macmillan Children's Book Group.

Daly, N. (1987). *Not so fast, Songololo.* New York: Puffin.

Davidson, M. (1969). *Helen Keller.* New York: Scholastic.

De Angeli, M. (1954). *Book of nursery and Mother Goose rhymes.* New York: Doubleday.

Delacre, L. (1989). *Arroz con leche: Popular songs and rhymes from Latin America.* New York: Scholastic.

Demi. (1994). *In the eyes of the cat: Japanese poetry for all seasons.* New York: Holt, Henry.

Demi. (1986). *Dragonkites and dragonflies: A collection of Chinese nursery rhymes.* San Diego: Harcourt, Brace.

Denenberg, B. (1991). *Nelson Mandela: "No easy walk to freedom."* New York: Scholastic.

De Paola, T. (1978). *Nana upstairs and Nana downstairs.* New York: Puffin.

de Paola, T. (1980). *The Lady of Guadalupe.* New York: Holiday House.

de Paola, T. (1981). *Now one foot, now the other.* New York: G. P. Putnam's Sons.

de Paola, T. (1983). *The legend of the Bluebonnet.* New York: Putnam.

De Paola, T. (1987). *Sing, Pierrot, sing.* San Diego: Harcourt Brace.

De Paola, T. (1991). *The legend of the Indian paintbrush.* New York: Putnam.

De Paola, T. (1992). *Strega Nona.* New York: Scholastic.

Der Manuelian, P. (1993). *Hieroglyphs from A to Z: A rhyming book with ancient Egyptian stencils for kids.* New York: Rizzoli Intl.

Durell, A., & Sachs, M., (Eds). (1990). *The big book for peace.* New York: Dutton Children's Books.

Edmonds, I. G. (1994). *Ooka the Wise: Tales of Old Japan.* North Haven, CT: Shoe String Press.

Emberley, R. (1989). *City sounds.* New York: Little.

Esser, D. C. Z. (1995). *Look to the light: A celebration of children and friendship.* Erie, PA: Fireside Gallerie.

Feelings, M. (1985). *Jambo means hello: Swahili alphabet book.* New York: Puffin.

Feelings, M. (1994). *Moja means one: Swahili counting book.* New York: Puffin.

Filipovic, Z. (1994). *Zlata's diary: A child's life in Sarajevo.* New York: Scholastic.

Fleischman, P. (1991). *The borning room.* New York: Scholastic.

Fox, M. (1989). *Wilfrid Gordon McDonald Partridge.* Brooklyn, NY: Kane-Miller.

Fox, M. (1991). *Possum magic.* San Diego: Harcourt Brace.

Fox, P. (1973). *The slave dancer.* New York: Dell.

Fralick, P. (1989). *Make it multicultural—Musical activities for early childhood education.* Hamilton, Ontario, Canada: Mohawk College.

Freedman, R. (1983). *Children of the wild west.* New York: Clarion.

Freedman, R. (1987). *Indian chiefs.* New York: Scholastic.

Freedman, R. (1988). *Buffalo hunt.* New York: Scholastic.

Freedman, R. (1992). *An Indian winter.* New York: Scholastic.

French, F. (1991). *Anancy and Mr. Dry-Bone.* New York: Little, Brown.

Friedman, I. R. (1984). *How my parents learned to eat.* Boston: Houghton Mifflin.

Fritz, J. (1983). *The double life of Pocahontas.* New York: The Trumpet Club.

Gaige, A. (1990). *We are a thunderstorm.* Kansas City, MO: Landmark Editions.

Gardiner, J. R. (1980). *Stone fox*. New York: HarperCollins.

Garland, S. (1993). *The lotus seed*. San Diego: Harcourt, Brace.

Gates, F. (1994). *Owl eyes*. New York: Lothrop, Lee, & Shepard.

George, J. C. (1991). *My side of the mountain*. New York: Puffin.

Gilman, P. (Adapt.). (1993). *Something from nothing*. New York: Scholastic.

Girard, L. W. (1986). *Adoption is for always*. Morton Grove, IL: Albert Whitman.

Girard, L. W. (1989). *We adopted you, Benjamin Koo*. Morton Grove, IL: Albert Whitman.

Goble, P. (1993). *The girl who loved wild horses*. New York: Macmillan Children's Book Group.

Golenbock, P., & Bacon, P. (1990). *Teammates*. San Diego: Harcourt Brace Jovanovich.

Greenfield, E. (1988). *Nathaniel talking*. New York: Writers & Readers.

Griego, M. C., Bucks, B., Gilbert, S., & Kimball, L. (1988). *Tortillitas para Maria: And other nursery rhymes, Spanish and English*. New York: Holt, Henry.

Groner, J. & Wikler, M. (1988). *All about Hanukkah*. Rockville, MD: Kar-Ben Copies.

Haley, G. E. (1988). *A story, a story*. New York: Macmillan Child Group.

Hamilton, V. (1982). *Sweet whispers, Brother Rush*. New York: Putnam.

Hartmann, W. (1994). *One sun rises: An African wildlife counting book*. New York: Dutton Child Books.

Haskins, J. (1992). *The day Martin Luther King, Jr., was shot: A photo history of the civil rights movement*. New York: Scholastic.

Heide, F., & Gilliland, J. H. (1995). *The day of Ahmed's secret*. New York: Morrow, William.

Heyer, M. (1989). *The weaving of a dream*. New York: Puffin.

Hillman, J. (1995). *Discovering children's literature*. Englewood Cliffs, NJ: Merrill.

Hirschfelder, A. B. & Singer, B. R. (1992). *Rising voices: Writings of young Native Americans*. New York: Macmillan Child Group.

Hoban, T. (1974). *Circles, triangles, and squares*. New York: Macmillan Child Group.

Hoban, T. (1987). *Under, over, and through*. New York: Macmillan Child Group.

Hoban, T. (1989). *Of colors and things*. New York: Greenwillow.

Hoban, T. (1991). *All about where*. New York: Greenwillow.

Hoberman, M. A. (1993). *Fathers, mothers, sisters, brothers: A collection of family poems*. New York: Puffin.

Howard, E. F. (1991). *Aunt Flossie's hats (and crab cakes later)*. New York: Houghton Mifflin.

Howe, J. (1987). *I wish I were a butterfly*. San Diego: Harcourt, Brace.

Huck, C. (1994). *Princess Furball*. New York: Morrow William.

Hudson, J. (1984). *Sweetgrass*. New York: Scholastic.

Hudson, W. (1993). *Pass it on: African-American poetry for children*. New York: Scholastic.

Hudson, W., & Wesley, V. W. (1988). *Book of black heroes from A to Z*. New York: Scholastic.

Hutchins, P. (1987). *Changes, changes*. New York: Macmillan Child Group.

James, M. (1992). *Shoebag*. New York: Scholastic.

Jassem, K. (1979). *Pocahontas: Girl of Jamestown*. Mahwah, NJ: Troll Associates.

Jeffers, S. (1991). *Brother Eagle, Sister Sky: A message from Chief Seattle*. New York: Scholastic.

Johnson, A. (1993). *Toning the sweep*. New York: Scholastic.

Johnson, J. W. (1993). *Lift every voice and sing*. New York: Scholastic.

Johnston, J. (1973). *They led the way: 14 American women*. New York: Scholastic.

Johnston, T. & De Paola, T. (1992). *The quilt story*. New York: Putnam.

Joosse, B. M. (1991). *Mama, do you love me?* New York: Scholastic.

Keats, E. J. (1976). *The snowy day.* New York: Puffin.

Keats, E. J. (1987). *John Henry: An American Legend.* (Edited by Anne Schwartz). Knopf Books for Young Readers. New York.

Kelly, E. P. (1956). *The trumpeter of Krakow.* New York: Scholastic.

Kimmel, E. (1985). *Hershel and the Hanukkah goblins.* New York: Scholastic.

Kimmel, E. A. (1988). *Anansi and the moss-covered rock.* New York: Holiday House.

Krauss, R. (1973). *I'll be you and you be me.* Freeport, ME: Bookstore Press.

Kroll, K. (1992). *Gonna sing my head off! American folk songs for children.* New York: Scholastic.

Kroll, V. L. (1994). *I wanted to know all about God.* Grand Rapids, MI: William B. Eerdmans.

Kuniczak, W. S. (1992). *The glass mountain: Twenty-six ancient Polish folktales and fables.* New York: Hippocrene Books.

Lacapa, M. (1992). *Antelope Woman: An Apache folktale.* Flagstaff, AZ: Northland.

Leigh, N. K. (1993). *Learning to swim in Swaziland: A child's eye view of a Southern African country.* New York: Scholastic.

Leitner, I. (1992). *The big lie: A true story.* New York: Scholastic.

Lester, H. (1992). *Me first.* Boston: Houghton Mifflin.

Lester, J. (1968). *To be a slave.* New York: Scholastic.

Lester, J. (1994). *How many spots does a leopard have and other tales.* New York: Scholastic.

Lewis, J. (1980). *The Chinese word for horse and other stories.* New York: Schocken Books.

Lewis, T. P. (1987). *Hill of fire.* New York: HarperCollins Children's Books.

Lionni, L. (1987). *Swimmy.* New York: Knopf Books for Young Readers.

Littledale, F. (1978). *The snow child.* New York: Scholastic.

Lobel, A. (1980). *Fables.* New York: Scholastic.

Lobel, A. (1994). *Away from home.* New York: Greenwillow.

London, J., & Pinola, L. (1993). *Fire race: A Karuk Coyote tale about how fire came to the people.* San Francisco, CA: Chronicle.

Longfellow, H. W. (1983). *Hiawatha.* New York: Dial.

Loomans, D. (1991). *The Lovables in the Kingdom of Self-Esteem.* Tiburon, CA: H. J. Kramer.

Loomis, C. (1994). *One cow coughs: A counting book for the sick and miserable.* New York: Ticknor & Fields.

Louie, A. (1990). *Yeh Shen: A Cinderella story from China.* New York: Putnam.

Lowry, L. (1989). *Number the stars.* South Holland, IL: Yearling.

Lukens, R. J. (1995). *Critical handbook of children's literature.* New York: HarperCollins.

MacDonald, M. R. (1992). *Peace tales: World folktales to talk about.* North Haven, CT: Shoe String Press.

MacLachlan, P. (1985). *Sarah, plain and tall.* New York: HarperCollins.

MacLachlan, P. (1993). *Journey.* New York: Dell.

Maddern, E. (1993). *Rainbow Bird: An Aboriginal folktale.* New York: Little, Brown.

Mado, M. (1992). *The animals: Selected poems.* New York: Macmillan Child Group.

Martin, R. (1992). *The rough-face girl.* New York: Putnam.

Mathis, S. B. (1986). *The hundred penny box.* New York: Puffin.

McCann, R. L. (1983). *Pie-Biter.* San Francisco: Design Enterprises of San Francisco.

McCarthy, R. F., et. al. (1993). *Grandfather Cherry Blossom.* New York: Kodansha America.

McCarthy, R. (1993). *The inch-high samurai.* New York: Kodansha America.

McCarthy, R., et. al. (1993). *The moon princess.* New York: Kodansha America.

McKissack, P., & McKissack, F. (1985). *The little red hen.* Chicago, IL: Children's Press.

McKissack, P. C. (1986). *Flossie & the fox.* New York: Dial Books for Young Readers.

McKissack, P. C., & McKissack, F. (1992). *Sojourner Truth: Ain't I a woman?* New York: Scholastic.

McNaught, H. (1982). *500 Palabras nuevas para ti: 500 words to grow on.* New York: Random House.

Meigs, C. (1933). *Invincible Louisa.* New York: Scholastic.

Mellonie, B., & Ingpen, R. (1983). *Lifetimes: The beautiful way to explain death to children.* New York: Bantam.

Mills, L. (1991). *The rag coat.* New York: Little.

Mitchell, M. K. (1993). *Uncle Jed's barbershop.* New York: Simon & Schuster Trade.

Moeri, L. (1980). *Star Mother's youngest child.* Boston: Houghton Mifflin.

Mori, K. (1993). *Shizuko's daughter.* New York: Ballantine.

Morimoto, J. (1988). *The inch boy.* New York: Puffin.

Morris, A. (1989). *Bread, bread, bread.* New York: Scholastic.

Moutoussamy-Ashe, J. (1993). *Daddy & me: A photo story of Arthur Ashe and his daughter Camera.* New York: Knopf.

Munsch, R. (1986). *Love you forever.* Scarborough, Ontario, Canada: Firefly Books.

Murphy, J. (1990). *The boy's war: Confederate and Union soldiers talk about the Civil War.* New York: Scholastic.

Musgrove, M. (1976). *Ashanti to Zulu: African Traditions.* New York: Dial Books for Young Readers.

Myers, W. D. (1991). *Now is your time! The African-American struggle for freedom.* New York: Scholastic.

Myers, W. D. (1993). *Malcolm X: By any means necessary.* New York: Scholastic.

Naylor, P. R. (1991). *Shiloh.* New York: Macmillan Children's Group.

Nicheodhas, S. (1965). *Always room for one more.* New York: Henry Holt.

Nodelman, P. (1992). *The pleasures of children's literature.* White Plains, NY: Longman.

Norton, D. E. (1987). *Through the eyes of the child: An introduction to children's literature.* Columbus, OH: Merrill.

Norton, D. E. (1990). Teaching multicultural literature in the reading curriculum. *The Reading Teacher, 44*(1), 28–40.

Nye, N. S. (1992). *This same sky: A collection of poems from around the world.* New York: Macmillan Child Group.

O'Dell, S. (1992). *Sing down the moon.* New York: Dell.

Opie, P. & Opie, I. (1992). *I saw Esau.* Cambridge, MA: Candlewick Press.

Osborne, M. P. (1989). *Favorite Greek myths.* New York: Scholastic.

Otto, S. (1990). *Aube Na Bing: A pictorial history of Michigan indians.* Grand Rapids, MI: Grand Rapids Intertribunal Council.

Otto, S. (1990). *Walk in peace: Legends and stories of the Michigan Indians.* Grand Rapids, MI: Michigan Indian Press.

Park, R. (1993). *Things in corners.* New York: Puffin.

Parks, R., & Haskins, J. (1992). *Rosa Parks: My story.* New York: Scholastic.

Paterson, K. (1990). *The tale of the mandarin ducks.* New York: Dutton Children's Books.

Paulsen, G. (1988). *Hachet.* New York: Puffin.

Paulsen, G. (1992). *The haymeadow.* South Holland, IL: Dell Yearling Books.

Paulsen, G. (1993). *The Monument.* New York: Dell.

Paulsen, G. (1993). *The River.* New York: Dell.

Pettit, J. (1993). *A place to hide: True stories of holocaust rescues.* New York: Scholastic.

Pfister, M. (1992). *The rainbow fish.* New York: Scholastic.

Pienkowski, J. (1994). *Bronto's brunch.* New York: Dutton Child Books.

Pienkowski, J. (1995). *Good night, moo!* New York: Dutton Child Books.

Polacco, P. (1992). *Chicken Sunday*. New York: Putnam.

Polacco, P. (1994). *Mrs. Katz and Tush*. New York: Dell.

Polacco, P. (1994). *Pink and Say*. New York: Philomel.

Potter, B. (1988). *Tales of Peter Rabbit and his friends*. Avenal, NJ: Random House.

Pragoff, F. (1995). *Baby days*. Old Tappan, NJ: Simon & Schuster.

Pragoff, F. (1995). *Baby plays*. Old Tappan, NJ: Simon & Schuster.

Pragoff, F. (1995). *Baby says*. Old Tappan, NJ: Simon & Schuster.

Pragoff, F. (1995). *Baby ways*. Old Tappan, NJ: Simon & Schuster.

Prelutsky, J. (1990). *Something big has been here*. New York: Scholastic.

Provenson, A. & Provenson, M. (1983). *The glorious flight: Across the channel with Louis Bleriot*. New York: Puffin.

Raimondo, L. (1994). *The little lama of Tibet*. New York: Scholastic.

Ransom, C. F. (1994). *Between two worlds*. New York: Scholastic.

Raphael, E., & Bolognese, D. (1994). *Sacajewa: The journey west*. New York: Scholastic.

Raschka, C. (1993). *Yo! Yes!* New York: Scholastic.

Redhawk, R. (1988). *ABCs the American Indian way*. Newcastle, CA: Sierra Oaks.

Reinstedt, R. A. (1992). *Tales and treasures of California's missions*. Carmel, CA: Ghost Town.

Rice, J. (1991). *Cajun alphabet: Full-color edition*. Gretna, LA: Pelican.

Ringgold, F. (1993). *Aunt Harriet's underground in the sky*. New York: Crown Brooks for Young Readers.

Robbins, R. (1960). *Baboushka and the three kings*. Boston: Houghton Mifflin.

Russell, D. L. (1991). *Literature for children*. White Plains, NY: Longman.

Sadler, C. E. (1985). *Heaven's reward: Fairy tales from China*. New York: Atheneum.

Sanford, D. (1985). *It must hurt a lot: A child's book about death*. Sisters, OR: Questar.

Santore, C. (1988). *Aesop's fables*. New York: JellyBean Press.

Say, A. (1990). *El chino*. Boston: Houghton Mifflin.

Say, A. (1991). *Tree of cranes*. Boston: Houghton Mifflin.

Say, A. (1993). *Grandfather's journey*. Boston: Houghton Mifflin.

Scheer, G. F. (1991). *Cherokee animal tales*. Tulsa, OK: Council Oak Books.

Schwartz, A. (1992). *And the green grass grew all around: Folk poetry from everyone*. New York: HarperCollins Children Books.

Schwartz, A. (1994). *Make a face: A book with a mirror*. New York: Scholastic.

Seeger, P. (1986). *Abiyoyo*. New York: Scholastic.

Seeger, P. (1994). *Abiyoyo*. New York: Macmillan Child Group.

Seuss, Dr. (1993). *Oh! The places you'll go!* New York: Random House Books for Young Readers.

Shulevitz, U. (1978). *The treasure*. New York: Eastern Press.

Small, D. (1985). *Imogene's antlers*. New York: Crown.

Smith, K. B. (1987). *Martin Luther King, Jr*. New York: Simon & Schuster.

Sneve, V. H. (1991). *Dancing teepees: Poems of American Indian youth*. New York: Holiday House.

Snyder, D. (1988). *The boy of the three-year nap*. Boston: Houghton Mifflin.

Soloff-Levy, B. (1991). *Succoth: A joyous holiday*. Mahwah, NJ: Watermill Press.

Soto, G. (1992). *A fire in my hands: A book of poems*. New York: Scholastic.

Soto, G. (1993). *Too many tomales*. New York: Putnam.

Speare, E. G. (1993). *The Sign of the beaver*. New York: Dell.

Spier, P. (1980). *People*. New York: Doubleday.

Spinelli, J. (1990). *Maniac Magee*. New York: Little.

Stanley, F. (1991). *The last princess: The story of Princess Ka'iulani of Hawaii*. New York: Four Winds Press.

Steptoe, J. (1987). *Mufaro's beautiful daughters*. New York: Lothrap, Lee, & Shepard.

Stinson, K. (1984). *Mom & Dad don't live together anymore.* Buffalo, NY: Firefly Books.

Stinson, K. (1991). *Mom and Dad don't live together any more.* Toronto, Ontario, Canada: Annick Press.

Sullivan, M. B., & Bourke, L. (1980). *A show of hands: Say it in sign language.* New York: J. B. Lippincott Junior Books.

Tangvald, C. (1988). *Mom & Dad don't live together anymore.* Elgin, IL: Cheriot Family.

Taylor, C. F. (Ed.). (1995). *The Native Americans: The indigenous people of North America.* London, England: Salamander.

Tomkins, W. (1969). *Indian sign language.* New York: Dover.

Tomlinson, C. M. & Lynch-Brown, C. (1996). *Essentials of children's literature.* Boston: Allyn & Bacon.

Tomlinson, C. M. & Lynch-Brown, C. (1996). *Essentials of children's literature.* (2nd ed.), New York: Little, Brown.

Turner, A. (1987). *Nettie's trip south.* New York: Macmillan.

Uchida, Y. (1993). *The bracelet.* New York: Putnam.

Vagin, V., & Asch, F. (1989). *Here comes the cat!* New York: Scholastic.

Walter, M. P. (1987). *Ty's one-man band.* New York: Macmillan Child Group.

Weeks, G. (1991). *Sleeping Bear: Its lore, legends, and first people.* Glen Arbor, MI: The Cottage Book Shop of Glen Arbor and the Historical Society of Michigan.

White, E. B. (1974). *Charlotte's web.* New York: HarperCollins Children's Books.

Willard, N. (1993). *The sorcerer's apprentice.* New York: Blue Sky Press.

Williams, S. A. (1992). *Working cotton.* New York: Harcourt, Brace.

Williams, V. B. (1991). *Cherry and cherry pits.* New York: Morrow, William.

Winter, J. (1988). *Follow the drinking gourd.* New York: Knopf.

Winthrop, E. (1979). *Journey to the bright kingdom.* New York: Scholastic.

Wisniewski, D. (1991). *Rain player.* Boston: Houghton Mifflin.

Wolkstein, D. (1979). *White Wave: A Chinese tale.* New York: HarperCollins Children's Books.

Wood, J. R. (1992). *The man who loved clowns.* New York: G. P. Putnam's Sons.

Wyndham, R. (1989). *Chinese Mother Goose rhymes.* New York: Putnam.

Xing, H. (1985). *Ma Ling and his magic brush.* Beijing, China: Foreign Languages Press.

Yashima, T. (1955). *Crow boy.* New York: Viking Child Books.

Yep, L. (1975). *Dragonwings.* New York: Scholastic.

Yolen, J. (1990). *The devil's arithmetic.* New York: Puffin.

Young, E. (1992). *Seven blind mice* New York: Putnam.

❖ Multimedia

Andersen, H. C. (1994). *Thumbelina* [CD-ROM]. WEA-Accolade.

Brown, M. C. (1993). *Arthur's birthday* [CD-ROM]. Novato, CA: Broderbund.

Get-Away Stories. *Annabel's dream of ancient Egypt* [CD-ROM]. Austin, TX: Multimedia Publishing.

Get-Away Stories. *Whale of a tale* [CD-ROM]. Austin, TX: Texas Caviar.

Kipling, R. (1991). *How the leopard got his spots* [Videocassette recording]. Microsoft.

Mayer, M. (1994). *Just Grandma and me* [CD-ROM]. Novato, CA: Broderbund.

Mayer, M. (1994). *Little monster at school* [CD-ROM]. Novato, CA: Broderbund.

Paulsen, G. (1988). *Hatchet* [Videocassette recording]. Ingram Entertainment.

White, E. B. (1990). *Charlotte's web* [Videocassette recording]. Ingram Entertainment.

AUTHOR/BOOK TALK PRESENTATIONS

NAME

BOOK TITLE   AUTHOR

EVALUATOR'S NAME

DATE

5	4	3	2	1
Excellent	Above Average	Average	Fair	Poor

1. Did the presenter appear comfortable and familiar with the book?

5	4	3	2	1

2. Was the presenter creative in the teaching approach (including visual aids and hands-on materials)?

5	4	3	2	1

3. Did the presenter provide an adequate introduction or background of knowledge in the presentation?

5	4	3	2	1

4. Were you enticed to read the book after hearing the presentation?

5	4	3	2	1

5. Did the presenter make adequate eye contact and use proper grammar?

5	4	3	2	1

6. Did the presenter apply the book to real-life situations?

5	4	3	2	1

7. Did the presenter encourage classroom participation?

5	4	3	2	1

Comments that would help to make the presentation even more effective:

CALDECOTT AWARD BOOKS

NAME

BOOK TITLE   AUTHOR

YEAR   PUBLISHER

AWARD WON AND YEAR OF AWARD

SUMMARY OF THE BOOK

1. What is the plot of the story?

2. How do the illustrations complement the setting, plot, and mood of the story?

3. What is the purpose for sharing this book with children or recommending that they read it?

4. How does the author develop the characters in the story? How do the illustrations enhance the characterization?

5. How might this book be classified (e.g., concept book, counting book, alphabet book . . .)?

6. Did the author employ a unique style or theme to capture the attention of the reader? If so, what was it?

7. Why do you believe this book qualifies as a children's book that is multicultural?

Additional comments:

CHAPTER BOOKS: NEWBERY AWARDS AND RECOMMENDED READINGS

NAME

BOOK TITLE   AUTHOR

YEAR   PUBLISHER

AWARD WON AND YEAR OF AWARD

SHORT NOVELS (FICTION)
1. Summary of the book (limit to one paragraph)

2. Describe what makes this selection multicultural.

SELECT THREE QUESTIONS TO ANSWER
1. How does the author effectively use characterization in the book? Who was your favorite character and why?

2. What is the purpose for sharing this book with children or recommending that they read it?

3. How did the author use theme to tie the plot, characters, and setting together to make a meaningful whole?

4. What in particular made you like or dislike this selection? (Please answer in reference to plot, characterization, setting, theme, style, illustrations, and application).

5. What questions came to your mind as you were reading?

6. How did you feel about the ending of the story? Did you agree with the author's choice of ending? Why or why not? How might you have changed it?

ACTIVITIES
1. Story pyramid
2. Web of literary elements
3. Story map
4. Venn diagram comparing literary elements or two characters in the book
5. Character web

(continued)

CHAPTER BOOKS: NEWBERY AWARDS AND RECOMMENDED READINGS, continued

NONFICTION SELECTIONS

Purpose/theme of the book—Explain how and why you would use this book in your classroom. (limit to one paragraph)

SELECT THREE QUESTIONS TO ANSWER

1. How did photos, charts, or illustrations help in the author's presentation?

2. What was the most interesting or surprising thing(s) you learned?

3. What questions did the book leave unanswered for you?

4. How would you evaluate the style and format of the book for children? Why?

ACTIVITIES

1. K-W-L chart
2. Sequence map

REQUIRED READINGS RESPONSE JOURNAL

NAME

BOOK TITLE   AUTHOR

YEAR   PUBLISHER

AWARD WON AND YEAR OF AWARD

SUMMARY OF THE BOOK

SELECT FROM ANY SIX (6) OF THESE STATEMENTS FOR RESPONSE:

1. A question I have is . . .

2. I began to think of . . .

3. I know the feeling of . . .

4. I love the way . . .

5. I realized . . .

6. I think . . .

7. If I were . . .

8. I'm not sure . . .

9. I predict . . .

10. My favorite character is . . .

11. I like the way the author . . .

12. I felt _____ when . . .

13. I wish that . . .

14. I was confused when . . .

15. This made me think of . . .

16. I wonder why . . .

17. I noticed . . .

REQUIRED READINGS RESPONSE JOURNAL, continued

18. I was surprised when . . .

19. I noticed . . .

20. I changed my mind about _____ because . . .

21. Why do you suppose . . .

22. I felt _____ at the end of the book because . . .

23. I never thought about . . .

24. I hope . . .

25. I wonder . . . What do you think? . . .

PART II

Integration of Children's Literature That Is Multicultural

It is necessary for educators to include children's literature that is multicultural within the existing curriculum
and plan of study that is accepted by the school district
in which they work. This integration can be best accom-
plished when teachers, students, and the community
understand what multiculturalism is and how to select
and evaluate appropriate children's books reflecting
diversity and pluralism. This portion of the text will
offer a definition of multiculturalism as it relates to children's literature. Also included are guidelines for identifying particular story elements and artistic elements,
as well as methods of choosing children's books that
reflect multiculturalism and testing their authenticity
and educational value.

CHAPTER 4

The responsibility of tolerance lies with those who have the wider vision.

George Eliot

What Is Multiculturalism?

▮ Self-esteem
▮ Family structure
▮ Ethnicity
▮ Gender equity
▮ Ageism
▮ Exceptionalities
▮ Values
▮ Socioeconomic status
▮ Communication, bilingualism, braille, sign

❖ How Do Educators Define Multiculturalism?

Despite all that has been written and researched, people in general—and educators in particular—continue to be confused about the definitions of multiculturalism and multicultural education. This text will use the terms synonymously.

The author offers her own definition on the basis of experience and a review of current literature.

Sleeter and Grant, in reviewing current literature, found that *"multicultural education* means different things to different people" (1987, p. 436). Teachers have been challenged in the identification of numerous terms that range from *multiethnic studies* to *antiracism* and finally to *education that is multicultural.*

James Banks, who usually refers to multiethnic studies rather than multicultural education, sees multicultural education as an *idea* or concept that involves all students, an *educational reform movement* that is imparting change, and also as an ongoing *process* that may never achieve actualization (Banks & Banks, 1989, p. 2). As an *idea,* Banks sees multicultural education as the affirmation of equal opportunity for all students to learn—regardless of background, gender, class, race, ethnicity, or culture. That idea also encompasses multiethnic education and global awareness as well as recognition of racism, prejudice, discrimination, equity, and values. In contrast, multiethnic education (as distinct from multicultural education) deals with the study of ethnic diversity in society—the histories, cultures, and experiences of ethnic groups (Darity, 1985). It does not address groupings based on gender, religion, ability, or social class (Bullard, 1992).

Two works from the late 1980s define multicultural education as a *process.* Ramsey, Vold, & Williams (1989) refer to multicultural education as a "process-oriented creation of learning experiences that foster awareness of, respect for, and enjoyment of the diversity of our society and world" (p. ix). Standifer (1987) has called it the "process which fosters the knowledge of, as well as the respect and appreciation for, the historical and contemporary conditions of men and women to society along with those educational processes that reflect the wide variety of roles open to all" (p. 472).

In *An Introduction to Multicultural Education,* James A. Banks (1994) reports on a study by Sleeter and Grant (1987) that determined that the "only commonality that the various definitions share is reform designed to improve schooling for students of color" (Banks, 1994, p. 16). More important than a standard definition of what constitutes multiculturalism are the goals and implications of multicultural education. This author has established her own set of goals for and implications of multicultural education as they connect and integrate with an educational philosophy and curricular practices.

Multicultural education affords all students the opportunity to view realistically the diversity of the American population and the world. As students' individual differences are identified and respected in today's elementary classrooms through the use of children's literature and up-to-date curricula, students and teachers will be involved in the *process* of multiculturalism that deals with the recognition of values, morality, attitudes, equity, and critical thinking.

Multiculturalism deals with both multiethnicity, with a focus on ethnic origins, and globalism, which emphasizes different countries and their contributions to the world in which we live. Drawing on this combination, multicultural education that is an integrated teaching process in an elementary classroom deals with ethnic groups, religious groups, gender, children's issues, handicaps and special needs, giftedness, ageism, and other important issues that influence and enhance the lives of our citizens.

Multiculturalism as an approach to learning is child centered. It begins with the child's understanding of self and the building of self-esteem, moves to an understanding and acceptance of others, and finally expands to a development of concern for larger problems and issues outside the child's immediate environment. This philosophy coincides with Christine Sleeter and Carl Grant's taxonomy, in which they have described the various multicultural education approaches currently being used, examined their applications, and analyzed them critically for shortcomings and oversights. Following are the five current approaches as described by Sleeter and Grant (1987):

1. *Teaching ethnically diverse groups.* This approach involves the assimilation of culturally diverse groups into the mainstream by providing instruction for transition into the traditional program.

2. *Human relations.* This approach imparts methodology for different groups to coexist cooperatively and gain better mutual understanding in the process.

3. *Single group studies.* This approach fosters cultural pluralism in the context of courses that deal specifically with particular groups' experiences, traditions, and contributions.

4. *Multicultural curriculum.* This approach creates a reflection of diversity through the promotion of cultural pluralism and social equality as school programs undergo change related to staffing, differentiated curriculum, and integrated instructional materials appropriate for all students.

5. *Education that is multicultural and social reconstructionist.* This approach to education prepares students to take action against inequity and injustice.

More recently, James Banks (1994) delineated the five dimensions of multicultural education. These are 1) content integration: how teachers use examples from various cultures within their content delivery; 2) the knowledge construction process: how teachers explain to their students that knowledge and understanding is influenced by assumptions, biases, and prejudices; 3) an equity pedagogy: when teachers use different teaching styles to accommodate different abilities and learning styles of their students; 4) prejudice reduction: attempting to change student attitudes

Multicultural Education Web

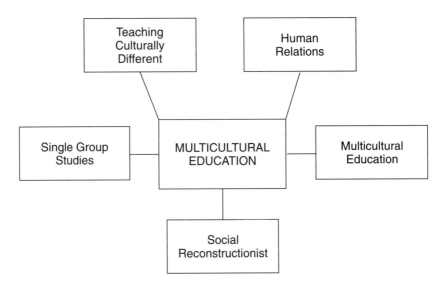

by use of teaching methods and materials; and 5) an empowering school culture and social structure: creating student leaders who reflect all different cultures, abilities and groups (p. 5). Teachers need to reflect on the ways they may be utilizing these various dimensions in their classrooms.

Because multiculturalism as a process exposes children daily to knowledge about themselves and others, young children in such an environment will become aware of the need to relate effectively with one another and to develop skills, attitudes, and abilities that help them function in a pluralistic society. As more and more early childhood curriculum is developed to respond to diversity issues, educators should consider at which level to begin and where to go. In any multicultural curriculum or program incorporating children's literature that is defined as multicultural, one should take into account James Banks's four levels of integration of content, described as follows:

Level 1, The Contributions Approach, which focuses on heroes, holidays and artifacts;

Level 2, The Additive Approach, which adds content, concepts, themes and perspectives without changing the structure of the curriculum;

Level 3, The Transformation Approach, which changes the structure of the curriculum in order to have students view concepts, views, events, and issues from the perspective of diverse groups;

Level 4, The Social Action Approach, where students show the decision-making process at work by investigating social issues and taking appropriate local and national action (Banks & Banks, 1989, p. 192).

It is apparent that James Banks's levels and Sleeter and Grant's taxonomy move in the same direction to accomplish educational goals related to multiculturalism. A multicultural curriculum is one that affords all students equal opportunity to excel. It encourages all students to acquire social skills, knowledge, and attitudes that will enhance their ability to live productively in a diverse society. As a cross-curricular approach that utilizes children's literature that is multicultural, it involves careful planning and serves the following goals:

1. Students will accept themselves both as individuals and as members of unique racial or cultural groups.

2. Students will begin or continue to accept others as members of different cultural, religious, ethnic, or gender groups, recognizing differences and similarities among people.

3. Students will increase their self-esteem as they begin to understand, recognize, and appreciate their own heritage.

4. Students will work cooperatively, developing interpersonal skills.

FIGURE 4–1 Sharing books with friends

5. Students will recognize the common bond of humanity among people of all cultures in a global society.

6. Students will identify commonly held stereotypes about groups or people.

7. Students will readily share information about diverse cultures with one another and with others outside the classroom.

8. Students will seek activity that will ultimately effect change for a more productive, cooperative, accepting society and world.

In order to train teachers more adequately to address and comprehend the process of multicultural education, critics and supporters alike have posed some questions. They are What curriculum is to be taught? Who is to be taught? and Who will teach multicultural education? (Yarbrough, 1992). Many national and state education groups and organizations have recognized the need to provide more resources and training for prospective and practicing teachers as they study and reflect on multicultural education. Still others have raised questions such as "What do teachers need to know to implement a multicultural curriculum?" (Derman-Sparks, 1989, p. 13). Should teaching emphasize information about other countries rather than people and the diversity of their cultures? Should there be a standardization of goals and activities that may take into consideration children's experiences and backgrounds and provide for multicultural education only where classrooms reflect diversity? Should the curriculum reflect differences in gender and physical ability as well as children's identity and attitude development and the impact of stereotyping, bias, and discrimination?

In response to these questions, Standifer (1987) notes and agrees with Derman-Sparks (1989) that in the early stages of teacher training, future teachers need to identify, accept, and recognize their own values and cultures. Only after educators have been able to identify and clarify their own feelings and perceptions about diversity can they help children do the same.

Teachers bring to the classroom their own perspectives, values, and dreams, which have direct influence on the attitudes of their students. For teacher training programs that include multiculturalism, James Banks (1991) recommends methods that help prospective teachers identify their ethnic and cultural identities by way of a topology of multicultural development. Following are the stages of this topology, applicable to both teacher and learner:

Stage 1: ethnic psychological captivity where the individuals internalize negative beliefs about themselves and their ethnic group;

Stage 2:   ethnic encapsulation where the individuals are ethno-centric and display separatist behaviors;

Stage 3:   ethnic identity clarification where the individuals accept themselves and positively identify attitudes toward group membership;

Stage 4:   biethnicity where individuals possess the attitudes, skills, and commitment needed to participate both within their own and with another cultural group;

Stage 5:   multiethnicity and reflective nationalism where individuals reflect on ethnic and national group identifications and can function within a range of ethnic and cultural groups within their nation;

Stage 6:   globalism and global competency where individuals extend these positive reflections about ethnic, national, and global identifications as needed to function in their nation and their world. (p. 142)

Classifications such as these stages and the taxonomies and levels discussed earlier help future and current teachers to become more global in their thinking and perspectives. Through the broadening of teacher attitudes and perspectives and the selection of children's literature that provides examples of diverse cultural groups and self-esteem building, the education of young children will be profoundly affected.

The foregoing has been a philosophical and research-based definition of multiculturalism. More specifically, this text will address the following areas as they relate directly to children, their literature, and their positive experiences in elementary education:

- Self-esteem
- Family structure
- Ethnicity
- Gender equity
- Ageism
- Exceptionalities
- Values
- Socioeconomic status
- Communication

Each of these terms is related directly to a multicultural curriculum that is delivered in an integrated fashion in an elementary setting. The remainder of the chapter will identify briefly, define in simple terms, and give selected examples of children's literature that promotes these concepts.

❖ Why Is the Self-Esteem of the Child So Critical in Multicultural Education?

When very young children begin the school experience, they know very little about others, but they know a great deal about themselves. Nevertheless, young children sometimes have limited acceptance of themselves. Here is where self-esteem building is so important to the learning process.

Goode (1973) defines self-esteem as "the judgment and attitude an individual holds toward himself" (p. 525). McCormick (1983) contends that as early childhood educators seek to develop positive self-esteem in young children, it is important to begin "where the child is" before the child can understand and relate to others.

There are various methods for integrating positive self-esteem building in the elementary setting:

▎ Creating positive self-images among children in the classroom by recognizing and celebrating differences and similarities
▎ Sharing experiences, talents, and hopes of all children each day
▎ Approaching classroom activities in a way that recognizes children as individuals; accepting and encouraging their personal feelings and methods
▎ Accepting one's own limitations and exceptionalities (important for both the students and the teacher)
▎ Participating fully in daily activities in order to enrich each learner's experience
▎ Exhibiting pride in personal work and accomplishments through demonstrations, displays, and dialogue
▎ Demonstrating self-control and self-discipline
▎ Showing a willingness to try new activities and challenges, to think creatively and take risks
▎ Expressing themselves as learners who are unique

These methods of allowing young children to build self-esteem can be facilitated through the use of children's literature that is multicultural. One example is Janice May Udry's *What Mary Jo Shared.* (1991), illustrated by Elizabeth Sayles. In this story about an African-American girl who never shared anything in school, elementary students discover that many children have the same fears about the sharing experience—trying to find something unique and special that others would admire. In the end, Mary Jo shares her father, Mr. William Wood, with her classmates. Teachers may find this story an effective introduction to an event in which parents are invited to school to share their interests, culture, hobbies, and experiences as models for the children. A lesson as simple as this can help children better understand that each class member has a desire to be special and that sharing of talents and special loves with others is one way to feel good about oneself.

FIGURE 4–2 Shared reading

❖ What Impact Does Family Structure Have on Children's Learning?

Beyond themselves, very young children identify most strongly with family members, the closest of whom are parents, siblings, and extended family members in the same household. As noted by Betsy West (1987),

Somewhere, sometime, concerned teachers have to let children know that there are different groupings of people called family, that love and care are the important elements in a family, that there are families without fathers, families without mothers, families of two adults of the same gender, and so on. (p. 126).

Although these issues tend to be controversial in today's society, they are real for the child, and teachers need to be very sensitive in dealing with the diverse family structures that are represented in an elementary classroom.

Although teachers are aware that for children self-esteem and self-worth are based on the attitudes of others, it is very important to be cognizant of the significant members of each child's family and of their effect on the child's learning. Likewise, parental or family involvement is a necessary element in the success of any multicultural program or any child's educational experience. Children are greatly influenced by family biases and prejudices and often share these attitudes openly in early childhood settings. On the other hand, when behaviors and attitudes of parents and family members are challenged through their children intentionally or unintentionally, cooperation between family and school is curtailed.

Partnership between the home and the school will be a critical factor in helping young children live and grow in a diverse world. As multicultural curriculum continues, through high-quality children's literature, to be refined and integrated within classrooms throughout the country, parents and other family members need to be consulted and involved in the multicultural program. Teachers can do this within their elementary classrooms by

- encouraging students to identify their own family structures,
- recognizing different family structures,
- allowing children to identify roles and stereotypes of individuals in family settings,
- understanding the various definitions that people around the world have for the term *family*, and
- identifying personal "roots" or developing a "family tree."

John Reynolds Gardiner's book *Stone Fox* (1980) is a wonderful story for middle elementary students. Through strife and thanks to determination, a young boy and his grandfather maintain their "family" and their home. Another book entitled *Families: A Celebration of Diversity, Commitment, and Love* by Jenness (1990) features the actual words of many children about their family structures, which include single parents, gay and lesbian parents, members of several cultures, foster children, only children, and extended families. Either of these stories could help children in an elementary setting become more cognizant of the love that is becoming the key to a consistent definition of family, rather than the stereotypical family structure reflected in some less current children's books.

❖ What Role Does Ethnicity Play in Children's Learning and Their Relationships to Books?

When educators think of multicultural education, they generally relate this thinking primarily to ethnicity. In this text, we will define *ethnicity* as "a term that has been used to include varied groupings based on national or linguistic background as well as religion, class, and regional identification" (Tiedt & Tiedt, 1986, p. 11).

The children in our elementary classrooms can be members of various ethnic groups. Boyer (1990) defines an ethnic group as "a group of people with a common heritage such as a geographic heritage (Poles, Swedes, Italians), which can be distinguished due to cultural and sociological traits" (p. 10). Such group membership, in combination with all other individual characteristics, influences the academic success of the elementary student. Early childhood recognition of diverse groups has been supported because, "it has been found that attitudes and understandings of children can be effectively guided at this early age with respect to differences among and between people of various cultures" (Dancy, 1987, p. 5).

Ethnic group membership can be addressed in the elementary classroom when teachers and students

- begin to understand the diversity in American culture;
- recognize the influence of various cultures on our everyday lives;
- locate the various cultural groups geographically in the world;
- identify the various ethnic groups represented in the classroom;
- invite others of different racial, cultural, and religious backgrounds (children or adults) to share with the class;
- work cooperatively with others, recognizing talents and needs;
- discover the origins of stories, games, foods, and festivals; and
- describe how others may feel in a given situation.

The folklore of the many ethnic groups is a wonderful resource for sharing ethnicity with children. *The People Could Fly: American Black Folktales,* written by Virginia Hamilton (1985) and illustrated by Leo and Diane Dillon, is a fine example of collected tales narrated in dialect to share with young children. Even teachers who are not of African-American ethnicity should attempt to read these short tales aloud, with much practice and great expression. Libraries and bookstores carry cassette versions for those who fail to master the storytelling art.

Another touching story is *Elijah's Angel* by Michael J. Rosen (1992), illustrated by Aminah Brenda Lynn Robinson. As a 9-year-old Jewish boy and a black Christian barber and wood carver become friends, they learn about each other's religious beliefs, fears, and joys. Both the author and the illustrator were acquainted with Elijah Pierce, who lived in Columbus, Ohio, and became the inspiration for this story. Through such children's books, young learners can discover their own ethnicity and that of others in a nonjudgmental fashion.

FIGURE 4–3 Discovering ethnicity

❖ What Do Educators Mean by Equity in the Classroom?

We have addressed the matter of ethnicity and the equity issue as related to ethnic group membership. In this section the primary concern is gender equity—equal opportunity for females and males in the classroom, the workplace, and society. Rather than create stereotypical situations for males and females, today's teachers can promote equity by offering young children well-rounded experiences that include hands-on activity, play, drama, cooperation, individualization and independent exploration, and active participation in math and science.

Leipzig (1987) remarks on the equity issue as it affects early childhood educators:

> When we talk about sexist childrearing, we're talking about something that goes far beyond isolated and superficial pieces of behavior, far beyond dressing girls in pink and boys in blue. This kind of experience becomes a lens through which children will see the world and themselves. (p. 43).

The ultimate goal and responsibility of the elementary school teacher is to offer support for all learners so that they, regardless of gender, can be satisfied, competent, well-rounded, and loving individuals in a very complex world. This can be achieved only when positive self-esteem is evident and when learners engage in cooperative, collaborative experiences as well as independent creative efforts. When these requirements are met, we have not limited the opportunity of either gender to become the best that they can be—whatever that may be.

Equity can be promoted in the elementary classroom when the following conditions exist:

▌ All learners are encouraged to be actively involved in the learning process.

▌ Both genders have positive role models exemplifying differentiated interests, occupations, abilities, and talents.

▌ Role-playing takes place.

▌ Participation includes small-group activity, cooperative learning, independent exploration, and creative problem solving.

▌ Stereotypical language referring to males and females is not acceptable in the classroom.

▌ Learning materials are appropriate, representing both genders equally.

Examples of appropriate materials are plentiful. Beverly Cleary has created an exuberant character, Ramona, in her series of books, _Ramona_

FIGURE 4–4 Increasing understanding and acceptance of differentiated roles in the classroom.

Quimby (1990) being one of the favorites. In this story Ramona's character supports her father's efforts to have a fulfilling job. Another book with a strong female protagonist is M. Hoffman's *Amazing Grace* (1991), in which an African-American girl named Grace works very hard to win the role of Peter Pan in the class musical. Continued exposure to plausible everyday situations for both genders will increase understanding and acceptance of differentiated roles in the classroom and the society at large.

❖ How Do Age and the Elderly Fit in Multiculturalism?

It is understood among adults that with age comes wisdom. Beyond the individual family that is often extended through aunts, uncles, grandparents, and others, the richness of our shared heritages has been passed down from generation to generation through our older people. The senior citizen population in this country is increasing as more and more people live beyond age 75 or 80. With this increase come the many issues that families and their children must deal with—failing health, disabilities and other limitations, extended care needs, Alzheimer's disease, and ultimately death. Many of these concerns are reflected in recent children's literature as the authors seek to offer real-life situations in story form for teachers, parents, and children at the elementary level.

Cultures have not always accepted aging in the same fashion. Whereas in Asian cultures elderly family members are revered, in other cultures, such as the Netsilik Eskimos who are nomadic and move to maintain their existence, the older members are sometime forgotten and left behind. The Netsilik Eskimos move from place to place and adhere to the belief that "the strong and productive members of the group are the most important for the survival of the family, and therefore, the older, weak people are expected to do all they can to help the strong" (*the Netsilik Eskimos*, 1969, p. 6). Due to the lifestyle of these people, "the old people are told in advance what their end is to be, and they submit peacefully without a word of recrimination. Sometimes, indeed, they are the first to suggest this end for themselves" (De Poncins, 1941, pp. 249–250). However, as Masha Kabakow Rudman (1995) states, "A society that excludes its elders deprives itself of first-hand encounters with the wealth of past experience these people afford, not only of world and local history but also of cultural and family roots" (p. 119).

Teachers can help students develop an appreciation for the contributions and rights of the aged by doing the following:

▮ Offering opportunities for children to interact with seniors in many different roles and capacities
▮ Regarding elderly people with dignity regardless of their situations
▮ Encouraging various forms of communication with elderly people so they may share stories, experiences, and history

■ Reducing the fear of becoming old and incapacitated through regular exposure to healthy, vibrant elderly members of society

■ Discussing the feelings of sadness and fear that arise when family members, particularly elderly ones, have died

■ Recognizing elders as a group of people with rights, abilities, and desires

Mem Fox's *Wilfrid Gordon McDonald Partridge* (1985) is a priceless book that uses Julie Vivas's illustrations to portray a group of elderly residents of a nursing home. Wilfrid's relationship with one of the women and his desire to help her recover her memory make this book very special. In Ackerman's *Song and Dance Man* (1988), the reader meets a grandfather who shares his dancing talents with his grandchildren. Both books show how the children love the elders as people, without consideration of their ages or limitations.

Although death should not be associated only with the elderly, it is appropriate to consider this issue when multiculturalism is integrated. Appropriate literature can help children as they progress through the stages of denial, fear, anger, guilt, grief, and acceptance. Leo Buscaglia's

FIGURE 4–5 Children's literature can help children as they progress through the stages of denial, fear, anger, guilt, grief, and acceptance.

The Fall of Freddie the Leaf: A Story of Life for All Ages (1982) is a simple story that follows the life and death of a leaf and his companions. The beauty of the words allows both young and old to relate it to real human life.

❖ Why Are Exceptionalities Included in Multiculturalism?

Educational trends have progressed from isolation of children with special needs or exceptionalities to mainstreaming and finally to inclusion. Mainstreaming gave students some opportunities to engage in learning experiences within "regular" classrooms when the students were mentally and/or physically capable. Now the trend is to encourage students with exceptionalities to be served through the regular curriculum and its delivery. The challenge for educators is adapting curriculum and delivery to meet these students' special needs. The area of exceptionalities falls under the umbrella of multiculturalism because of the need to address prejudices and biases that might arise from the inclusion of these students.

As with death, parents and even educators may experience particular stages of loss when faced with accepting an exceptional child. Such a child may have learning problems, attention difficulties, social problems, emotional limitations, hearing or vision loss, motion limitations, and communication difficulties. Gifted students likewise fall into the category of exceptionality since often their high levels of intelligence, creativity, and originality make them considerably different learners in a traditional classroom setting. Certainly, such special needs or circumstances lead to reactions including fear, rejection, adaptation, and acceptance among children in the elementary classroom. Teachers face the challenge of preparing their classrooms for these circumstances. Following are some ways for educators to promote acceptance of exceptionalities:

- Encourage awareness of the special needs of each individual.
- Express worries, fears, misunderstandings, and confusion about exceptionalities.
- Provide effective role models of successful individuals who have coped with special needs.
- Eliminate inappropriate labeling of individuals and groups with special needs.
- Role-play and dramatize exceptionalities to gain a better understanding of limitations and feelings.
- Select stories and other works of literature that portray special needs people in successful, productive roles.

A children's book that uses folklore to encourage acceptance and understanding of blindness is *The Seeing Stick* by Jane Yolen (1977), enhanced

FIGURE 4–6 Seeing takes on many dimensions.

by powerful illustrations. In this story the emperor's blind daughter wishes to see, and the emperor announces to his kingdom that the people must find the solution. Finally, after many failed attempts, an old man uses a carving stick to show the princess how to see the world. In the end it is revealed that the old man is also blind. The story's powerful simplicity helps youngsters better understand blindness and realize that seeing takes on many dimensions.

❖ Why Must Values Be Addressed in Multiculturalism?

Whenever teachers express themselves in a personal way to their students, they express their personal values. As they move throughout the classroom and offer kindness and compassion, they infuse values into their teaching. As role models, teachers promote positive values for the young people they reach.

Values as related to multiculturalism refers particularly to the elimination of prejudgment, bias, and racism. Working independently or cooperatively, children learn to treat one another with justice and fairness. Inequity is unacceptable.

Educators can help to develop positive values in elementary students by doing the following:

- Encouraging children to recognize and develop appreciation of many cultures
- Demonstrating the value of refraining from prejudgment
- Identifying the many contributions of various cultures to our society
- Allowing children to recognize and identify prejudice concerning individuals
- Allowing children to recognize and identify discrimination against individuals
- Encouraging students to recognize and identify racial and gender inequity

A contemporary young adolescent novel embodying positive values is *Maniac Magee* by Jerry Spinelli (1990). As the reader follows the main character through a number of personal struggles and adventures with many people and situations, bias, prejudice, and inequity are evident. This is a highly effective piece of literature that helps inspire students to work toward a social-reconstructivist society.

❖ What Effect Does Socioeconomic Status Have on Children's Learning?

In the past twenty-five years, American society has undergone many socioeconomic changes. The educational system had previously been structured for delivery to middle-class Americans—a rather stereotypical image of a two-parent family with adequate income being produced by the principal earner as father and homeowner. The mother might have helped with support for extras, which would include such items as higher education for the children.

Today's educators face a more fluid socioeconomic picture. A family's situation in a particular economic level (i.e., lower, middle, upper) depends on such factors as income, residence, profession, and level of education. With contemporary developments including technological advances, changing family status, careers requiring relocation, and the prominence of equity issues (feminine and minority), the middle class as we have known it has begun to shrink. Instead, teachers face an increase in numbers of poor and disadvantaged youth in the elementary schools.

With these demographic changes come such concerns as health care, abuse (physical, mental, and substance), neglect, inadequate housing, poor nutrition, and negative educational experiences as they relate directly to learning opportunity and socioeconomic status. People under economic pressure are not necessarily those who would fit the lower-class stereotype. Some may be affluent adults who have suddenly lost their jobs and the ability to provide for their families as they have been accustomed to doing. Some may suddenly find themselves heading single-parent households and not receiving adequate child support to maintain their previous middle-income status. With the steady influence of technology and mass communication, many jobs are being eliminated and companies downsizing, putting executives out of work. Those who survive the cuts may be so overworked that they cannot provide the kind of parenting that is necessary to develop confident, competent children within a family.

Teachers who recognize these challenges can help children in the elementary classrooms adjust to the changes by taking the following measures:

- Noting the similarities and differences among all people in the country and the world
- Engaging children in cooperative learning experiences
- Selecting materials and activities that show males and females in equal roles
- Inviting parents to become partners in their children's education through literacy programs, visitation, and sharing
- Providing positive role models of adults other than parents so that other caretakers are recognized and accepted
- Providing extended school care experiences for children whose parents and caregivers work beyond the school day
- Providing additional experiences for children whose parents and caregivers cannot take them to sporting, cultural, and recreational events
- Utilizing alternative assessment that involves observation, informal assessment, demonstration, portfolios, and communication skills

One good book that addresses some socioeconomic issues is *Tar Beach* by Faith Ringgold (1991). It is the story of a young girl in Harlem who dreams of the day when she can be free enough to be anything she wishes to be. Images of the inner city and expressed concerns about belonging and employment security are real in this book for young children. The illustrations, in their vitality, won the Caldecott Honor Award for the author/illustrator, who tells her own story.

Because today's educators face a student population subject to rapid changes in socioeconomic status, they must remember to teach all students without concern that background or experience will limit academic successes. Instead, teachers should have confidence in the level of experience that children can have within the classroom through effective, appropriate children's literature that is multicultural.

❖ How Do Children of the World Communicate in Different Ways?

When all other issues have been addressed, communication between children in the elementary classroom becomes the final concern. Language differences and limitations due to such handicaps as hearing loss and blindness can determine acceptance of oneself and others. The same is true for the child who must use a communication board or other device to express feelings and needs. Computerization and technology have enhanced alternative communication with such resources as audio- and videocassettes, CD ROMs, and communication screens.

Following are differentiated learning activities that involve varied communication in the elementary classroom:

- Describing objects, places, and events verbally
- Participating in class discussions
- Speaking in front of small or large groups
- Recognizing the importance of nonverbal communication
- Role-playing
- Thinking critically
- Engaging in creative problem solving
- Brainstorming, webbing, illustrating
- Identifying diverse communication systems
- Attempting communication in a second language
- Comparing and contrasting various communication forms
- Listening and responding to music and art of diverse cultures

ALIKI (1993) dedicates her book *Communication* to all "the tellers and listeners of the world" (p. vi). Through picture, symbol, and word, she explains that communication is a complicated process that takes many acceptable forms, such as verbal expression, body language, Braille, laughter, and crying. She concludes with the statement that communication means knowing that you are not alone. Surely multiculturalism across all of the issues addressed in this chapter includes the learner's belief that he or she is not alone but is special and valued as a loving person in the elementary classroom.

❖ Summary

Multiculturalism has many definitions. It is most commonly regarded as an idea or concept, an educational reform movement, and/or a process of teaching. It encompasses issues of self-esteem, family structure, ethnicity, gender equity, ageism, exceptionalities, values, socioeconomic status, and communication differences. Children's literature is the vehicle through which multiculturalism can be integrated within the regular curriculum and content. Today's teachers will attempt to make their students become more aware of themselves and others and then become agents of social change in the world.

❖ Reflections and Questions to Consider

1. What is multicultural education? Who are some of the noted authorities in this area?

2. How can teachers integrate multiculturalism within the classroom? What role does children's literature play?

3. Select a particular children's book that is multicultural. Design a lesson for sharing the book with your students in order to move them through one of the developmental stages of multicultural awareness. Share this lesson with your fellow students/colleagues.

❖ Children's Literature Cited

Ackerman, K. (1988). *Song and dance man.* New York: Alfred A. Knopf.

ALIKI. (1993). *Communication.* New York: Scholastic.

Buscaglia, L. (1982). *The fall of Freddie the Leaf: A story of life for all ages.* Thorofare, NJ: Slack.

Cleary, B. (1990). *Ramona Quimby.* New York: Morrow.

Fox, M. (1985). *Wilfrid Gordon McDonald Partridge.* New York: Kane Miller.

Gardiner, J. R. (1980). *Stone Fox.* New York: HarperCollins.

Hamilton, V. (1985). *The people could fly: American black folktales.* New York: Alfred A. Knopf.

Hoffman, M. (1991). *Amazing Grace.* New York: Dial.

Jenness, A. (1990). *Families: A celebration of diversity, commitment, and love.* Boston: Houghton Mifflin.

Ringgold, F. (1991). *Tar Beach.* New York: Scholastic.

Rosen, M. J. (1992). *Elijah's angel.* San Diego, CA: Harcourt Brace.

Spinelli, J. (1990). *Maniac Magee.* New York: Scholastic.

Udry, J. M. (1991). *What Mary Jo shared.* New York: Scholastic.

Yolen, J. (1977). *The seeing stick.* New York: Crowell.

❖ References

Banks, J. A. (1989). Integrating the curriculum with ethnic content: Approaches and guidelines. In J. A. Banks & C. A. Banks (Eds.). *Multicultural Education: Issues and Perspectives.* Boston: Allyn & Bacon.

Banks, J. A. (1991). Teaching multicultural literacy to teachers. In J. Marshall & J. T. Sears (Eds.), *Teaching Education* (pp. 135–144). Columbia, SC: University of South Carolina Press.

Banks, J. A. (1994). *An introduction to multicultural education.* Boston: Allyn & Bacon.

Banks, J. A., & Banks, C. A. (Eds.). (1989). *Multicultural education: Issues and perspectives.* Boston: Allyn & Bacon.

Boyer, J. B. (1990). *Curriculum materials for ethnic diversity.* Lawrence, KS: University of Kansas, Center for Black Leadership Development and Research.

Bullard, S. (1991). Sorting through the multicultural rhetoric. *Educational Leadership, 49* (4), 4–7.

Dancy, E. (1987). *Multicultural early childhood resource guide.* Albany, NY: New York State Education Department.

Darity, E. R. (1985). *Multiethnic perspectives on education.* Paper presented at the national conference of the National Association for Women Deans, Administrators, and Counselors, Milwaukee, WI.

De Poncins, Gontran. (1941). *Kabloona.* New York: Reynal & Hitchkock.

Derman-Sparks, L., and the A.B.C. Task Force. (1989). *Anti-bias curriculum: Tools for empowering young children.* Washington, DC: National Association for Young Children.

Goode, C. (Ed.) (1973). *Dictionary of education.* New York: McGraw Hill.

Finazzo, D. A. (1991). *About me and others: A multicultural education curriculum.* Unpublished manuscript.

Finazzo, D. A. (1992). The effects of a multicultural curriculum on the attitudes of first grade students (Doctoral dissertation, Indiana University of Pennsylvania, 1992). *Dissertation Abstracts International.*

Leipzig, J. (1987). Helping whole children grow: Nonsexist childrearing for infants and toddlers. In B. Neugebauer (Ed.), *Alike and different: Exploring our humanity with young children* (pp. 36–45) Redmond, WA: Exchange Press.

McCormick, T. E. (1983, November). *No one model American family: A necessary understanding for effective multicultural education programs for young children.* Paper presented at the annual meeting of the National Association for the Education of Young Children, Washington, DC.

The Netsilik Eskimos on the Sea Ice. (1969). Man: A Course of Study, no. 7. Cambridge, MA: Educational Development Center.

Ramsey, P. G., Vold, E. B., & Williams, L. R. (1989). *Multicultural education: A source book.* New York: Garland.

Rudman, M. K. (1995). *Children's literature: an issues approach.* White Plains, NY: Longman.

Sleeter, C. E., & Grant, C. A. (1987). An analysis of multicultural education in the United States. *Harvard Educational Review, 57* (4), 421–442.

Standifer, J. A. (1987). The multicultural, nonsexist principle: We can't afford to ignore it. *Journal of Negro Education, 56,* 471–474.

Tiedt, P. L., & Tiedt, I. M. (1986). *Multicultural teaching.* Boston: Allyn & Bacon.

West, B. (1987). Children are caught—between home and school, culture and school. In B. Neugebauer (Ed.), *Alike and different: Exploring our humanity with young children.* (pp. 124–135). Redmond, WA: Exchange Press.

Yarbrough, L. (1992, January/February). Three questions for the multiculturalism debate. *Changes,* pp. 64–69.

CHAPTER 5

The only sense that is common in the long run, is the sense of change . . . and we all instinctively avoid it.

E. B. White

Selecting and Evaluating Children's Literature That Is Multicultural

▌ Distinguishing story elements
▌ Critical thinking

❖ **What Literary Elements Are Evident in Children's Literature That Is Multicultural?**

Literature written specifically with children in mind has been classified according to genre. It also may be classified according to the literary elements that are present within each work. Identifying these elements in children's books involves examining the printed text to see how the words of the author relate specifically to

▌ character,
▌ theme,
▌ plot,
▌ setting, and
▌ style.

Each of these story elements will be defined in this chapter, with specific children's literature selections cited as appropriate examples of high-quality use of those elements. Likewise, lessons that focus on the development of literary elements using particular children's books will be featured within this section.

How Is Characterization Developed?

In children's literature that is multicultural, as in other children's stories, *characterization* involves the development of the main and supporting characters—people, animals, or creatures—within the story. The main character generally has a problem to solve, and his or her relationships with the environment, other people, and events determine the outcome of the story.

Characters are most commonly identified as *protagonist/antagonist* and *main character/supporting character*. The *protagonist* is portrayed as the "good" or "positive" force in the story. The *antagonist*, who often occupies an equally important role, is the "bad" or "evil" element. Both types need not be present in every story; this is totally dependent upon the genre of the book (see chapter 3).

The *main character* is that person, animal, creature, or inanimate object upon whom or which the story is based. As children read books for pleasure and information, the main characters receive most of their attention.

Supporting characters or minor characters are those whose presence enhances the story line and helps in the development of the main character and the action. They receive more limited attention because the author is unable to develop them to the extent that the main character is developed. Sometimes these lesser characters are depicted as "flat" or one-dimensional. Thus, a supporting character may have one role or one noted dimension or characteristic that qualifies the character for the role in the story. Such a character tends to take the typical evil part, the simpleton role, or the role of the sarcastic, mean person. Examples are Aunt Spiker and Aunt Sponge in the fantasy *James and the Giant Peach* (Dahl, 1961).

On the other hand, well-rounded characters are those who are depicted with many traits. As main characters they often undergo change in the course of the story, becoming more fully developed and demonstrating many different traits through various means. James of *James and the Giant Peach* (Dahl, 1961) is one such character. He interacts with many different creatures and, in the process of this interaction, becomes more accepting of himself and his circumstances. The changes in his feelings and personality make him a *dynamic* rather than a *static* character. Throughout the story the aunts are static in that they remain mean, bitter, and self-centered. They can also be considered *foils* for James as they embody the complete opposites of his personality and traits.

Characterization is developed in many ways:

1. through dialogue;
2. through thoughts of the character and others;
3. through action;
4. through descriptive words, phrases, and narration of the author; and
5. through illustrations within the book and on the cover.

In the animal fantasy *Charlotte's Web*, E. B. White (1952) does a remarkable job of developing characterization. (This work also qualifies as a children's book that is multicultural because it deals with the issues of self-esteem, acceptance of others, and death of a friend.) The character of Wilbur the pig, the main character, is developed through his dialogue with other animals and the others' dialogue about him. Likewise, the story's plot or action helps the reader understand who Wilbur is as he moves around the barnyard and the fair. Wilbur is often found alone, thinking of his life and relationships; in such scenes the main character's thoughts enhance his development. Detailed descriptions enable the reader actually to visualize Wilbur under certain circumstances. Finally, cover illustrations and others within the book help clarify the image of the main character in the reader's eyes.

It is most important in multicultural children's selections that the characters not be depicted in stereotypical fashion. Stereotypical, flat characters are those cast in images that are commonplace and predictable. The danger in character development is to portray certain groups of people in certain ways—for example, strong males and weak females; athletic and rhythmic African-Americans; intellectual Asians; lazy and unpunctual Latinos; hot-tempered Italians; savage Native Americans; frugal Jews; inactive, failing elderly people. It is crucial for readers to examine characters for well-roundedness and to recognize the limited extent to which the author has developed certain characters.

What Types of Themes Are Evident in Culturally Diverse Children's Books?

The theme of a book defines its purpose for the reader. It is the underlying message or main idea that pervades the story. Very often, by the nature of its genre (i.e., fantasy or realistic fiction), the theme is very evident and well defined; it is direct and explicit for the reader. By contrast, in many works for adults, the theme is less evident and obvious; rather, it is subtle and implied by the author.

As young readers look for the theme, the teacher may ask them to consider the following questions:

▪ What is the author trying to say in the story?
▪ What message do you get from the story?

- Why might the author want to share this story or tale with you?
- What ideas or thoughts seem to be carried throughout the story?
- Does the author leave you with special thoughts, ideas, worries, fears, or morals after reading the story?

Sometimes more than one theme is evident in a book. One such story is *Old Turtle* by Douglas Wood (1992). The story is a fable with a peaceful message about cooperation in the world. Within it are values-related themes of conservation, collaboration, recognition of differences and similarities among people, and belief in a higher being. In discussion groups and with questions to guide critical thinking, children can determine the implied theme(s) of such a book.

Following is a lesson based on the children's book *Tikki Tikki Tembo* by Arlene Mosel (1968). Participating in this lesson, children are likely to identify the theme of the story on their own as well as to use it as a model for their own writings.

FOCUS

Reading—DRTA, prediction, guessing, cause-effect maps, summarizing, following directions, sequencing

Rationale

The purpose of this lesson is to provide a connection between Chinese folklore and DRTA (Directed Reading-Thinking Activity) through the use of a predictable book.

SUBJECT/CONTENT AREA

Reading

Goals

To provide various graphic organizers in relation to folklore in order to enhance and improve comprehension for elementary readers.

Objectives

The students will help in the reading of a selection and predict what will happen next by making good guesses based on what has already occurred in the story.

The students will create cause-effect maps as a group.

The students will retell the story, noting proper sequence.

The students will use a summarizing spinner to choose a topic for communication and write about that topic in their journals.

The students will participate in a directed cooking activity, following specific directions for a Chinese dish.

Terms/Vocabulary

Honored

Heir

Predicting

Guessing

Tikki tikki tembo—no sa rembo—chari bari ruchi—pip peri pembo

Chang

Festival of the Eighth Moon

Cause-effect

Bao (steamed buns)

Steamer

Materials

Tikki Tikki Tembo by Arlene Mosel (1968)

Experience paper

Summarizing spinners

Refrigerated biscuit dough

Pork sausage (½ lb.)

Garlic

Onion

Cornstarch

Vegetable oil

Steamer

Journals

Readiness/Motivation

Reiterate to the students the importance of folktales and of Chinese culture. Show the book *Tikki Tikki Tembo,* and ask if any students recognize it. If some do, simply ask them not to tell the whole story yet because the whole group will be doing a new and different activity with the story even though some may have heard it before. In introducing the story, encourage the students to look at the pictures and think about who might be in the story, where it might take place, and what might be happening. Inform students that knowing the purpose—listening for cause and effect—will aid them in their reading. As a culminating experience, the students will be able to engage in another important cultural activity—cooking some Chinese food. Be sure to ask if any of them have eaten in a Chinese restaurant and if they have noticed things that may be different there.

Procedures/Instructions

1. After all students have arrived, join the group for a story. Ask students to restate the characteristics of folktales. Ask students to relate the importance of folklore in Chinese society even today.

2. Show the book *Tikki Tikki Tembo.* Pass out multiple copies of the book. By a show of hands, have students indicate if they have seen the book before. If they have, remind them that they must not tell the ending of the story to their friends but instead must listen very carefully for specific purposes—which will be described a bit later. Those who have read the book before may be chosen to help read the story aloud for the group.

3. Ask students to define the word *predict.* Ask them likewise to define *guess.*

4. Inform the students that, as they look at the pictures in the book, they are to help predict or guess what the story may be about. Ask the following questions:

   What is the setting?

   Who is in the story?

   When does it take place?

   Where does it take place?

   What is the problem in the story?

   How is the problem solved?

   What type of ending might this story have?

5. Record these answers on chart paper before reading the story with the students.

6. Periodically, throughout the reading, choose students who have indicated that they are familiar with the story to read aloud. Stop occasionally to ask questions regarding their predictions.

7. Continue the reading to verify predictions.

8. At the conclusion of the story, ask students to retell the story using their books as a guide.

9. Record the summary line by line on chart paper. As students add lines, ask the following questions where appropriate:

   What was the Chinese custom for naming sons a long, long time ago?

   What is a custom?

   What were the names of the two sons, and what did they mean?

   Who is the Old Man with the Ladder?

   How does the Old Man with the Ladder get the water out of Chang?

   What is the Festival of the Eighth Month?

   How fast did Chang run for help when Tikki Tikki Tembo fell into the well?

   What made Chang out of breath?

What does his mother call Chang?

How do you think she feels about him?

What happened to Tikki Tikki Tembo after he fell into the well?

How long did it take for him to get better?

What is the point of the story?

10. As lines are added, use questions that involve predicting and verifying.

11. At the completion of the retelling, ask students if they know what a cause is. Ask these questions:

What do we mean when we say "cause"?

Define *effect.*

Can you look at these events and identify a cause and then an effect?

12. As students identify each cause and effect, connect them with arrows on the chart paper for all to see.

13. Instruct students to return to their small assigned groups to work on their summarizing spinners, choosing the one or two areas that they would most like to write about in their journals. While some students are writing and others are completing story illustrations, others will engage in a cooking activity in the kitchen area. Be sure to connect this cooking activity to the story and the mentions of the festival and the foods that are shared at that time.

14. Follow the recipe for Bao (steamed buns). Instruct students to follow you as you model. Put buns into the steamer for the designated time. Serve them, when cooked, with iced tea and fortune cookies.

Recipe for Bao (steamed buns)

1 tube of refrigerated biscuit dough

$\frac{1}{2}$ pound of frozen ground breakfast sausage, defrosted

1 tablespoon oil

$\frac{1}{3}$ cup chopped onion

1 clove chopped garlic

2 tablespoons cornstarch

1 cup water

In a wok, brown the breakfast sausage, oil, onion, and garlic. Allow to cool. Mix cornstarch and water until thickened. Combine cornstarch mixture and sausage mixture, and warm until the sauce is thick. Remove from stove. Separate the dough into biscuits, and roll into round flat shapes with rolling pin. Drop a teaspoon of the sausage mixture into each biscuit, then pinch and twist to close. To cook, place the biscuits into steamer for about 10 minutes. If steamer is not available, place on ungreased cookie sheet and bake at 350° until lightly browned. Serve immediately.

Student Evaluation

Students will be evaluated on the ability to recall the story details in order orally within the group. Students will be evaluated on the ability to make predictions and back their predictions with facts from the story. Further evaluation will be made as they point out cause-effect relationships within the details. As the students go back to their small groups, they will be observed as they stay on task to write in their journals. By properly following directions, they will find success in the creation of Chinese Bao.

What Is the Plot of the Story?

The plot of any children's book is the action of the story. It is the described set of events that span the beginning, middle, and end of the book. The plot includes the details in a sequence. It is the way in which the main character moves through the story to deal with other characters, situations, problems, and environments to get to the end and ultimately solve the problem. The plot is the method by which the main character deals with conflict, whether that conflict be internal (within the self) or external (with other people, circumstances, issues, situations, or environments).

Plots can have many possible structures (Russell, 1991; Hillman, 1995):

- Dramatic/linear
- Parallel
- Episodic
- Circular/cumulative

A story with dramatic/linear structure involves a conflict centered on the main character. The story follows a predictable progression, starting with descriptions of the setting and characters and the beginnings of the action. Somewhere in the middle of the story, the action moves toward a major conflict or climax, which leads toward a sense of resolution at the end. Figure 5–1 illustrates this plot structure.

Parallel plots develop in the same fashion as linear plots, but with two or more plots running simultaneously, commonly evolving toward similar endings or resolutions. Russell (1991) cites the example of the classic story *Blueberries for Sal* by Robert McCloskey (1993), in which the theme is separation, anxiety, and fear. The actions of the two main characters—a little girl and a bear cub, both without caregivers—coincide, with the plots very similar and reaching the same resolution. The parallel structure might be illustrated as shown in figure 5–2.

Plots that are episodic comprise segments that are rather self-standing, often seen as separate episodes or pieces of action that constitute the chapters of a book. Two books about young girls and their lives, *Little*

FIGURE 5–1 Dramatic/linear plot structure

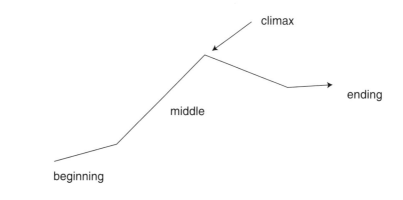

Women (1868) by Louisa May Alcott and *Little House in the Big Woods* by Laura Ingalls Wilder (1953), are great examples. The episodic plot structure is illustrated in figure 5–3.

In the final pattern, cumulative or circular plot development, certain events build upon one another as the original idea persists and other items, ideas, phrases, or occurrences are added one by one. This structure is common in predictable children's picture books as well as in some of

FIGURE 5–2 Parallel plots

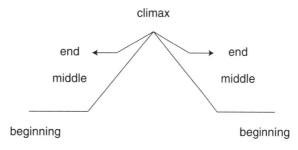

FIGURE 5–3 Episodic plots

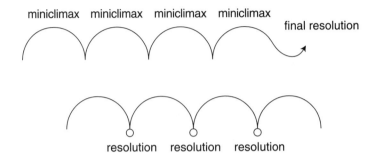

the traditional folktales of various cultures. Figure 5–4 illustrates the cumulative plot structure.

The following lesson plan shows how the book *Weaving of a Dream: A Chinese Folktale* (by Marilee Heyer (1986) can help children become aware of characterization, plot, and theme.

FOCUS

Reading—story frame creation, comparing/contrasting

Rationale

The purpose of the lesson is to pass on a portion of the Chinese culture through the tradition of the Chinese folktale—the essence of the culture being based on

FIGURE 5–4 Cumulative or circular plot development

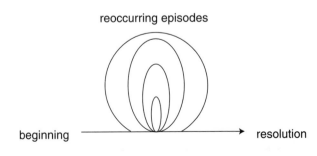

interpersonal relationships and certain ways of living, acting, and dealing with other people.

SUBJECT/CONTENT AREA

Reading

Goals

To provide an opportunity for elementary youngsters to use high-quality literature from a culture different from their own to identify the major elements of folklore through a story map that schematizes setting, problem, goal, episodes, and resolution.

Objectives

The students will demonstrate increased knowledge about Chinese culture through exposure to and discussion of Chinese folklore.

The students will be able to practice listening skills.

The students will be able to develop the ability to organize thoughts through use of a story map.

The students will identify the major elements of Chinese folklore: setting, problem, goal, episodes, and resolution.

The students will be able to strengthen their writing skills.

The students will create book covers, using wallpaper and panda bear patterns, for their personal books.

Terms/Vocabulary

Story map
Setting
Problem
Goal
Episodes
Resolution
Collage
Compare/contrast
Embroidery
Brocade
Sun Mountain
Leme
Letuie
Leje
Widow
Crone

Materials

> *Weaving of a Dream* by Marilee Heyer (1986)
>
> Experience paper
>
> Lightweight cardboard (10 in. by 12 in.)
>
> Wallpaper Sample books
>
> Glue
>
> Scissors
>
> Journals

Readiness/Motivation

Reestablish student schemata by reviewing those thinking processes that the children may have used in the area of reading folklore—retelling, Big Book, prediction, guessing, summarizing, cloze, cause/effect. Ask students to relate again the things that make Chinese folklore important to that culture, and draw a comparison with the importance of folklore to American culture. Begin the lesson by telling the students that, through listening and careful observation of beautiful pictures, they will learn more Chinese folklore.

Procedures/Instructions

1. Establish the purpose of the lesson and the sequence of the morning's events by listing them on the experience paper.

2. Announce to students that they will be listening to a story about an old widow and her special gift of weaving. They are to listen particularly for story details that will be discussed later. They are also to look very carefully at the pictures.

3. Read *Weaving of a Dream.*

4. Throughout the story, refer to artifacts in the classroom that help to develop schemata—robe, name chops, brocades, embroidered slippers. Name chops are prints in the Chinese culture that are made of wood and reflect the name and/or interest of an individual.

5. Use contextual clues to have students help define *embroidery, brocade, crone,* and *widow.*

6. When the reading is finished, ask students to recall the story by completing as a group the story frame: setting (characters, time, and place), problem, goal, episodes, and resolution. Record this information on the chart paper.

7. Explain to students that, whenever they have trouble recalling a story, they may use the story map frame to organize their thoughts.

8. Give students a break for water and stretching.

9. Finally, explain how students will make their own book covers out of cardboard and wallpaper. Each student receives two pieces of lightweight cardboard and

three pieces of wallpaper of his or her choice. Two pieces of wallpaper are used to cover the cardboard; the third is used as a base for the panda bear patterns. Cut two pieces of wallpaper about ½ inch larger (all around) than the cardboard base. Cut corners of the wallpaper and then fold sides of wallpaper over edges to cover up the board. Use glue to hold in place. Use a hole punch to make two or three holes in each. Using creativity and personal design, students can make the covers of their choice for their own books.

Student Evaluation

Students will be evaluated on active participation in the group creation of the story map (see figure 5–5). Through their journal writings, students can be observed using all of the story elements as they "tell" their own versions of stories they have created. Oral response will be the criterion for student evaluation by the teacher.

How Does the Setting Influence Multicultural Children's Literature?

Setting is defined as the time and place of a story. Whether or not the plot follows any of the previously mentioned patterns, the setting in a multicultural book plays an important part. The importance of details in the setting depends on the genre of the book. In folklore, it is acceptable to share "once upon a time" tales in which place and time may not be of primary concern. However, children's literature that is multicultural includes stories whose settings reflect diverse cultures and places and help to tell the truth about people and their lives.

FIGURE 5–5 *Weaving of a Dream* story map

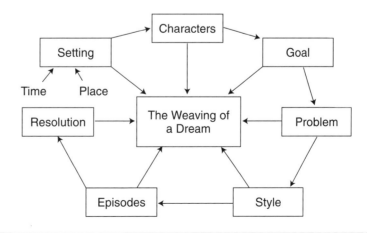

Settings in historical fiction and realistic fiction must reflect fact rather than stereotypical or inaccurate descriptions of places and times, whether current or past. Whatever the setting, the feelings aroused in the reader by descriptions of place and time help further to create the story. In other words, the setting, however integral or incidental, establishes the mood within which the plot takes place.

In Gary Paulsen's books about survival, time and place set the stage for the conflict that faces young men growing up in contemporary times. Gary Paulsen in *Hatchet* (1988) has the main character, Brian Robeson, see this setting:

> For a good distance, perhaps two hundred yards, it was fairly clear. There were tall pines, the kind with no limbs until very close to the top, with a gentle breeze sighing in them, but not too much low brush. Two hundred yards up there seemed to be a belt of thick, lower brush start-ing—about ten or twelve feet high—and that formed a wall he could not see through. It seemed to go on around the lake, thick and lushly green, but he could not be sure. (p. 62).

This well-described setting helps the character and the reader identify with the situation at hand—a young boy facing the family trauma of divorce and stranded alone after a plane crash in the wilderness. The out-comes of stories that depict realistically children dealing with controver-sial issues depend on adequate setting descriptions.

How Does Style Affect the Meaning of a Book?

Authors of children's books have varying styles. As in all written forms, the writer must set a mood or feeling; this is the style of the book. The reader is encouraged to ask,

- What do I feel as I am reading this book?
- What does the author do to make me feel a certain way when I read this book?
- How does the author use language to affect the telling of the story?
- Does the author use certain techniques to make me feel a certain way when I read this book?
- Do I notice different language sounds or word meanings when I am reading this book?
- Can I notice humor—or, instead, sadness—when I am reading?

All of these questions address the subject of style. Throughout the read-ing of a book, children and teachers will notice that the author may use certain language patterns to express the feelings of the characters, set the scene, and direct the action. Some of the language may be figurative, with the author saying one thing and meaning something quite different. Metaphors and similes may be used to make comparisons between characters and events. Other figurative tools such as personification (where inanimate objects take on human characteristics), alliteration (where beginning sounds of words are repeated), and assonance (where repetitive vowel sounds are evident in words and sentences) help to establish the written style.

Some styles reflect humor; others are quite serious. With the choice of style, the author determines how the message will be sent to the reader. Use of a particular dialect also can be regarded as the writer's style. Virginia Hamilton uses African-American dialect, personification, and humor to retell the folktales of He Lion, Bruh Bear, and Bruh Rabbit in *The People Could Fly* (1985). The use of dialect strengthens the story as the reader hears, " 'Listen,' said He Lion, and then he roared: 'ME AND MYSELF. ME AND MYSELF. Nobody tell me what not to do,' he said. 'I'm the king of the forest, *me and myself* ' " (p. 8).

As the style of Hamilton's work helps convey the historical aspect of the African-American heritage, the style of Kate Waters and Madeline Slovenz-Low's *Lion Dancer* (1990) gives a good flavor of the Chinese heritage. The day-to-day life of Ernie Wan is shown through his words as translated by the authors and through the vivid photographs of Martha Cooper. The style—short, poignant sentences likened to the speech of a very young Chinese boy—is authentic, simple, and informative. The following is a lesson that could be used to introduce this story to young children.

FOCUS

Reading—Question, Answer, Detail; Sequencing; Tracing; Fine Motor Coordination

Rationale

The purpose of this lesson is to encourage student exploration and appreciation of traditional Chinese celebrations through different facets of culture (history, art, customs, religious practices, foods, and games) and to help students discern commonalities and differences between Chinese and American celebrations, all through the use of literature.

SUBJECT/CONTENT AREA

Reading

Goals

To expose students to the culminating experience that joins all areas of Chinese culture—the festival—in order to bring closure to a study of ways the Chinese have contributed in all facets to our society today

To develop in elementary students the ability to use QAD (Question, Answer, Detail) in reading nonfiction

To provide students with sequencing practice that is not limited to putting story parts in order

Objectives

The students will learn that the Chinese engage in different kinds of celebrations.

The students will compare the Chinese new year celebration with celebrations in the United States.

The students will ask questions, give answers, and add details to information regarding the Chinese new year festival.

The students will actively put events in proper order for the five days of the Chinese new year.

The students will explain the significance of paper cutting in China.

The students will demonstrate the art of paper cutting, creating their own designs or tracing using the folding or unfolded technique.

Terms/Vocabulary

Bai-nien (Happy New Year)
Po-po (boiled dumplings)
Dragon dance
Lion dance
"Money tree"
Paper cut
Question
Answer
Detail
Sequencing

Materials

Lion Dancer by Kate Waters and Madeline Slovenz-Low (1990)

Origami paper

Construction paper

Scissors

Experience paper

Patterns and models

Glue

Readiness/Motivation

Students are to recall special holidays that are celebrated in the United States. Prompt them with these questions:

How do we celebrate . . . ?

What kinds of special things do your family members do on that holiday?

What makes a festival or holiday special?

Why do people celebrate?

As students complete their answers, ask them to look around the room for signs of Chinese festivals and holidays—lanterns, dragons, kites, paper cuttings, foods. Inform students that they will read about the Chinese new year and then have an opportunity to create their own paper cuts.

Procedures/Instructions

1. Introduce the concepts of festival and celebration to the large group of youngsters. Ask students to name American celebrations and festivals. Generate questions about the celebrations, making the discussion more personal:

How does your family celebrate . . . ?

Why do we celebrate . . . ?

Which is your favorite celebration and why?

2. Explain that the Chinese people also have built their culture around celebrations and festivals. Some are much like ours, and others are very different. For instance, Chinese people do not celebrate birthdays as we do. Instead, they celebrate only for the very old and do so by offering them plain noodles—for a "long life." Explain that the group's task will be to learn about the Chinese new year and compare it to their own.

3. Read the story. Restate the purpose for reading—listening and reading for the events and their sequence (order) and recalling specific details.

4. Read aloud and call on volunteers to read as well. Note the photographs.

5. Upon completion of the book, draw three columns labeled "Question," "Answer," and "Detail" on a piece of chart paper. Ask the students questions about an event or day in the festival. Fill in the columns on the chart paper with your questions, the students' answers, and supporting details.

6. Pass out sentence strips to individuals. Ask them to stand and read their strips aloud. Explain that they must help to put the events in the proper order.

7. Tape the strips on the paper in order as students give them to you.

8. Mention the importance of following a sequence. Explain to students that they will have an opportunity to create paper cuts if they follow the correct sequence.

9. Demonstrate the procedure for making various paper cuts.

10. Break into small groups and pass out construction paper, scissors, and patterns (teacher-made designs of animals, objects, and people that the students may trace and cut or use as models for their own designs).

11. Circulate as students work independently.

12. When every student has had a chance to make a paper cut, display the student work.

Student Evaluation

Students will have an opportunity to read orally and will thus be evaluated. As students progress in individual work, the teacher will make candid observation of students in action—cutting and folding paper. Cooperation in the group effort using the QAD method will be observed.

It is clear to the reader of children's books that the literary elements of characterization, setting, plot, theme, and style affect the delivery of the story and the way it is understood. The authenticity and appearance of culturally diverse themes and characters are also very critical in contemporary education, and they foster the continuation of multicultural historical perspectives in our schools. Although the elements just discussed deal with the use of words in text, illustrations and other visual elements play an important role as well.

FIGURE 5-6 Literary elements of a book

LITERARY ELEMENTS

Element	What is it?	What is its value?	How is it seen?
Character	Who, what is in the story	Answers "Who?" or "What?" Establishes someone/something for children to relate to personally; shows personality and relationships with others	Person/animal/thing can be seen as protagonist or antagonist, can be main or supporting characters
Plot	The action of the story; includes the beginning, middle, and ending; the climax is the culmination point	Establishes the pattern of the events of the story; encourages retelling by students; gives a type of chronology	Can be complex, with multiple plots, or simple, with action moving to a logical conclusion and resolution by the main character(s); sequential and predictable; conflict of man vs. nature

FIGURE 5-6 Continued

LITERARY ELEMENTS

Element	What is it?	What is its value?	How is it seen?
Theme	The message the author has for the reader; why the book was written; the main idea or central purpose	Establishes the mood of the story; sets the purpose; can help the reader see the "truth" in the world and establish values	Can be directly or indirectly stated (implied), as a moral
Point of view	The speaker or narrator of the book	Shares the thoughts of the writer through the text itself; events and feelings are explained, expressing the inner thoughts of the author	First person: telling a personal narrative; third person who is omniscient: knowing the thoughts of all the characters from an outsider's viewpoint; implied speaker: a person's character is not directly stated but can be construed by author's ideas; the reader may also be implied if the author wants the reader to have a certain attitude while reading
Setting	Where the story takes place; time and place	Distinguishes among past, present, and future and familiarizes students with known and unknown places in their world	Can be imaginative or real depending upon the genre; events are sequential; sets the historical background; may be symbolic if fantasy
Style	The way the author uses words to share the message	Encourages children to look at the various ways language can be shared	Through humor, rhyme, song, drama, poetry, repetition

What Are Visual Elements in Culturally Diverse Children's Books?

Directly connected with the printed text are the illustrations of children's books. In books for young children, much of the mood is conveyed through the visual elements. Certainly characterization is enhanced by pictures, as is setting.

Following are the most common visual elements:

- Line
- Color
- Shape
- Texture
- Arrangement
- Total effect
- Style

FIGURE 5–7 Visual elements of a book

VISUAL ELEMENTS

Element	What is it?	What is its value?	How is it seen?
Line	Visible/invisible lines that can be part of a total picture	Directs to points of interest or shows movement	Horizontal, vertical, bold, or fine
Color	The hues and shadows that are seen within the art itself	Sets the mood of the story and the tone of the work	Warm, cool, black/white/pencil
Shape	The formation of lines in a closed fashion	Outlines objects, projects feelings of the artist	Geometric, curving, symmetrical
Texture	The blending of line, color, and shape to make the art take on a fuller dimension	Establishes reality of the characters, setting	Three-dimensional, feathery, cross-hatched
Medium	The type of material/approach of the art	Provides a variety of ways to express the story	Pen and ink, oil, watercolor, paper cut, print
Style	The particular way the artist shares the story and feelings	Expresses the uniqueness of the artist and encourages student self-expression	Realistic, impressionistic, computerized

---

Each of these visual elements will be defined and described very briefly. Connections will be made with quality children's literature illustrations and with the personal testimonies of the artists about their works.

Line in illustrations means the placement of marks on the paper, generally as outlines of characters, animals, scenes, and separations. Lines may appear thin and delicate, giving a sense of fragility to the page, or bold and dark, showing force, fear, and determination. Movement on the page is determined by the vertical and horizontal placement of lines. Russell Freedman's illustrations of Native American life in such books as *Buffalo Hunt* (1988) share the peacefulness of a land of the past with the use of horizontal lines in the fusion of the skyline and the countryside.

Color also sets the mood of a story. Illustrators make strong decisions about feelings when they select bold, bright colors as opposed to muted ones. The cultures of people are reflected strongly through color, as Hamilton chose to do with *The People Could Fly* (1985). Whereas the front cover is in color, the inside pages are black and white, perhaps to depict the conflicting feelings and lives of the black and white folk portrayed through the animal tales. A similar technique was used in the counting book illustrated by Tom Feelings, *Moja Means One: Swahili Counting Book* (Feelings, 1971). These examples show subtle ways to distinguish culture. In other culturally diverse children's selections, the vivid colors of the cultures are apparent—the earthy yellows, browns, oranges, and golds of the Native Americans; the softly colored and subtle quilting reflecting the Jewish people; and the bright greens, blacks, and reds of the Africans.

Finally, Leo Lionni makes a strong statement about friendship, cooperation, and togetherness with *Little Blue and Little Yellow* (1959). Blobs of color jump around the pages as children discover how their personal colors can perhaps blend and be beautiful when love is present.

When readers note the shapes in illustrations, they look at the way lines connect to create forms of some sort. These are often angular or rounded. The rounded shapes of objects, faces, and scenes elicit warm emotions in the reader. The angular, squarish, or rectangular shapes may serve as frames to complete a work, or they may be bold, creating in the reader a feeling of intensity about the situation. One cannot help but note the framing of pictures in the retelling of the English legend *St. George and the Dragon* by Margaret Hodges (1994). This effect causes the reader to feel the confinement of the people as the story progresses.

Texture is the sense of physical touch that the reader experiences by looking at illustrations. Pictures can show the appearance of fur, fabric, sand, or wood. Maurice Sendak extends this gift of texture to the reader of *Where the Wild Things Are* (1963) as the monsters seem to come alive on the pages and the child becomes aware that all children have fears and sometimes react inappropriately to directions from caregivers.

Often the arrangement of illustrations within the book affects the meaning and mood of the work. Through purposeful placement of pictures or figures, the illustrator helps direct the reader's attention to important items, characters, and events.

The total effect of the art work derives from the combination of the lines, colors, shapes, texture, and style of the artist. The style of the artist depends on the medium used. Some artists produce pen-and-ink sketches, many use watercolors and pastels, and still others try collages or montages and graphics or photography. They may seem most comfortable expressing themselves through cartoon drawings in which certain features of the characters and images are highly exaggerated for effect. Much of the artwork associated with the retellings of traditional folklore is representative of the cultural folk art indigenous to the culture and peoples featured. More traditional styles are those known as expressionism (use of paints, exaggerated details of images), impressionism (softness through color and light that produces fantasy images), and surrealism (placement of objects in weird, strange positions to create suspense, drama).

The lesson plan that follows features *The Girl Who Loved Wild Horses* (Goble, 1993). Throughout this Native American folk piece, pictures with

FIGURE 5–8 Visual elements comparison by Stephanie

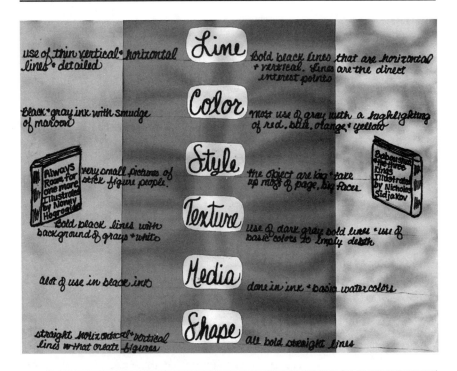

FIGURE 5-9 Visual elements comparison by Cathy

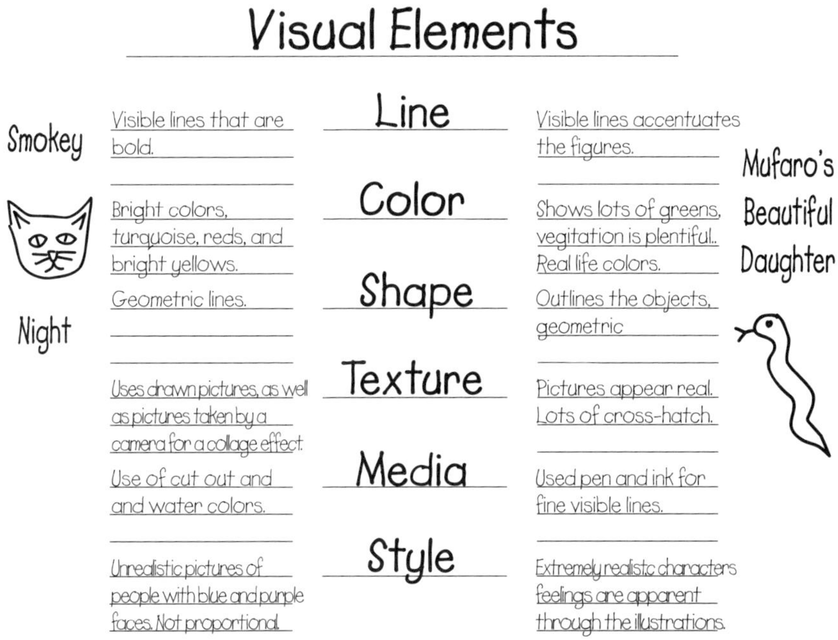

Visual Elements

Smokey	Visible lines that are bold.	**Line**	Visible lines accentuates the figures.	Mufaro's
	Bright colors, turquoise, reds, and bright yellows.	**Color**	Shows lots of greens, vegitation is plentiful. Real life colors.	Beautiful
Night	Geometric lines.	**Shape**	Outlines the objects, geometric	Daughter
	Uses drawn pictures, as well as pictures taken by a camera for a collage effect.	**Texture**	Pictures appear real. Lots of cross-hatch.	
	Use of cut out and and water colors.	**Media**	Used pen and ink for fine visible lines.	
	Unrealistic pictures of people with blue and purple faces. Not proportional.	**Style**	Extremely realistic characters feelings are apparent through the illustrations.	

---

black and/or white backgrounds, often as large as full page, help readers understanding the Native American people and their explanations of earth, creatures, and humanity.

FOCUS

Reading—characterization

Rationale

The purpose of the lesson is to expose students to the Native American culture while giving them opportunity to interact with one another in exploring characterization.

SUBJECT/CONTENT AREA

Reading—age level: 8- to 9-year-olds

Goals

To provide a view of the folklore of Native Americans and the development of characterization in children's literature.

Objectives

The students will read a folktale about Native Americans.

The students will be able to develop an appreciative attitude toward Native Americans through exposure to their culture.

The students will determine how the characters are developed in the story.

The students will create a visual piece that shows the moods and feelings that are developed through the story and its characters.

Terms/Vocabulary

Folktales
Characters

Materials

The Girl Who Loved Wild Horses by Paul Goble (1993)

Drawing paper

Markers, pencils, colored pencils

Readiness/Motivation

Ask students to recall what they know about folktales. What are some folktales that they remember? What are the common elements of folktales? What types of messages do people get from folktales? Finally, what do students think might be included in a Native American folktale?

Procedures/Instructions

1. Gather all students in a comfortable area for reading and sharing.

2. Before reading, ask the students to help you predict what might happen in a story entitled *The Girl Who Loved Wild Horses.* Record their responses on the board or on experience paper.

3. Explain that the group will read this retelling of a folktale in order to understand better the culture of Native Americans and also to try to describe characters and feelings in the story.

4. Read the story to the group. Be sure to share the illustrations and note that the book won an award (the Caldecott) for its illustrations.

5. At the conclusion of the story, share the visual that shows the horse and descriptors of the characters and their feelings. Encourage the students to be creative in making their own visual presentations of similar ideas.

6. When students have completed their projects, display them and have students explain their projects to one another.

FIGURE 5–10 *The Girl Who Loved Wild Horses* student artwork by Scott

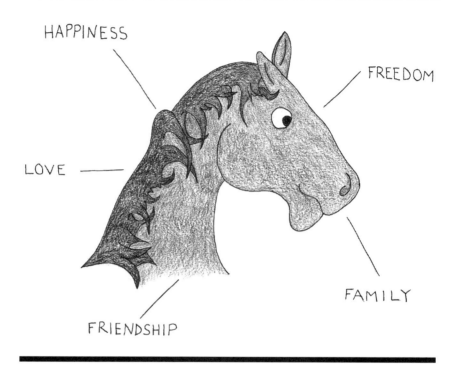

HAPPINESS

FREEDOM

LOVE

FAMILY

FRIENDSHIP

Student Evaluation

Students can be evaluated by their peers who will give them feedback on how well they could retell the story with visuals.

Lisa Campbell Ernst, children's writer and illustrator of *When Bluebell Sang,* explains that children should approach their own art as professional artists do: "Rejoice in who you are! It is your uniqueness that will breathe life into your art" (Cummings, 1992, p. 44). Viewing the works of these artists is as important for children as reading high-quality stories in print—both serve as models for children as they attempt to write and illustrate their own creations. They also help children become better trained in the critical analysis of texts and pictures.

❖ What Is the Importance of Critical Thinking in Selecting Children's Literature?

Educators who use children's literature in their classrooms must decide what books are appropriate to share with their students. A critical analysis of text, illustrations, themes, and style helps to determine book selection. Input from children, parents, and the community lends to credible, careful choices.

❖ Testing the Authenticity of Children's Books

When selecting children's literature for use at school and at home, it is very important that we train ourselves as educators and our students to become critical thinkers. Such thinkers seek the truth and ask many types of questions. Asa G. Hilliard III boldly states the importance of critical thinking:

> We say that the search for truth is our highest goal for students. To foster it, we must facilitate in students the assumption of a critical orientation. Of course, criticism implies an awareness of all cultural alternatives and a thoughtful and honest examination of those alternatives. No cultural tradition can be regarded as immune to criticism. (p. 13).

To look critically at children's books takes courage and training by our faculties. When teachers seem more confident in this process, they in turn pass the critical ability on to their students.

When evaluating the authenticity of children's books that are multicultural, it is often necessary to do the following:

- Seek the advice of experts or those who themselves have culturally diverse backgrounds
- Begin with the original stories of the culture being investigated, rereading original folktales and legends of the early development of the people
- Match retold versions with originals to check authenticity
- Select texts and books that feature culturally diverse groups in active rather than passive roles

Critical readers ask three different types of questions about what they read—factual/literal, interpretive, and evaluative. Factual or literal questions are ones that entail investigation and simple truth. The answers are direct and reflect "who, what, where, when" organizational thinking. There is generally only one correct response to a factual question. Interpretive questions are more open-ended. Many answers may be correct because the reader answers "why" or "how." In testing authenticity of works, the reader may ask, "Why did the main character respond in this way in this folktale?" Evaluative questions place the reader in the story or situation. The responses to these questions relate directly to the reader's personal experiences as connected to the story. Such a question might be, "If you were the protagonist in this story, would you have made the same decision? Why or why not?"

❖ Traditional versus Multicultural Viewpoints

Multicultural curriculum and its delivery have been the subject of much discussion. Many members of ethnic groups support the notion of "centric" curriculum, where students of culturally diverse backgrounds learn about their own particular cultures. Asante (1992) believes that "by 'centering' their students of color, teachers can reduce feelings of dislocation engendered by our society's predominantly 'white self-esteem curriculums'" (p. 28). Students in this type of environment become empowered with their knowledge of their own cultures, and teachers become more understanding of their students through total immersion in the cultural exposure of the students. On the other hand, some educators support educational environments that encourage teachers who "are also responsible, in a highly multireligious and multiethnic society, for creating and cultivating common ground through the literature they teach in all its many forms" (Stotsky, 1992, p. 56). These educators contend that all students need to see the contributions of all cultural groups—majority and minority alike—to their world.

❖ What Constitutes Appropriate Children's Literature?

The first portion of this chapter outlined the literary and visual elements that are common in children's literature. Certainly, as teachers evaluate books for their classrooms, they should endeavor to identify these elements as major components of text and story. Beyond this examination, it is important to ask further questions about books that we choose for our children to read. The questions in the following outline are adapted from criteria developed by James B. Boyer (1990), Bonnie Neugebauer (1987), and Louise Derman-Sparks and the A.B.C. Task Force (1989). Another writer who encourages recognition and awareness of cultural diversity is Stacey York. Her *Roots & Wings* (1991) is particularly valuable to early childhood educators who need to understand the basics of multiculturalism at that level and know how to integrate it effectively in their educational facilities.

Questions for Evaluating Children's Literature That Is Multicultural
The story itself

- Does the story include real and authentic characters?
- Are the actions of the characters true-to-life and not stereotypical?
- Are different cultures portrayed in a positive fashion?
- Within the story, do the characters develop and grow in acceptable ways?

▌ Is the story one that would instruct readers who are not members of a particular group, culture, or population in a way that would increase understanding and acceptance?

▌ Does the story help members of the group or culture portrayed become more proud of their own heritage or background?

▌ Does the language in the book properly reflect the speech of the people featured?

▌ Does the book avoid negative or "loaded" language that slants the story?

▌ Are all characters—males, females, and members of particular groups—featured fairly and equally?

The illustrations

▌ Do the illustrations represent authentic physical characteristics of people of diverse cultures in a natural way?

▌ Do the illustrations complement the story and enhance its telling?

▌ Does the style used by the illustrator correspond to the story?

The author/illustrator

▌ What experiences has the author/illustrator had to prepare him or her for the publishing of this book?

▌ Does the author attempt to share his or her personal values with the reader?

▌ What qualifies the author/illustrator to write or portray this story?

The book itself

▌ What is the copyright date, and does that date have any effect on the authenticity and truth of the book?

▌ What reviews of the book have been issued by various groups, whether representing ethnicity, gender, age, or education?

▌ How might this book be used to enhance children's understanding of themselves and others?

▌ How might this book be integrated into the regular curriculum?

▌ How readily available is this book for sharing with children, parents, community groups, and teachers?

▌ Does the book present information that can be used for further investigation, questioning, exploration, and critical analysis?

▌ Does the book encourage students to become more socially conscious?

How Can We Encourage Student Responses?

It is appropriate to have students themselves help in the evaluation of their reading materials. Teachers may use various methods to encourage student response. One method is the response journal, a small notebook or paper booklet that the student may use to reflect on the story while reading. Students may write their personal, self-generated feelings, or they may be directed to respond to particular questions about the story that the teacher has selected. In any case, both types of responses should receive written "answers" from the teacher. If students write their responses on only one side of the paper, the teacher can use the remaining space to further the dialogue. It is most effective to respond by asking questions such as, "Why did you feel this way after reading this particular section?" "Why do you think so?" "What in the story made you react this way?"

Another response technique is the reading log, which is also open-ended. Reading logs are children's lists of the books that they have chosen to read and the key ideas, thoughts, and reactions that they might have concerning those books. Having access to these reading logs allows the teacher to read candid reviews of the books that children self-select.

What about Censorship of Children's Books?

It is the belief of this writer that censorship of children's books limits our teaching capacities. Barbara Elleman, the editor of *Book Links*, also thinks that students should be allowed to make their own decisions about books, with the guidance of a concerned, qualified educator:

> Books containing these or any stereotypes shouldn't necessarily be dismissed because of their failings; instead the portrayals should be talked about with children. They should know that one can be neat and still be nice, that affluence isn't always corrupt, that someone from a monied family isn't necessarily a snob. Stereotypes won't disappear by sweeping them under the rug; they are best met head-on through discussion and sharing. It's another reason to read with and to children. (Elleman, 1994, p. 4)

Sometimes we sell our children short by not giving them opportunity to look more closely at books that we might question for authenticity and value. Very young children easily recognize that all the brothers look alike in *The Seven Chinese Brothers* by Margaret Mahy (1990). Although the illustrations are stereotypical, the folktale remains valid, and children need to have the opportunity to explore the possibility of that validity. Likewise, the tale *Seven Blind Mice* by Ed Young (1992) features a resolution with the discovery made by a "white" mouse. It would seem a more powerful learning experience for children if they could encounter this discovery when reading and then dialogue about what it might mean and how they might feel after thinking about it.

Another controversial book is *Sylvester and the Magic Pebble* by Steig (1988). Students reading this book will soon discover that Sylvester's mother is represented in a stereotypical fashion—apron and all. Nevertheless, the illustrations have been recognized with the Caldecott Award. On the other hand, the female protagonist in *Sarah, Plain and Tall* (MacLachlan, 1987) is hardly the typical female portrayed in early times. She is creative, dynamic and bold.

It is important that young children see literature from many perspectives and become more critical readers and thinkers in the process. We are not necessarily doing them a favor when we, as teachers, always decide what is appropriate for them to read.

Finally, a survey instrument (pages 151–160) that may be used to elicit responses from young children about themselves and others before they are exposed to children's literature that is multicultural. The same instrument could be used as a post-reading evaluative tool when the teaching and sharing have been completed.

FIGURE 5–11 *Sarah Plain and Tall* web by Susan

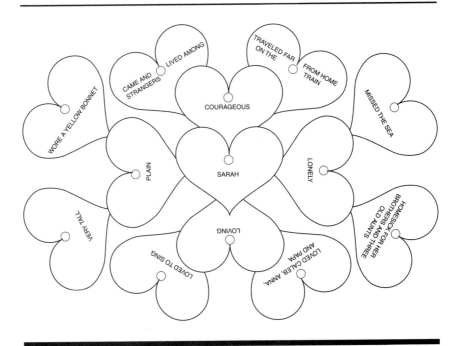

ABOUT ME AND OTHERS:
A MULTICULTURAL EDUCATION INSTRUMENT

Part I Demographics

(Information to be supplied by the evaluator *)

Date _____*   Evaluator* _____

Student number _____

Name of school _____

Location of school*:
   urban
   rural
   suburban
   out of the U.S.

Oral questions to be asked by evaluator

1. How old are you?

   I am _____ years old.

2. What grade are you in?

   I am in the _____ grade.

3. Do you live in an apartment, a house, a trailer, or any other type of building?

   I live in a(n) _____ .

4. Who do you live with?

   I live with   _____

                      _____

                      _____

                      _____
                      (Suggest: family members)

5. What language do you use at home?

   I speak _____ at home.

ABOUT ME AND OTHERS:
A MULTICULTURAL EDUCATION INSTRUMENT (continued)

6. What language do you use at school?

   I speak _____ at school.

7. Do you go to a church, a synagogue, or some other place to pray?

   I go to a _____ .

8. To what ethnic or racial group do you and your family belong?

   I am _____ . (reflects ethnic group)

   or

9. What color is your skin?

   The color of my skin is _____ .

Part II Self-Esteem

Directions: Circle the face that most reflects how you feel about each of the following statements:

   1. Sharing with others makes me feel . . .

   2. When I think of my family, I feel . . .

ABOUT ME AND OTHERS:
A MULTICULTURAL EDUCATION INSTRUMENT (continued)

3. When I think about my race (or ethnic group), I feel . . .

4. At home, I feel . . .

5. With my friends, I feel . . .

6. When my family members do not speak like my teacher, I feel . . .

ABOUT ME AND OTHERS:
A MULTICULTURAL EDUCATION INSTRUMENT (continued)

7. When I speak English at home, I feel . . .

8. When I am with friends who are most like me, I feel . . .

9. When I am with people different from me, I feel . . .

PART III Diversity and Biases

10. When I see people from other countries in different clothes, I feel . . .

ABOUT ME AND OTHERS:
A MULTICULTURAL EDUCATION INSTRUMENT (continued)

11. When I see children in wheelchairs, I feel . . .

12. When I see blind people, I feel . . .

13. When I see people from other countries with families different from mine, I feel . . .

14. When my friends speak a different language, I feel . . .

ABOUT ME AND OTHERS:
A MULTICULTURAL EDUCATION INSTRUMENT (continued)

15. When I see people who have a different color of skin than my skin, I feel . . .

16. When I try to speak a different language, I feel . . .

17. When I play with African-American children, I feel . . .

18. If Chinese people were to come to dinner at my house, I would feel . . .

ABOUT ME AND OTHERS:
A MULTICULTURAL EDUCATION INSTRUMENT (continued)

19. When my friends say that Mexican children are always late, I feel . . .

20. When my friends say that old people are mean, I feel . . .

21. When my teacher says that girls can be anything that boys can be, I feel . . .

22. When my friends say that boys are stronger than girls, I feel . . .

ABOUT ME AND OTHERS:
A MULTICULTURAL EDUCATION INSTRUMENT (continued)

23. When my friends say that girls are smarter than boys, I feel . . .

24. If Tom, who has brown skin, lived next door to me, I would feel . . .

25. If Elaine, whose father wears a little black hat and goes to the temple, were invited to my birthday party, I would feel . . .

26. If Rico, who does not speak English, tried to play with me on the playground, I would feel . . .

ABOUT ME AND OTHERS:
A MULTICULTURAL EDUCATION INSTRUMENT (continued)

27. If Jeremy, who lives only with his mother, wanted me as a partner, I would feel . . .

28. When the teacher assigns Sarah, who is in a wheelchair, as my partner, I feel . . .

29. When children in my class laugh at children who look different from me, I feel . . .

30. When my friends are not nice to Daniel, who has on old clothes, I feel . . .

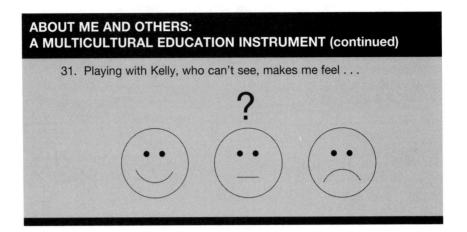

ABOUT ME AND OTHERS:
A MULTICULTURAL EDUCATION INSTRUMENT (continued)

31. Playing with Kelly, who can't see, makes me feel . . .

❖ Summary

Each book includes specific story elements of character, theme, plot, setting, and style. Illustrations may also be present to enhance the story line. The artistic elements, including color, shape, texture, and style, reflect the uniqueness of the artist as related to the telling of the story. As teachers look at children's literature, it is important that they regard the authenticity of books as well as the accuracy of their portrayals of diversity and cultural pluralism. Some works of children's literature have become controversial and inappropriate. Training young children to become critical thinkers and readers will help to alleviate this problem.

❖ Reflections and Questions to Consider

1. Select a particular author, and find at least four examples of his or her work. Compare the literary elements as the author has progressed through his or her career.

2. Select several illustrators and examples of their work. Create a visual representation of the artistic elements that you have viewed to share with your group.

3. Using the criteria presented in this chapter, review a new children's literature piece to see how it fits into the category of children's literature that is multicultural.

4. Explain the introductory quote, *"The only sense that is common in the long run, is the sense of change . . . and we all instinctively avoid it,"* as it relates to this chapter.

❖ Children's Literature Cited

Alcott, L. M. (1868). *Little women.* New York: Little, Brown.

Cummings, P. (1992). *Talking with artists.* New York: Bradbury.

Dahl, R. (1961). *James and the giant peach.* New York: Knopf.

Ernst, L. (1992). *When Bluebell sang.* New York: Macmillan Children's Book Group.

Feelings, M. (1971). *Moja means One: Swahili counting book.* New York: Dial.

Freedman, R. (1988). *Buffalo Hunt.* New York: Holiday House.

Goble, P. (1993). *The girl who loved wild horses.* New York: Macmillan Children's Book Group.

Hamilton, V. (1985). *The people could fly: American black folktales.* New York: Alfred A. Knopf.

Heyer, M. (1986). *Weaving of a dream: A Chinese folktale.* New York: Viking Children's Books.

Hodges, M. (1984). *St. George and the dragon.* Boston: Little, Brown.

Lionni, L. (1959). *Little blue and little yellow.* New York: Astor-Honor.

MacLachlan, P. (1987). *Sarah, plain and tall.* New York: HarperCollins Children's Books.

Mahy, M. (1990). *The seven Chinese brothers.* New York: Scholastic.

McCloskey, R. (1993) *Blueberries for Sal.* New York: Puffin.

Mosel, A. (1968). *Tikki Tikki Tembo.* Austin, TX: Holt, Rinehart & Winston.

Paulsen, G. (1988). *Hatchet.* New York: Puffin Books.

Sendak, M. (1963). *Where the wild things are.* New York: HarperCollins.

Steig, W. (1988). *Sylvester and the magic pebble.* New York: Simon & Schuster.

Waters, K., & Slovenz-Low, M. (1990). *Lion dancer.* New York: Scholastic.

White, E. B. (1952). *Charlotte's web.* New York: Harper & Row.

Wilder, L. I. (1953). *Little house in the big woods.* New York: Harper & Row.

Wood, D. (1992). *Old Turtle.* Duluth, MN: Pfeifer-Hamilton.

Young, E. (1992). *Seven blind mice.* New York: Philomel, Putnam.

❖ References

Asante, M. K. (1991). Afrocentric curriculum. *Educational Leadership, 49*(4), 28–31.

Boyer, J. B. (1990). *Curriculum materials for ethnic diversity.* Lawrence: The University of Kansas Press.

Derman-Sparks, L., and the A.B.C. Task Force (1989). *Anti-bias curriculum: Tools for empowering young children.* Washington, DC: National Association for the Education of Young Children.

Elleman, B. (1994, May). Handling stereotypes. *Book Links,* pp. 4.

Hilliard, A. G., III (1992). Why we must pluralize the curriculum. *Educational Leadership, 49*(4), 12–16.

Hillman, J. (1995). *Discovering children's literature.* Edgewood Cliffs, NJ: Prentice-Hall.

Neugebauer, B. (1987). What are we really saying to children? Criteria for the selection of books and materials. In B. Neugebauer (Ed.), *Alike and different: Exploring our humanity with young children,* (pp. 136–138). Redmond, WA: Exchange Press.

Russell, D. L. (1991). *Literature for children: A short introduction.* New York: Longman.

Stotsky, S. (1992). Whose literature? America's! *Educational Leadership, 49*(4), 53–56.

York, S. (1991). *Roots & Wings.* St. Paul, MN: Redleaf Press.

Curricular Applications
of Multicultural Literature

The elementary school setting and a philosophy of integrating reading, writing, speaking, and listening across all curriculum areas lend themselves well to the inclusion of a multicultural view of teaching and learning. Multicultural education affords all students the opportunity to view realistically the diversity of the American population and the world. As students' individual differences are identified and respected, students and teachers become involved in the multicultural education process, which deals with recognition of values, morality, attitudes, equity, and critical thinking.

Multicultural education deals with both multiethnicity (which focuses on ethnic origin) and globalism (which emphasizes different countries and their contributions to the world in which we live). With this combination, the integration of cultural study into regular curriculum focuses on ethnic groups, religious groups, gender equity, communication differences, physical and academic challenges, ageism, socioeconomic status, and other important issues that influence and enhance the lives of our citizens.

The multicultural approach to learning is child centered. It begins with the child's understanding of self (building of self-esteem), moving to an understanding of others, and finally expanding to an acquisition of concern for larger problems and issues outside the child's immediate environment. Although thematic units are often a means of delivering information in multicultural education, the approach can be employed on a daily basis, letting students be exposed to diverse cultures; become aware of the need to relate effectively with one another; and develop skills, attitudes, and abilities that help them function in a pluralistic society. All of these developments are facilitated through the use of children's literature that is multicultural.

This part of the book is activity oriented. The activities it includes are designed for the beginning as well as the experienced teacher, the parent, and/or the college student in teacher training. The lessons have been researched, tested, and demonstrated at urban, rural, and suburban sites as well as shared with preteaching college students. Therefore, the lessons include simple directions and terminology. The author of the text is coming from the perspective that even when resources and experiences are limited, multicultural awareness can be built and enhanced for all teachers, students, and parents through children's literature and the use of these lessons.

Within each chapter in part III, the curricular area will be defined as it relates directly to the first two parts of the book. If future teachers are at all apprehensive about using these lessons, they should first refer to chapters 1 through 5 for the content behind multiculturalism as well as the methodology related to children's literature. These lessons can also serve as models for future lessons. The reader is welcome to adapt them to suit different audiences, age levels, books, and themes.

The chapters in part III will also address the implications of the implementation of a multicultural cur-

FIGURE 6–1 Reading by myself

riculum approach. Ultimately, activities that include children's literature that is multicultural and that fit the curricular parameters are offered for the reader's use and reference. Reflection questions and summaries do not follow these chapters because the practicum and application portions of each chapter would consist in the teaching of the lesson itself.

A multicultural curriculum is one that affords all students equal opportunity to excel. It encourages all students to acquire social skills, knowledge, and attitudes that will enhance their ability to live productively in a diverse society. As a cross-curricular process, it is based on careful planning. Each of the chapters that follow will attempt to address the following student outcome goals:

1. Students will accept themselves both as individuals and as members of unique racial or cultural groups.

2. Students will begin or continue to accept others as members of different cultural, religious, ethnic, or gender groups, recognizing differences and similarities among people.

3. Students will increase their self-esteem as they begin to understand, recognize, and appreciate their own heritages.

4. Students will work cooperatively, developing interpersonal skills.

5. Students will recognize the common bond of humanity among people of all cultures in a global society.

6. Students will identify common stereotypes that are held about groups or people.

7. Students will readily share information about diverse cultures with one another and with others outside the classroom.

CHAPTER 6

Promoting Positive Self-Esteem

In the definition of multiculturalism, self-esteem is an integral element. Chapter 4, entitled "What Is Multiculturalism?" reminds us as educators that the attainment of positive self-esteem can only enhance understanding of oneself and others.

This chapter addresses the area of self-esteem as it could be approached in an elementary classroom. It restates the definition of self-esteem and presents teacher and student objectives and straightforward lesson plans. (Refer to chapter 4 for more theoretical background information and additional examples of children's literature that can be used in the elementary setting.)

❖ Definition and Implications

As young children begin to examine themselves and to ask and answer the question, "Who am I?" they develop their self-concepts. A child's evaluation of this self-concept in comparison to others and the expectations that the child and others have for him or her determine the child's self-esteem. Thus, self-esteem is the dimension of evaluation, positive or negative, of the child's self-concept (Harter, 1985; Rosenberg, 1985). Having high self-esteem means that children accept themselves readily and are satisfied with themselves as they are. By contrast, those who exhibit low self-esteem see a gap between who they are and what they would like to be. In such a case satisfaction is missing, and the child may feel less valuable (Bee, 1989). In *Developing Roots & Wings: A Trainer's Guide to Affirming Culture in Early Childhood Programs,* Stacey York (1991) states that "the early years are the years in which we need to help children develop a positive racial identity, cultural awareness, and social skills" (p. 12). Noticing themselves and recognizing their own personal beings as valuable and unique is so essential for young children in our schools.

Promoting positive self-esteem is critical in the early stages of learning. This can be done for each child in the following ways:

1. By creating a positive self-image
2. By sharing
3. By approaching activities as an individual
4. By accepting one's own limitations and exceptionalities
5. By participating in daily activities
6. By exhibiting pride in work and accomplishments

As teachers work at developing more positive self-esteem in their students, the implications become clear. Students with higher self-concepts are generally more successful academically. They also feel that they have internal locus of control, meaning that they determine their own behaviors and attitudes for success and are not controlled solely by outside forces. They make friends more easily and retain them longer. Their relationships with family members are more positive. These students are more positively motivated and less likely to be depressed (Bee, 1989; Rosenberg, 1985).

The activities included in this chapter encourage students to increase self-concept and awareness by doing the following:

1. Perform tasks as an individual
2. Share information with the group
3. Participate in daily activities
4. Demonstrate self-control
5. Show willingness to try new activities
6. Define a personal work space that will not interfere with others
7. Demonstrate pride in work
8. Express oneself as "one of a kind"

❖ Lesson Plans

Lessons presented in this chapter will include the following elements:

Rationale, a statement that describes the purpose of the lesson (why and how it applies to multicultural integration within the curriculum)

Subject/content area that will be covered with the lesson

Age level for which the lesson would be most appropriate (The concepts and ideas could be upscaled or downscaled depending upon the group of children and the level of expertise and comfort of the instructor; age levels were chosen instead of grade levels because many educational settings have moved toward multiage groupings)

Goals that the teacher would set in regard to curricular infusion

Objectives for student competencies that could be demonstrated, observed, and measured

Materials that would be best used in the lesson

Terms/vocabulary that would be introduced, reviewed, or integrated within the lesson;

Readiness/motivation, which involves setting the stage for the lesson and creating an atmosphere for learning for all students whatever their schemata (past experiences and prior knowledge)

Procedures/instructions, which delineate all the directions for carrying on the lesson (Within each step, the instructor can evaluate success or further document student progress as he or she sees fit)

Student evaluation, which includes methods of assessing student performance of competencies and objectives

LESSON PLAN 1—CREATING A COMMUNITY QUILT: LEARNING ABOUT OURSELVES AND OTHERS

Rationale

The purpose of this lesson is to provide students with an opportunity to identify themselves as individuals within their home structures, classroom setting, and cultural backgrounds, ultimately building upon their self-esteem.

Subject/Content Area

Language arts and fine arts

Age Level

4- to 7-year-olds

Goals

To have students accept themselves both as individuals and as members of unique racial or cultural groups

To have students begin or continue to accept others as members of different cultural, religious, ethnic, or gender groups—recognizing differences and similarities among people

To have each student express him- or herself as "one of a kind"

To have students identify their own family structures and members

To have students discover the origin of games.

Objectives

1. The students will listen to a selection about a particular quilt and then construct a classroom quilt that reflects themselves, their families, their community, and their school.

2. The students will become more aware of Russian culture by constructing dolls that "nest" (or fit inside one another) out of styrofoam cups.

3. Students will sort by size.

Materials

The Keeping Quilt by Patricia Polacco

Unbleached muslin cut to 4- by 4-inch squares (3 per child)

Quilted backing

Binding

White paper cut to 4- by 4-inch squares (3 per child)

Fabric crayons

Iron

Scraps of cloth from home

Thread

Yarn

3 styrofoam cups for each child (varied sizes)

Markers

Readiness/Motivation

Begin the lesson by reading the literature selection. If a quilt is available to show students before the reading, share it with them. Ask if any of them have seen a quilt or have one at home. Ask if they know who might have made the quilt and if it has any special story or pieces. Tell the students that they will be listening to a story about a very special quilt and how it came to be so special. Give them a purpose for listening by announcing that later the group will be constructing a quilt just like the one in the story.

Procedures/Instructions

1. Before reading the story, locate Russia on the map or globe. Tell the students that they will be hearing about children who have come from that country and have a Russian cultural heritage. Ask the class to listen to the story for things that make these children similar to children in this country.

2. Read the selection and share the pictures.

3. Ask the students to list ways in which children and families in the story are similar to children in this country. Write these answers on the board or on chart paper.

4. Explain to the students that they will be working together to make a classroom quilt that tells all about who they are and where they live.

5. Distribute fabric crayons and white paper (3 pieces each) to the children. Ask each child to draw a picture of only him- or herself on one piece, filling up the paper and *not writing his or her name on the paper as yet.* After the pictures are completed, tell the students to turn the papers over and write their names clearly *in pencil on the back.* Then take the papers to the window and turn them so that the colored sides face the front and the names appear backward. Have the children trace their names *in crayon* on this side.

6. Collect the papers, turn them colored-side down, and gently iron them onto the muslin fabric. The image that was colored should transfer, and the name should appear correctly. **Remember: Only what is drawn in color will show up on the fabric.**

7. Repeat the process with a second piece of paper. This time have the children draw the members of their families.

8. Have children color the third piece to show their community and school.

9. Ask the students to bring in scraps of old clothing or blankets that can be added to the quilt. Cut these in 4- by 4-inch squares. Arrange all of the squares in a decorative fashion, and sew them together to make a quilt. (You may want to ask a parent volunteer to do this in the classroom.)

10. Cut the quilted backing to match in size, and pin it to the sewn squares. Border the quilt with the binding. The children can help finish the quilt by sewing and tying yarn knots in the corners.

GAME: Nesting Dolls

Country/Culture: Russia

Directions:

1. Display a set of wooden Russian nesting dolls, if available. Explain their use in play by children in Russia.
2. Distribute 3 styrofoam cups per student—1 large, 1 medium, and 1 small.
3. Using felt-tip markers, decorate the cups as people.
4. Allow students to play with the decorated cups and sort them according to size.

Resource: Polacco, Patricia, *The Keeping Quilt.* New York: Simon and Schuster Books for Young Readers, 1988.

LESSON PLAN 2—RECOGNIZING HOW WE ARE ALIKE AND DIFFERENT: TRAVEL TO AND FROM SCHOOL, NEAR AND FAR

Rationale

The purpose of this lesson is to provide students with an opportunity to identify themselves as individuals within their school structure and cultural background and to share that information with other groups of children near and far.

Subject/Content Area

Language arts and social studies

Age Level

3- to 7-year-olds

Goals

To have students accept themselves both as individuals and as members of unique racial or cultural groups

To have students begin or continue to accept others as members of different cultural, religious, ethnic, or gender groups—recognizing differences and similarities among people

To have each student express him- or herself as "one of a kind"

To help increase students' self-esteem through recognition of their own heritages and cultural backgrounds

To have students communicate in writing about themselves

To have students locate various cultural groups in the world

Objectives

1. Students will become aware of various types of transportation available to students as they go to school all over the world.
2. Students will identify the way they go to school daily.
3. Students will communicate by mail with students near and far about how they go to school.

Materials

This Is the Way We Go to School by Edith Baer

Postcards or letter paper and envelopes

Experience paper

Markers

Readiness/Motivation

Before reading the book *This Is the Way We Go to School,* have the children think about how they got to school that day. On experience paper, write down their responses—for example, "Johnny rode the bus to school today. Sarah walked to school today. . . ."

Procedures/Instructions

1. Share the book *This Is the Way We Go to School* with the children. Tell them that they will be hearing how children around the world go to school each day.
2. Involve the students in the reading by showing them the many pictures and the map at the end of the book.
3. Inform the students that they will be able to share information about how they each go to school with other children their age and grade in a different place.
4. Give each child a postcard or a piece of writing paper and an envelope. (You will need to work with another teacher or teachers in appropriately matched school districts to procure a list of student first names and a corresponding teacher's name and address for mailing.)
5. Encourage each student to copy the sentence that was written about how he or she got to school that day and to illustrate the sentence on the postcard or stationery.
6. Have each student address the card or letter by writing the heading, "Dear . . . (first name of the pen pal child)."
7. It is hoped that this activity can become the beginning of a lasting correspondence exchange between the students.

Resource: Baer, Edith, *This Is the Way We Go to School.* New York: Scholastic, 1990.

LESSON PLAN 3—"PROUD TO BE MYSELF": RECOGNIZING ONE'S OWN SPECIAL TRAITS

Rationale

The purpose of this lesson is to give students an opportunity to recognize and express how they are unique and important individuals.

Subject/Content Area

Language arts and fine arts

Age Level

7- to 8-year-olds

Goals

> To have the students accept themselves both as individuals and as members of unique racial or cultural groups
>
> To have the students work cooperatively, developing interpersonal skills
>
> To have the students perform tasks as individuals
>
> To have the students share information with the group
>
> To have each student express him- or herself as "one of a kind"
>
> To have the students treat one another fairly and justly
>
> To have the students recognize prejudice concerning individuals
>
> To have the students recognize discrimination against individuals

Objectives

1. Students will express verbally and in writing how they perceive themselves to be special and unique.
2. Students will illustrate how they perceive themselves to be special and unique.

Materials

> 12-inch by 18-inch drawing paper
>
> crayons or markers
>
> *Fritz and the Beautiful Horses* by Jan Brett

Readiness/Motivation

Ask the students if they have ever felt left out of a group of their friends. Encourage the students to tell how they felt during that time. Then explain that this kind of thing happens to most everyone but that it is very sad. Introduce the book

Fritz and the Beautiful Horses. Tell the students that they will be hearing about a special horse and that the horse experiences some of the same bad feelings they all have had at one time or another.

Procedures/Instructions

1. Read the book *Fritz and the Beautiful Horses.*

2. On completion of the reading, ask the students to answer the following questions:

   Describe the horses in the walled city.

   What was different about Fritz?

   What was Fritz's wish?

   What happened in the story to change the children's feelings about Fritz?

   How did the people feel about Fritz at the end of the story?

3. Ask the children to discuss the importance of the way people look and appear to others. Describe the prejudice and discrimination that some groups of people encounter because of the way they look, the color of their skin, their families, or their sex. Encourage the children to bring these ideas out in the discussion.

4. Explain that each of us is very important as an individual.

5. Ask the children to think how they are special. What makes them so unique and special to this class and to their families?

6. Give each child a piece of drawing paper and have each one illustrate the way in which he or she is special. Have those who are able write their names and the sentence, "I am special." Some children may ask you to help them extend the sentence by telling how they are special.

7. Share the drawings within the group and display them for all to see.

Resource: Brett, Jan, *Fritz and the Beautiful Horses.* Boston: Houghton Mifflin, 1981.

LESSON PLAN 4—"WHAT 'COLOR' AM I?" WHAT DIFFERENCE DOES THAT MAKE?

Rationale

The purpose of this lesson is to give students an opportunity to discuss and discover how skin color often makes us feel about ourselves and others.

Subject/Content Area

Language arts

Age Level

7- to 8-year-olds

Goals

To have the students begin or continue to accept others as members of different cultural, religious, ethnic, or gender groups—recognizing differences and similarities among people

To have students increase their self-esteem as they begin to understand, recognize, and appreciate their own heritages

To help students identify common stereotypes that are held about groups or people

To help each student express him- or herself as "one of a kind"

To have students demonstrate how differences in our lives are enriching

To help students identify the uniqueness of people, places, things, and animals

To help students describe how others may feel in a given situation

To help students learn the value of not making prejudgments

To help students recognize and identify racial inequity

To have students participate in class discussions

Objectives

1. Students will discover the different skin "colors" of the children in their class and yet realize how much alike the students are in the classroom.
2. Students will write very short stories that tell who they are.

Materials

You Be Me—I'll Be You by Pili Mandelbaum

Primary paper and pencils

Readiness/Motivation

Before reading the story, ask the children if they had ever wished they were someone else at any time of their lives. Encourage them to tell about the feeling and explain what they think caused them to feel that way at the time. Explain that that they will be hearing a story about a little girl who wishes she could be someone else.

Procedures/Instructions

1. Read the book *You Be Me—I'll Be You.* Be sure to share the pictures with the children.
2. After the story, ask the children to form a circle. Have them all put their hands in the middle of the circle. Tell the children to look carefully at the colors of skin that they see in the circle.

3. What do they notice? Are all the colors the same? Does having white skin really mean that one's skin is white? What about a person who is said to have black skin? How do they compare?

4. Ask the children whether it makes any difference if our skins are different in color. Encourage free discussion.

5. At the conclusion of the discussion, tell the students that they need to tell about who they are. Ask them to include what they look like, what they like to do, what their favorite things are, who is in their families, what they do best, and what makes them unique or different from anyone else.

6. Have nonwriters dictate their stories to you. Then read their words together.

7. Encourage beginning writers to try to write the words, even if only the beginning and ending sounds of the words.

8. Have the students share their writings during sharing time.

Resource: Mandelbaum, Pili, *You Be Me—I'll Be You.* Brooklyn, NY: Kane/Miller, 1990.

LESSON PLAN 5—"I'D RATHER BE ME!"

Rationale

It is important for children to realize that it is better to be yourself than to try to be someone you're not.

Subject/Content Area

Reading, art, and values (specifically, the value of being oneself)

Age Level

6- to 9-year-olds

Goals

> To expose the children to a sense of self-worth and acceptance

> To demonstrate that what one wishes for is not always the best choice

Objectives

1. The students will design lists or sets of drawings explaining why it is good to be themselves.

2. The students will create an "I Like Being Me Because . . ." poster to be displayed in the hallway.

Materials

White poster board for each child

Paint, paintbrushes, markers, pencils, scissors, tissue paper, and crayons for each child

Plain white writing paper

Smocks (to cover/protect clothing)

Where the Wild Things Are by Maurice Sendak

Readiness/Motivation

Tell the class a story about something you pretended to be because you didn't want to be yourself. Ask the students if they have ever wished they were something or somebody else. Mention that you know a little boy named Max who felt the same way.

Procedures/Instructions

1. Gather the children together in the reading area and go through the readiness procedure just described.

2. Introduce the book *Where the Wild Things Are* to the children. Begin reading. When you come to the section that is wordless, ask the students to make up text for that part.

3. When you reach the part of the story where Max leaves the wild things, ask the children why they think Max is leaving. Lead them into the idea that he wants to be Max again and misses his family.

4. After finishing the story, talk about why Max may have wanted to be someone else for a while. Ask the students whether they think he preferred being a wild thing or preferred just being Max. What makes them infer the latter? Why would he rather be Max?

5. Instruct the children to return to their seats while one student passes out writing paper. Tell the children that they are to brainstorm in writing or in pictures why it is good to be them, what makes them happy to be themselves.

6. When the students have finished their brainstorming activity, pass out the poster board, markers, smocks, and paints. Instruct the students to use their ideas and create posters that complete the title phrase "I like me because . . ." Be sure to write the title on the board and remind the children to write it somewhere on their posters.

7. Offer students the opportunity to create hand puppets to go along with Max and the monsters he met one night. Using paper bags or poster board and various other materials, students can create puppets to help them retell the story or to help share the reasons why they like themselves.

8. Closure: When the painting is finished, have the children put their posters and puppets aside to dry. Each child should be responsible for cleaning up after him- or herself. Remind the children to rinse their brushes and wipe off their tables. After each area is clean, discuss some of the reasons the children like being themselves. Do not treat any answer as conceited or silly. Encourage all children to input at least one reason.

FIGURE 6–2 Bag puppet

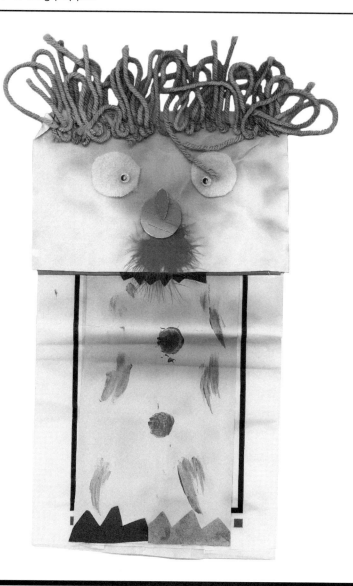

FIGURE 6-3 Finger puppet

Student Evaluation

The students will not be evaluated with assigned grades or plus marks. Instead, this activity will give the teacher a sense of where the students stand in terms of self-esteem and self-concept. The teacher can work from these results to help the children who do not feel that they have much that is special and good in their lives.

Printed with permission by Marie Brown Forst, an undergraduate student at Edinboro University of Pennsylvania.

Resource: Sendak, Maurice, *Where the Wild Things Are.* New York: Harper & Row, 1963.

❖ Related Bibliography

Baer, E. (1990). *This is the way we go to school.* New York: Scholastic.

Bee, H. (1989). *The developing child.* New York: Harper & Row.

Brett, J. (1981). *Fritz and the beautiful horses.* Boston: Houghton Mifflin.

Harter, S. (1985). Competence as a dimension of self-evaluation: Toward a comprehensive model of self-worth. In R. L. Leahy (Ed.), *The development of the self* (pp. 57–121). Orlando, FL: Academic Press.

Mandelbaum, P. (1990). *You be me—I'll be you.* Brooklyn, NY: Kane/Miller.

Polacco, P. (1988). *The keeping quilt.* New York: Simon & Schuster Books for Young Readers.

Rosenberg, M. (1985). Self-concept and psychological well-being in adolescence. In R. L. Leahy (Ed.), *The development of the self* (pp. 205–246). Orlando, FL: Academic Press.

Sendak, M. (1963). *Where the wild things are.* New York: Harper & Row.

York, S. (1991). *Developing roots & wings: A trainer's guide to affirming culture in early childhood programs.* St. Paul, MN: Redleaf Press.

CHAPTER 7

Recognizing Similarities
and Differences

Multiculturalism, by definition (refer to chapter 4, "What Is Multiculturalism?"), deals with the comparing and contrasting of peoples. Our roles as educators include the recognition and celebration of diverse children in our classrooms. More than that, we serve as models for our children as we help them understand how all of us are similar and yet so unique and different.

The purpose of this chapter is to expand on the differences among peoples noted theoretically in chapter 4. Here specific children's books dealing with diversity and similarity are presented as an integral part of day-to-day teaching practice.

Rudine Sims Bishop, cited by Micklos (1995/96), concurs that multicultural children's literature is the vehicle for children's understanding of diversity: "Children's literature can show readers how they are connected to one another through common emotions, needs, and desires, while also helping them appreciate the differences among people" (p. 8). The children's books and activities that follow are prime examples of alternative methods for sharing what children and adults know about different populations. These books reflect not only contrasting views but also comparative ones.

❖ Definition and Implications

Applying multicultural literature in the everyday elementary curriculum allows the educator and the students to view the similarities and differences among individuals and groups in our country and in the world. It is crucial that the building of awareness of diversity begin simply and slowly in the classroom itself as students and teachers identify first who they are and then how they share many of the same interests, goals, physical attributes, and basic needs.

Gibson (1984) has reflected on the process that a person must follow to become more multicultural, a method of perceiving, evaluating, believing, and doing. In the context of that process, the lessons presented in this chapter, which focuses on similarities and differences, challenge our young people to view themselves as individuals, as family members, as members of their classes and schools, as community members, and as contributing members of a diverse global society. In order to become convinced that all people share certain basic characteristics and needs, they can explore these commonalities through literature. Gudykunst and Kim (1984) describe the multicultural person as one who "possesses an intellectual and emotional commitment to the fundamental unity of all humans and, at the same time, accepts and appreciates the differences that lie between people of different cultures" (p. 230). The question becomes how to bring about this cognitive and emotional sensitivity.

Elementary children can become more cognizant of their similarities while celebrating their differences by engaging in the following activities in school and at home:

1. Noting likenesses and differences
2. Comparing and contrasting
3. Participating with others in common activities
4. Identifying uniqueness in people, places, things, and animals
5. Describing objects that are similar or different

The implications of creating a classroom where students possess both a stronger awareness of themselves as individuals and a sense of similarities and differences in lifestyles, learning styles, and customs reach beyond the elementary classroom setting. Acceptance and tolerance would be visible results of curricular approaches that dealt with both similarities and differences rather than emphasizing only one or the other. Separatism and stereotyping would be less prevalent in schools that reflected and rejoiced in both the individuality and the commonality of human beings.

Activities outlined in this chapter will focus on the positive effects of recognition of similarities and differences among children and humans in general. Students will be encouraged to do the following:

1. Note likenesses and differences
2. Compare and contrast events
3. Compare and contrast stories
4. Participate with others in common activities
5. Identify activities that are common to all people
6. Demonstrate how differences in our lives are enriching
7. Identify the uniqueness of people, places, things, and animals

❖ Lesson Plans

Lessons presented in this chapter will include the following elements:

Rationale, a statement that describes the purpose of the lesson (why and how it applies to multicultural integration within the curriculum)

Subject/content area that will be covered with the lesson

Age level for which the lesson would be most appropriate (The concepts and ideas could be upscaled or downscaled depending upon the group of children and the level of expertise and comfort of the instructor; age levels were chosen instead of grade levels because many educational settings have moved toward multiage groupings)

Goals that the teacher sets in regard to curricular infusion

Objectives for student competencies that could be demonstrated, observed, and measured

Terms/vocabulary that would be introduced, reviewed, or integrated within the lesson

Materials that would be best used in the lesson

Readiness/motivation, which involves setting the stage for the lesson and creating an atmosphere for learning for all students whatever their schemata (past experiences and prior knowledge)

Procedures/instructions, which delineate all the directions for carrying on the lesson (Within each step, the instructor can evaluate success or further document student progress as he or she sees fit.)

Student evaluation, which includes methods of assessing student performance of competencies and objectives

LESSON PLAN 1—FUN WITH NURSERY RHYMES FROM MANY PLACES

Rationale

The purpose of this lesson is to provide students an opportunity to compare and contrast traditional nursery rhymes of their own culture with those of the Chinese culture.

Subject/Content Area

Language arts, fine arts, and physical education

Age Level

6- to 9-year-olds

Goals

> To have students accept themselves both as individuals and as members of unique racial or cultural groups
>
> To have students begin or continue to accept others as members of different cultural, religious, ethnic, or gender groups—recognizing differences and similarities among people
>
> To have students work cooperatively, developing interpersonal skills
>
> To have students readily share information about diverse cultures with one another and with others outside the classroom
>
> To have students note likenesses and differences
>
> To ask students to compare and contrast stories and events
>
> To have students participate with others in common activities
>
> To have students read and develop appreciation of multicultural literature
>
> To have students demonstrate nonverbal communication

Motivation/Readiness

Ask the students if they can name any common nursery rhymes—for example, "Mary Had a Little Lamb." (If the students cannot name any examples, then recall some from your own memory and ask them if they have heard any of these popular rhymes. Tell the students that these rhymes are commonly called nursery rhymes.) Then share the Chinese nursery rhyme book with the children, explaining that it includes common rhymes from the country and culture of China. Refer particularly to the rhyme concerning the dragon (see the Dragon's Tail game later in the lesson). Encourage the students to compare and contrast the rhymes they know with these rhymes.

Game: Chinese Jump Rope

Country/Culture: China

Objectives:

1. Students will construct a Chinese jump rope out of rubber bands.
2. Students will chant their names in English and Chinese as well American and Chinese nursery rhymes while jumping with the rope.

Materials

Rubber bands in various sizes

Chinese Mother Goose Rhymes by Robert Wyndham

Procedures/Instructions

1. Give each student at least 25 or 30 rubber bands (largest sizes are best).
2. Demonstrate to students how to intertwine the rubber bands using slip-knots.
3. Continue until the bands form a rope at least 6 feet long. Connect the ends to make a circle.
4. To play, have one child stand at one end and one at the other, with bands around the ankles.
5. The third player steps in and out of the rope, hopping while doing so.

Game: Dragon's Tail

Country/Culture: China

Objectives

1. Students will work cooperatively to add parts to the dragon's tail in a Chinese game.
2. Students will relate the dragon's tail game to the Chinese nursery rhyme about the dragon.

Materials

Outdoor play area

Ropes to mark boundaries or chalk to draw lines on the playground

Procedures/Instructions

1. Establish boundaries within which children must stay.
2. Select one student to be the "dragon," whose goal is to catch another child and add to the dragon's length.
3. As additional children are added to the "dragon," they must hold hands with the "dragon" and use the free hand to catch another classmate.

4. The "dragon" may split into smaller dragons to snare runners, but a unit must always include at least two players.

5. When only one runner is left, that child becomes the new "dragon."

Resource: Wyndham, Robert, *Chinese Mother Goose Rhymes.* New York: Philomel Books, 1968.

LESSON PLAN 2—KIDS AND ADULTS: I GUESS WE ARE A LOT ALIKE, BUT . . .

Rationale

Children need to learn to be able to perceive similarities and differences among people of various ages.

Subject/Content Area

Reading, social studies; concept of story, similarities and differences, the sociology of families

Age Level

7- to 9-year-olds

Goals

To expose children to the world of similarity and difference

To allow children the experience of listening to and analyzing a story

To allow children the experience of investigating the past

Objectives

1. The students will join the class in group discussion about the meaning of the story.

2. The students will create questions that they would like to ask their caregiver(s) about his or her (their) childhood(s).

3. The students will interview their caregiver(s) and report the findings in their journals.

4. The students will have the option of sharing what they have learned with the class.

Terms/Vocabulary

Helm
Porpoise
Jig
Typhoon

Materials

Humphrey's Bear by Jan Wahl

Unlined white paper

Pens, pencils, markers, crayons, and other writing implements

Student journals

Readiness/Motivation

Ask the students if any of them have anything in common with the adults they live with. If no students answer, talk about what you have in common with the people or person you lived with as a child (hair color, grouchiness, etc.). If some students do answer, discuss the similarities.

Procedures/Instructions

1. Gather the students together in the reading area of the room. Follow the readiness procedure just described.

2. Introduce the book *Humphrey's Bear.* Tell students the title and the author of the book. Ask them what they think the book will be about from looking at the front cover.

3. Open the book and begin reading the story to the class. Explain the vocabulary words as they appear in the text.

4. When you have reached the last page, ask the students what they think Humphrey's father meant when he said, "I used to sail with him, too." Accept many answers. If no child mentions that the bear used to belong to Humphrey's father, refer the children to the line in the text that states, "It had been Humphrey's father's bear long ago."

5. Ask the students how they think the father's words made Humphrey feel. Discuss the idea that all adults once were children and that they too had stuffed animals and played with their imaginations.

6. Bring up the idea that adults a long time ago did many things that children still do today: They played baseball, they played house. Ask the children what types of activities their parents and caregivers did when they were small.

7. Have the children resume their seats and get out pencils, pens, markers, or crayons. Tell them to think about questions they could ask the adults in their homes about the adults' childhoods long ago. Pass out paper, and tell the children to write their questions on the paper. Also, tell them to include questions asking what types of activities children do today that the adults didn't do when they were young.

8. Have each child interview an adult in his or her home (or some other adult friends) and write down the findings in their journals within the next week.

9. Closure: When the children have finished the interview assignment, invite them to share with the class what they have found.

Student Evaluation

The students will be evaluated on the effort they put into designing questions and recording responses. If a child's parent or caregiver is unresponsive, suggest that the student ask someone in the school, such as the principal or the office secretary, about his or her childhood.

Resource: Wahl, Jan., *Humphrey's Bear. New York: Holt, Henry,* 1989.

Printed by permission of Marie Brown Forst, an undergraduate student at Edinboro University of Pennsylvania.

LESSON 3—THE PEOPLE I KNOW AND THOSE BEYOND . . .

Rationale

The purposes of this lesson are to expose students to different groups or sets of people in the world and within their own country and to have them share similarities and differences and identify the groups that exist within their own class.

Subject/Content Area

Language arts, math

Age Level

6- to 10-year-olds

Goals

To have students accept themselves both as individuals and as members of unique racial or cultural groups

To have students begin or continue to accept others as members of different cultural, religious, ethnic, or gender groups—recognizing differences and similarities among people

To have students recognize the common bond of humanity among people of all cultures in a global society

To have the students recognize and identify objects in a set

To have students recognize the following set designations of people: race, religion, age, sex, education, culture, physical ability

To help students note likenesses and differences

To ask students to identify activities that are common to all people

To have students identify the uniqueness of people, places, things, and animals

To have students locate various cultural groups in the world

Objectives

1. Students will identify various cultural groups and their likenesses and differences.
2. Students will construct a collage of faces, places, clothing, and homes, comparing and contrasting.
3. Students will sort their own shoes according to style, color, presence or absence of laces, and so on.
4. Students will create a graph depicting the groups reflected in their class.

Materials

People by Peter Spier

12-inch by 18-inch paper

Glue

Scissors

Magazines/pictures

Shoes from individuals

Motivation/Readiness

Have all the children sit in a large circle, on the floor, on carpeting, or on chairs. Ask the children to look around them and observe some things that are the same about all the children in the circle. What did they see? Did they notice that all the children are wearing clothing? Did they notice that all the children have shoes on? Explain that the group will be reading a book that tells about the many kinds of people in the world and notes how they are alike and how they are different. Ask the children to listen very carefully so that they can share about these similarities and differences.

Procedures/Instructions

1. Read the selection *People.* After reading, ask the children to tell in what ways they saw that people in the world are alike. Write a heading "Alike," and list the similarities on the board or on chart paper as the children express their ideas.
2. Ask the children to tell how the people in the world are different. Write these ideas under the heading "Different."
3. Announce that the class will be looking very carefully at how the children in the class are alike and different. First ask the children to remove their shoes and put them in the middle of the circle. Ask for help putting the shoes in separate groups—all the shoes with laces, all those with buckles, all those that slip on, and all those with velcro fasteners (if any). Then sort the shoes again, this time by color. You may also sort by size. For each sorting, make a simple bar graph to display the number of students making up each group.

4. Repeat the same exercise using other sorting criteria: eye, hair, and skin color; languages spoken at home; and, possibly, the number of people in the family. Talk about the differences and likenesses in the groups as they are displayed in graph form.

5. Give the children old magazines, newspapers, and catalogs. Have them cut out pictures and create a large group collage that illustrates the diverse groups of people in the world.

Resource: Spier, Peter, *People.* New York: Doubleday, 1980.

LESSON 4—A LESSON IN CAUSE AND EFFECT: TALKING IT OVER

Rationale

The purpose of this lesson is to provide a connection between Chinese folklore and DRTA (Directed Reading Thinking Activity) through the use of a predictable book.

Subject/Content Area

Language arts

Age Level

8- to 11-year-olds

Goals

To have students begin or continue to accept others as members of different cultural, religious, ethnic, or gender groups—recognizing differences and similarities among people

To encourage students to work cooperatively, developing interpersonal skills

To have students use words to describe objects, places, and events

To ask students to participate in class discussions

To have students read and develop appreciation of multicultural literature

Objectives

1. The students will help in the reading of a selection and predict what will happen next by making good guesses based on what has already occurred in the story.

2. The students will create cause-effect maps as a group.

3. The students will retell the story, noting proper sequence in a story map.

Materials

Tikki Tikki Tembo by Arlene Mosel (1989)

Experience paper or chalkboard

Markers

Motivation/Readiness

Show the children the book *Tikki Tikki Tembo.* Ask the students if they recognize it. If some do, then simply ask them not to tell the whole story as yet because the group will be doing a few new activities based on the story even though some may have heard it before.

Ask the children if they know where China is on the map or globe. Have someone point it out for the others. Tell the children that the story *Tikki Tikki Tembo* takes place in China and is a folktale. Ask the children if they know what a folktale might be. Explain that it is a story told and retold for many years by the people of a certain group or culture. (A folktale may be told to explain why things happen—for instance, why the moon shines at night or why the stars are configured as they are—or just to tell something funny to others.) This story explains how Chinese children get their names.

In introducing the story, encourage the students to look at the pictures and think about who might be in the story, where it might take place, and what might be happening. Inform the students that knowing the purpose—listening for *why* (cause) and *what happens* (effect)—will help them understand the story. As a culminating experience, students will be creating cause-effect charts and story maps about the setting, problem, goal, episodes, and resolution of the story.

Procedures/Instructions

1. Gather all students together for the reading of the story. Remind them that the story is a Chinese folktale or an example of Chinese folklore.

2. Show the book *Tikki Tikki Tembo.* By show of hands, have students indicate if they have seen the book before. If they have, remind them that they must not tell the ending of the story to their friends but instead should listen very carefully for the purpose of explaining what happens and why (cause and effect). Students who have heard the book before may be helpful in involving the group in saying the predictable portions aloud.

3. Ask the students to define the word *predict.* Write down their ideas. Ask them likewise to define *guess.*

4. Inform the students that, as they look at the pictures in the book, they are to help to predict or guess what the story may be about. Ask the following questions:

   What is the setting?

   Who is in the story?

When does it take place?

Where does it take place?

What is the problem in the story?

How is the problem solved?

What type of ending might this story have?

5. Record the answers to these questions on chart paper before reading the story with the students.

6. Periodically throughout the reading, encourage students to join in during the predictable portions of the story. Stop occasionally to ask questions regarding their predictions.

7. Continue the reading to verify predictions.

8. At the conclusion of the story, ask the students to retell it, using the book as a guide.

9. As the students help to develop the story map as illustrated in figure 7-1 (on the board or on chart paper), ask the following questions where appropriate:

What was the Chinese custom for naming sons a long, long time ago?

FIGURE 7–1 Venn diagram

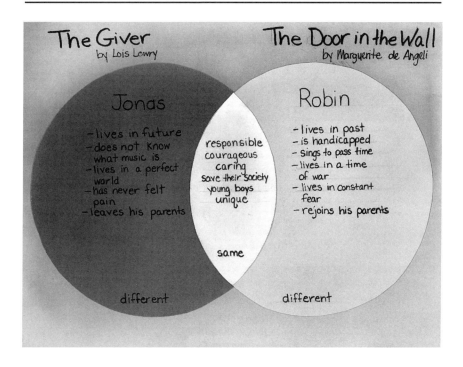

What is a custom?

What were the names of the two sons, and what did they mean?

Who was the Old Man with the ladder?

How did the Old Man with the ladder get the water out of Chang?

What is the Festival of the Eighth Month?

How fast did Chang run for help when Tikki Tikki Tembo fell into the well?

What made Chang out of breath?

What did Chang's mother call him?

How do you think she felt about him?

What happened to Tikki Tikki Tembo after he fell into the well?

How long did it take for him to get better?

What is the point of the story?

10. At the completion of the retelling, ask students if they know what a cause is:

What do we mean when we say "cause"?

Tell what an effect is.

Can you look at the episodes and tell the causes and effects?

11. As students identify each cause and effect, connect them with arrows on the board or paper for all to see. Display the chart.

Resource: Mosel, A., *Tikki Tikki Tembo,* New York: Holt, Henry, 1989.

LESSON PLAN 5—WITH LOVE, FROM ALL OF US . . .

Rationale

The purpose of this lesson is to give students an opportunity to see that, although there may be many different cultures, all people show their love for others in the same way.

Subject/Content Area

Language arts

Age Level

All elementary; 6- to 12-year-olds

Goals

To have the students begin or continue to accept others as members of different cultural, religious, ethnic, or gender groups—recognizing differences and similarities among people

To help students recognize the common bond of humanity among people of all cultures in a global society

To help students readily share information about diverse cultures with one another and with others outside the classroom

To have students communicate verbally with classmates

To have students note likenesses and differences

To have students identify activities that are common to all people

To help students locate various cultural groups in the world

Objectives

1. Students will express verbally and in writing what love or loving is to them.

2. Students will recognize that love is expressed in similar ways in many different cultures.

Materials

> *Loving* by Ann Morris
>
> Blank Big Book
>
> Crayons or markers

Readiness/Motivation

Show the children that you care for them by giving each one a special hug to start the day. Explain that, in our culture, this gesture is a way to show that we care for or love someone. Ask the children to tell how their family members show that they love one another.

Procedures/Instructions

1. Display the book *Loving.* Read it and share the pictures with the children.
2. During the reading, ask the students if they do any of the things that they see in the book.
3. Upon completion of the reading, explain that the students will work together to create a Big Book that tells what "loving is . . ." to them.
4. Allow each student a page to illustrate and write a description of loving as it applies to him or her. (Students may have to dictate their sentences to you for writing.)
5. When the book is completed, share it with the group and compare it to the book *Loving.*

Resource: Morris, Ann, *Loving.* New York: Lothrop, Lee & Shepard Books, 1990.

LESSON PLAN 6—COMPARING AND CONTRASTING . . .

Rationale

The purpose of this lesson is to give students an opportunity to compare and contrast characters in stories that reflect diversity issues.

Subject/Content Area

Language arts

Age Level

Upper elementary; 10- to 12-year-olds

FIGURE 7–2 Book/movie Venn diagram

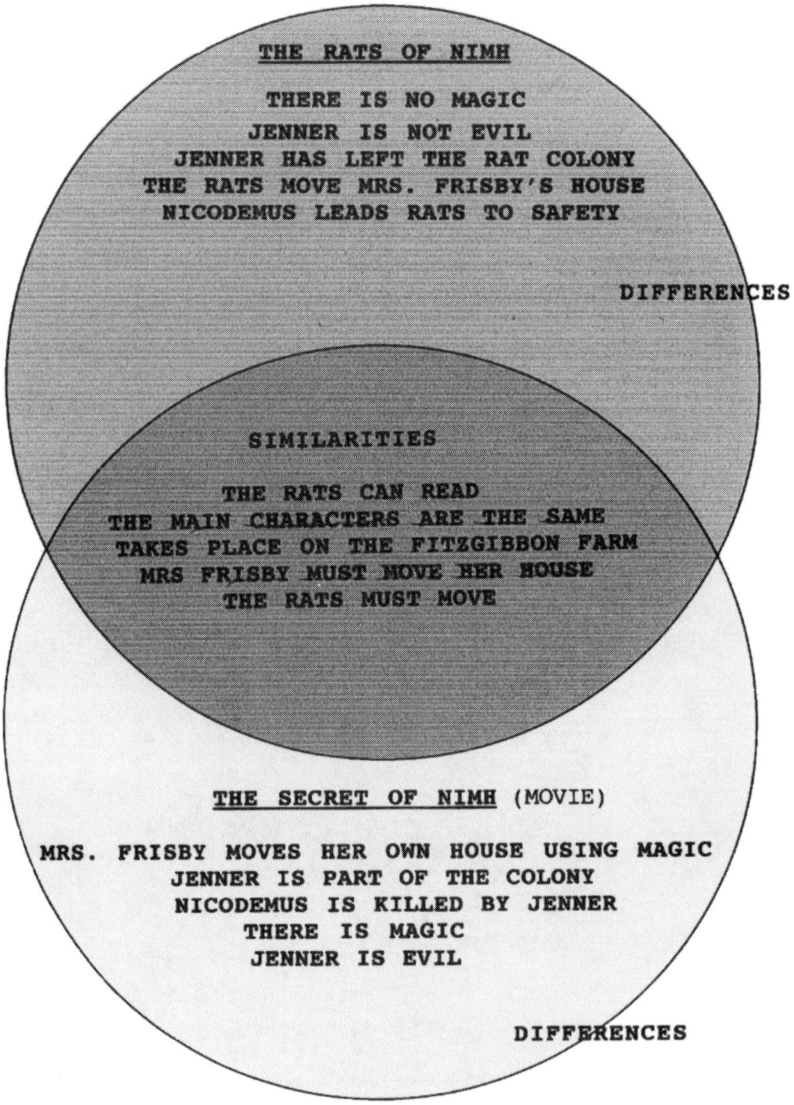

THE RATS OF NIMH

THERE IS NO MAGIC
JENNER IS NOT EVIL
JENNER HAS LEFT THE RAT COLONY
THE RATS MOVE MRS. FRISBY'S HOUSE
NICODEMUS LEADS RATS TO SAFETY

DIFFERENCES

SIMILARITIES

THE RATS CAN READ
THE MAIN CHARACTERS ARE THE SAME
TAKES PLACE ON THE FITZGIBBON FARM
MRS FRISBY MUST MOVE HER HOUSE
THE RATS MUST MOVE

THE SECRET OF NIMH (MOVIE)

MRS. FRISBY MOVES HER OWN HOUSE USING MAGIC
JENNER IS PART OF THE COLONY
NICODEMUS IS KILLED BY JENNER
THERE IS MAGIC
JENNER IS EVIL

DIFFERENCES

Goals

To have the students begin or continue to accept others as members of different cultural, religious, ethnic, or gender groups—recognizing differences and similarities among people

To help students recognize the common bond of humanity among people of all cultures in a global society

To have students note likenesses and differences

Objectives

1. Students will create Venn diagrams of characters in stories that they have read that reflect diversity.

2. Optional: Students will compare and contrast the book itself with the visual and oral presentation of a video of a story that is culturally diverse.

Materials

Paper, white and construction (various colors)

Crayons, colored pencils or markers

Computer, disk, word processing program

Overhead transparency sheets

Readiness/Motivation

Assemble a small group of students. Have them discuss what for them constitutes a book that deals with diversity issues. Ask one student to record the information that is generated in the group. Have the students think about what makes the ideas of diversity common and what makes them different.

Procedures/Instructions

1. Tell students that they each will have an opportunity to visit the library and select two books that deal with diversity issues (ethnic groups, handicaps, gender equity, contributions of various cultures, etc.). They may choose to work in pairs, with each partner selecting only one book.

2. After the selections are made, encourage students to read the books, looking for a main character in the story that especially intrigues them.

3. Explain, upon completion of the reading, that the students will work together as partners to create a Venn diagram that shows how the main characters in the two books are similar and different. Students can collaborate on the selection of these books.

FIGURE 7–3 *Number the Stars* and *The Upstairs Room* "compare and contrast" Venn diagram by Dana

---

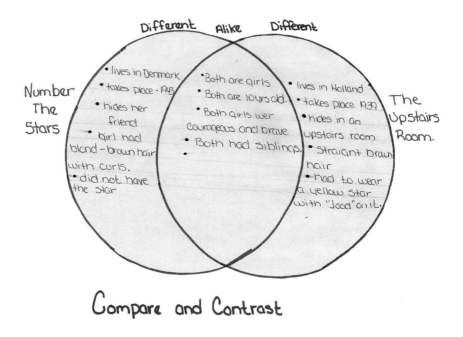

Compare and Contrast

---

4. Students may *also* explore whether or not their particular books have been made into movies. If so, the students can do a comparison/contrast to see how the book and the movie versions are alike and different.

5. Upon completion of their Venn diagrams, have students share their books and visuals with the group.

❖ Related Bibliography

Bennett, C. (1990). *Comprehensive multicultural education.* Boston: Allyn & Bacon.

Gibson, M. (1984). Approaches to multicultural education in the United States: Some concepts and assumptions. *Anthropology and Education Quarterly, 15*(1), 99–120.

Gudykunst, W. B., & Kim, Y. Y. (1984). *Communicating with strangers: An approach to intercultural communications.* New York: Addison-Wesley.

FIGURE 7–4 *Bridge to Terabithia* and *Where the Red Fern Grows* "compare and contrast" Venn diagram by Jennifer

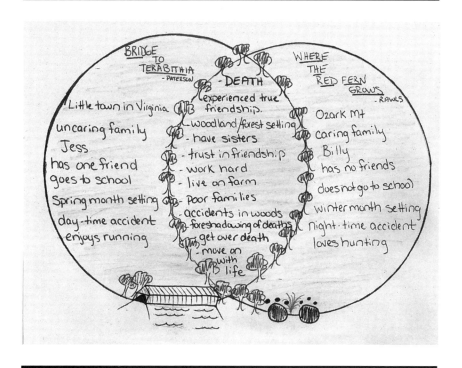

Micklos, J. Jr. (1995/96, December/January). Multiculturalism and children's literature. *Reading Today*, pp. 1, 8.

Morris, A. (1990). *Loving*. New York: Lothrop, Lee, & Shepard.

Mosel, A. (1989). *Tikki Tikki Tembo*. New York: Holt, Henry.

Orlick, T. (1978). *The cooperative sports and games book*. New York: Pantheon.

Spier, P. (1980). *People*. New York: Doubleday.

Wahl, L. (1989). *Humphrey's bear*. New York: Holt, Henry.

Wyndham, R. (1968). *Chinese Mother Goose rhymes*. New York: Philomel Books.

CHAPTER 8

Accepting Cultural Pluralism

The definition of multiculturalism in part speaks to the issue of many cultures combining to form a better society. This forging and fusing of many different approaches to life can be referred to as *pluralism.* Unlike the "melting-pot" theory (see chapter 2), which discouraged individuals from retaining their heritage and roots, cultural pluralism recognizes that in diversity lies strength and in acceptance of different races, ethnicities, languages, and cultures lie understanding and growth.

Seeing other cultures represented in books that they read, children will soon see themselves and others in what they read. Supporting this idea is IRA President Dolores B. Malcolm, who states, "Only through the acceptance of the presence of 'all' will the true concept of pluralism be realized. . . . Every culture has a heritage, and all children need to know and respect their own heritage and that of other people" (Micklos, 1995/96, p. 8).

❖ Definition and Implications

Cultural pluralism implies that recognition and acceptance of particular ethnic groups are very important for a functioning society. Teachers who attempt to prepare their elementary students for a world that is diverse and cooperative will need to be aware of how cultural pluralism is defined and how it can be addressed within their curricula.

Nieto (1992) defines cultural pluralism as "a model based on the premise that all newcomers have a right to maintain their languages and cultures while combining with others to form a new society reflective of all our differences" (Nieto, 1992, p. 307). She also observes that this model has been referred to at various times as the *salad bowl, mosaic,* or *tapestry* (see chapter 4 of this text for definitions and explanations of these terms). With this definition in mind, the educator who is the pure pluralist may desire a classroom that serves only a specific group or ethnic population so that the members of that group will begin to understand and accept themselves better as ethnic group members within the larger society. In fact, some pluralists believe that only people who are members of the group in question should teach about ethnicity (Howard, 1993).

The environment of the ethnic group will tend to provide support for the individual whose language and customs are different from those of the mainstream. Research by James A. Banks (1994) has shown that members of various ethnic groups (more commonly referred to as minority groups) who espouse the pluralistic viewpoint believe that their populations are well ordered and structured but different in their approaches to language, lifestyle, values, and group relationships.

In contrast, the educator who looks at curriculum and students from an assimilationist perspective will see the national culture as most prevalent and regard the microcultures as nonfunctioning or deprived or deficient unless they become part of the norm. Here the primary focus is on the need to recognize the commonalities of the peoples of the nation and the world and not to devote much attention to their differences. In this view, recognition of differences can only cause dissention and controversy.

The teacher who integrates multiculturalism within his or her curriculum combines some of the assimilationist with some of the pluralist. Multiculturalism reflects both positions without taking extreme and radical stands on the issues. The educator who uses the multicultural approach tends to see the importance of common group membership, with group members constantly aware of their personal heritages and ethnic group participation contributions. Thus, the teacher who applies this theory within the elementary classroom "believes that the curriculum should reflect the cultures of various ethnic groups *and* the shared national culture" (Banks, 1994, p. 131).

This chapter stresses the importance of cultural pluralism but from the perspective of the multicultural educator rather than that of the pure cultural pluralist. The activities outlined here are designed around the following goals:

1. Understanding diversity in American culture
2. Recognizing the influence of various cultures on our everyday living
3. Locating various cultural groups in the world
4. Discovering the origins of stories, games, and foods

When educators look very carefully at the implications of incorporating cultural pluralism into their daily teaching, they must understand that they are on ground that has rarely been explored. Most schools and administrators will respond to expressions of the need for including cultural pluralism by stating that their school populations do not reflect diversity and that, therefore, there is no need to be concerned with pluralism. On the contrary, in schools where diversity is not prevalent, the lack of knowledge of other cultures implies fear because fear, anger, and reactionary behaviors arise from lack of knowledge about someone or something. As our students can use technology to contact people across continents, they need to understand how people of different cultural groups celebrate, pray, communicate, eat, learn, work, and live. Indeed, they need to know how they themselves came to celebrate, pray, communicate, eat, learn, work, and live in their own homes through their personal heritages and cultural backgrounds. This personal exploration, as well as the exposure to the lives and backgrounds of others, can only make learning experiences richer and more rewarding.

In order to make students more aware of the importance of cultural pluralism (as opposed to separatism or elitism), the activities in this chapter will encourage students to do the following:

1. Describe how others may feel in a given situation
2. Invite others (children or adults) of different racial, cultural, or linguistic backgrounds to share with them
3. Work cooperatively with others
4. Recognize the influence of various cultures on our everyday living
5. Locate various cultural groups in the world
6. Discover the origins of stories
7. Discover the origins of games
8. Discover the origins of foods and festivals
9. Identify their own cultures

❖ Lesson Plans

Lessons presented in this chapter will include the following elements:

Rationale, a statement that describes the purpose of the lesson (why and how it applies to multicultural integration within the curriculum)

Subject/content area that will be covered in the lesson

Age level for which the lesson would be most appropriate (The concepts and ideas could be upscaled or downscaled depending upon the group of children and the level of expertise and comfort of the instructor; age levels were chosen instead of grade levels because many educational settings have moved toward multiage groupings.)

Goals that the teacher would set in regard to curricular infusion

Objectives for student competencies that could be demonstrated, observed, and measured

Materials that would be best used for the lesson

Terms/vocabulary that would be introduced, reviewed or integrated within the lesson

Readiness/motivation, which involves setting the stage for the lesson and creating an atmosphere for learning for all students whatever their schemata (past experiences and prior knowledge)

Procedures/instructions, which delineate all the directions for carrying on the lesson (Within each step, the instructor can evaluate the success or further document student progress as he or she sees fit.)

Student evaluation, which includes methods of assessing student performance of competencies and objectives

LESSON 1—SHARING OF STORIES AND OURSELVES: A LESSON ABOUT NATIVE AMERICANS, RELATIONSHIPS, AND PERSONAL LIMITATIONS

Rationale

The purposes of this lesson are to recognize the importance of culture shared from generation to generation through stories, to encourage participation in the Native American culture, and to become more acceptant of personal handicaps.

Subject/Content Area

Language arts, storytelling, and fine arts

Age Level

8- to 10-year-olds

Goals

To have students work cooperatively, developing interpersonal skills

To have students identify common stereotypes that are held about groups or people

To encourage students to recognize and develop appreciation of many cultures

To have students participate in verbal sharing

To have students communicate verbally with class members

Objectives

1. Students will share stories or tales as Native Americans would have done by using a sharing stick.
2. Students will create a rainbow of color.
3. Students will create a counting rope for all the stories and cultures shared.

Materials

Long stick

Rope

12-inch by 18-inch construction paper (white, fingerpaint paper)

Paints (watercolor, fingerpaint)

Knots on a Counting Rope by Bill Martin Jr. and John Archambault

*Recommended additional readings about Native Americans: *The Star Maiden* by Barbara Juster Esbensen and *Turquoise Boy: A Navajo Legend* by Terri Cohlene

Motivation/Readiness

Discuss with children their methods of sharing with the class (e.g., "show and tell"). Tell the children that they will be hearing a story about a young boy and an old man who share with each other in a new way.

Procedures/Instructions

1. Read the selection *Knots on a Counting Rope*. Ask the children to listen to the story to hear how the old man and his grandson share with each other. (Students are to share with one another while passing the stick.)
2. As students share daily or at times agreed upon within the classroom, the large stick is to be held by the person who is speaking. While that person is

holding the stick, all attention is to be given that speaker; no one is to interrupt until the speaker's time is up or the sharing is finished. The stick is passed to the next speaker when it is his or her turn to share. This technique can be employed in sharing or any other time that it would be beneficial to listen to one person's comments at a time.

3. Another Native American custom is the counting rope featured in the reading selection. Inform the students that, each time the class reads a book about a different group or culture, a knot will be tied on the large rope. It will be interesting to see how many knots have been tied by the end of the year. Suggested follow-up books are *The Star Maiden* by Esbensen and *Turquoise Boy: A Navajo Legend* by Cohlene.

4. As a concluding follow-up to the story, have the children join as a group to make a large mural of a rainbow—a group effort that shows "the blue of the morning . . .", the red off . . . , and so on. Display the mural for all to see, calling it "The Rainbow of Our Eyes."

Resource: Martin, Bill Jr., and Archambault, John, *Knots on a Counting Rope.* New York: Henry Holt, 1990.

Game: Trick the Dancer

Country/culture: Northwestern Native American/Indian tribes

Objectives

1. The students will demonstrate cooperation, agility, and listening skills.

Materials

A drum and a drummer

Directions

1. The drummer plays while the players move in a circle to the beat.

2. When the drum stops suddenly, all players must freeze in position. Anyone who moves, twitches, or slips is out.

3. Each time the drummer stops, someone is caught until at last there is only one player. That player is the winner.

Resources: Cohlene, Terri, *Turquoise Boy: A Navajo Legend.* Mahwah, NJ: Watermill Press, 1990.
Esbensen, Barbara Juster, *The Star Maiden.* New York: Little Brown, 1988.

LESSON PLAN 2—FAIRY TALES FROM OTHER LANDS; COMPARING AND CONTRASTING

Rationale

The purpose of this lesson is to provide students an opportunity to compare and contrast different genres of various cultures around a central theme—for example, "Little Red Riding Hood" and *Lon Po Po.*

Subject/Content Area

Language arts and fine arts

Age Level

8- to 11-year-olds

Goals

> To have students work cooperatively, developing interpersonal skills
>
> To have students begin to recognize the common bond of humanity among people of all cultures in a global society
>
> To help students note likenesses and differences
>
> To have students compare and contrast events
>
> To have students compare and contrast stories
>
> To have students demonstrate how differences in our lives are enriching
>
> To have students identify the uniqueness of people, places, things, and animals
>
> To help students discover the origins of games

Objectives

1. Students will compare and contrast the story "Little Red Riding Hood" with a Chinese folk version of that tale called *Lon Po Po.*
2. Students will engage in a language experience activity in which they will write and draw how the stories are alike and different.
3. Students will play the Chinese game of hopscotch, recognizing the origin of the popular international game.

Materials

> Language experience paper
>
> Markers
>
> *Lon Po Po* by Ed Young

Optional: *Tikki Tikki Tembo* by Arlene Mosel

Readiness/Motivation

Ask the children to recall the story of "Little Red Riding Hood." Have the children retell the story as a group. Record their story on the board or on experience paper. Tell the children that they will be hearing a different version of the story as it is often told in China (you may want to have a map or globe available to point out that country's location).

FIGURE 8–1 *Lon Po Po* story map by Andria

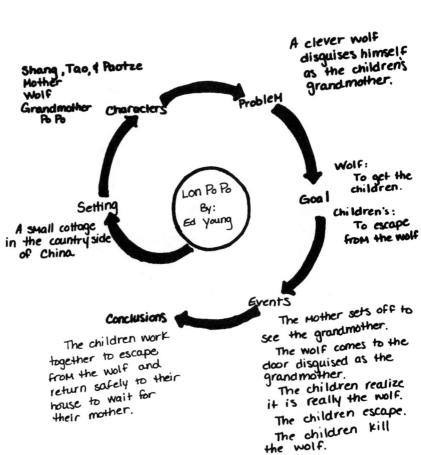

Procedures/Instructions

1. Read the story *Lon Po Po.* Show the pictures and encourage interaction with the book. Ask the children to describe what they see on each page, and have them try to explain the artist's purpose for this type of illustration.

2. After the reading is completed, tell the students that the group will be writing down the things that make this story similar to "Little Red Riding Hood" and the things that make it different.

3. Write the word "Alike" on one sheet of experience paper, and write "Different" on the other sheet.

4. Ask the students to list ways in which the two stories are alike. Write these responses on the first paper. If some students are able to write some of the words or phrases, allow them to do so on the paper. You may also have them draw pictures to show what they mean.

5. Ask the students to list ways in which the two stories are different. Write these responses on the second sheet of paper.

6. Share the responses with the entire group.

7. Engage in the game of hopscotch, which originated in China.

8. As a further follow-up activity, encourage children to read *Tikki Tikki Tembo* by Arlene Mosel and compare that tale to a more traditional folktale they may know.

Resources: Mosel, Arlene, *Tikki Tikki Tembo,* Austin, TX: Holt, Rinehart, & Winston, 1968.
Young, Ed, *Lon Po Po.* New York: Philomel Books, 1989.

Game: Hopscotch

Country/Culture: China

Objectives

1. Students will demonstrate gross motor activity and ability and recognition of progression.

Materials

Tape, chalk, or stick

Sidewalk, play yard, or playground

Pebbles, stones, or bottle caps for markers

Procedures/Instructions

1. Draw a pattern with 10 squares using chalk, a stick, or tape on a fairly smooth surface.

2. Number the squares from 1 to 10.

3. All markers (potsie) are put on the first square at the beginning. Play begins when the first player hops on one foot in each of the squares, beginning with square 2.

4. The player continues until he or she misses by stepping on a line or falling.

5. If the player reaches 10 without missing, he or she can choose a square for a private house and mark it. No one else can step on this square.

6. The player with the most private houses is the winner.

Resource: Young, Ed, *Lon Po Po*. New York: Philomel Books, 1989.

Game: Ribbon Dance

Country/Culture: China

Objectives

1. Students will engage in the traditional ribbon dance of the Chinese.

Materials

Dowel rods (2 feet in length)

Ribbon (of durable material)

Colored plastic tape

thumbtacks

Directions

1. Distribute one dowel rod per child, and instruct the children to wrap the rods with the colored plastic tape.

2. Each student is then to tack a yard of ribbon to the dowel with a thumbtack.

3. Students engage in the ribbon dance by holding the dowels above their heads and making circular motions. They may also make circular motions on either side of their bodies, being aware of the presence of others and allowing for plenty of room. When these simple moves are perfected, students may attempt to make figure eight motions in front of their bodies or at their sides. Play Chinese music in the background as motivation for movement.

LESSON PLAN 3—KEEPING A DIARY, IN GOOD TIMES AND BAD

Rationale

The purpose of this lesson is to expose students to different cultures through the actual words of children and to their fears, struggles, and lives that endured through war.

Subject/Content Area

Language arts and social studies

Age Level

10- to 12-year-olds

Goals

> To have students begin to recognize the common bond of humanity among people of all cultures in a global society
>
> To help students note likenesses and differences
>
> To have students compare and contrast events
>
> To have students compare and contrast stories
>
> To have students demonstrate how differences in our lives are enriching
>
> To have students describe how others would feel in certain situations
>
> To have students describe how they would feel in certain situations

Objectives

1. Students will compare and contrast the stories of two young women as they describe themselves in their diaries.
2. Students will engage in a language experience activity in which they chart how the stories are alike and different.
3. Students will construct their own personal diaries of their daily lives and compare them with the books they have read.

Materials

> Language experience paper
>
> Markers
>
> *Anne Frank: The Diary of a Young Girl* by Anne Frank
>
> *Zlata's Diary* by Zlata Filipovic
>
> Small spiral notebooks
>
> Computer disks
>
> World map and globe

*Optional books: *My First Chanukah* by Tomie de Paola
      Light Another Candle: The Story and Meaning of Hanukkah, by Miriam Chalkin

Readiness/Motivation

Ask the students to share what they may remember about Germany, Hitler, and the Jewish people who lived in Europe. Ask students if they can describe the

Holocaust. Using chart paper, record their answers. Ask students if they recall information about Bosnia and the children there. (You may want to have a map or globe available to point out these locations.)

Procedures/Instructions

1. Explain to the students that they will have the opportunity to hear you read two books that are true stories of children who lived in war-torn places and wrote their stories. Introduce *Anne Frank: The Diary of a Young Girl* and *Zlata's Diary*. At this point, tell the students to explain the difference between a diary and a story or novel.

2. Read portions of the books aloud daily to the students. (Complete one book before beginning the second.) Assign students certain pages to read on their own. Encourage reluctant readers to read orally as partners or to read aloud with parents or other adults at home. Explain to the students that, while the books are being read, they are to be keeping daily diaries of their own—diaries that describe their feelings, fears, worries, joys, and wishes and that should remain private unless they want to share them with you as the teacher. Allow students to keep their diaries on paper (in notebooks) or on the computer on separate disks.

3. Write the word "Compare" on one sheet of experience paper. Write "Contrast" on the other sheet.

4. Ask the students to list ways in which the two diaries are alike. Write the responses on the first paper. Allow the students to do this writing.

5. Ask the students to list ways in which the two diaries are different. Write these responses on the second sheet of paper.

6. Share and discuss the responses with the entire group.

7. Engage in a follow-up discussion that relates to the students' own journals and the feelings they had while writing. How do their journals/diaries compare to those of the two girls who wrote the books? Why are diaries so important for the preservation and documentation of history? What historical events would the students want their children and grandchildren to remember about their own times? Why?

8. As additional follow-up, encourage the students to read and reference the following books: *My First Chanukah* by Tomie de Paola and *Light Another Candle: The Story and Meaning of Hanukkah* by Miriam Chalkin.

Resources: Filipovic, Zlata, *Zlata's Diary*. New York: Scholastic, 1994.
Frank, Anne, *Anne Frank: The Diary of a Young Girl*. New York: Simon & Schuster, 1952.

Game: Dreidel Spinning Game

Country/Culture: Jewish

Objectives

1. Students will take turns spinning a top device that is traditionally used in the Jewish culture.

Materials

Dreidel or ordinary top

Paper and pencil for recording scores

Directions

1. Draw a circle on a piece of paper or on the ground.
2. Mark the circle into 8 equal preshaped wedges, and number the wedges 1 through 8.
3. Taking turns, students place the dreidel in the center of the circle and spin. The number landed on is the score.
4. The game continues until all players have had 5 or 6 turns. The highest scorer is the winner.

Resources: de Paola, Tomie, *My First Chanukah.* New York: G. P. Putnam's Sons, 1989.

Chalkin, Miriam, *Light Another Candle: The Story and Meaning of Hanukkah.* Boston, MA: Clarion Books, 1981.

❖ Related Bibliography

Banks, J. A. (1994). *Multiethnic education: Theory and practice.* Boston: Allyn & Bacon.

Chalkin, M. (1981). *Light another candle: The story and meaning of Hanukkah.* Boston, MA: Clarion.

Cohlene, T. (1990). *Turquoise boy: A Navajo legend.* Mahwah, NJ: Watermill Press.

De Paola, T. (1989). *My first Chanukah.* New York: G. P. Putnam's Sons.

Esbensen, B. J. (1988). *The star maiden.* New York: Little, Brown.

Filipovic, Z. (1994). *Zlata's diary.* New York: Scholastic.

Frank, A. (1952). *Anne Frank: The diary of a young girl.* New York: Simon & Schuster.

Howard, G. R. (1993). Whites in multicultural education: Rethinking our role. *Phi Delta Kappan* (75), 36–41.

Martin, B. Jr., & Archambault, J. (1990). *Knots on a counting rope.* New York: Henry Holt.

Micklos, J. Jr. (1995/1996, December/January). Multiculturalism and children's literature. *Reading Today,* pp. 1, 8.

Mosel, A. (1968). *Tikki Tikki Tembo.* Austin, TX: Holt, Rinehart, & Winston.

Nieto, S. (1992). *Affirming diversity.* New York: Longman.

Orlick, T. (1978). *The cooperative sports and games book.* New York: Pantheon.

Young, E. (1989). *Lon Po Po.* New York: Philomel Books.

CHAPTER 9

Seeing Diversity in Families

Teachers of the twentieth and twenty-first centuries are hearing politicians cry out about the demise of the family unit. We are faced with creating a family unit of our own in the elementary classroom—a place of community, understanding, and compassion. In the making of such a community, we need to recognize the diversity in existing family structures.

The authors of *Knowing and Serving Diverse Families* refer to many different cultural and ethnic groups and the various acceptable ways to live within those groups. They contend that for us as educators, "though each of us views a situation through eyeglasses colored by the culture within which we were born and reared, understanding gradually comes through cross-cultural contacts, studies, and observations, and a more enlightened and objective view generally develops" (Hildebrand, Phenice, Gray, & Hines, 1996, pp. 10–11). They further explain that we cannot expect families to be alike but rather that diversity is life giving and important. In fact, the definition of family varies from group to group, individual to individual, culture to culture. For some of us, the family is a group of individuals, whereas for others, it can include a place or area of gathering. In all cases, as teachers and caregivers of the young, we are challenged with recognizing the various types of families and family memberships.

This chapter serves as an introduction to that process. It will look at the definition of family in a traditional sense—a group of individuals with common ties and residence. It will briefly address methods of encouraging young children to be more comfortable about their families through use of children's books and activities.

❖ Definition and Implications

The family has traditionally been the mainstay of the individual in our country. As the individual in childhood recognizes first himself or herself, one first recognizes the relationships with others closest to him or her—the family members. In early days, this family provided security, love, shelter, and care. In other words, the family was sufficient to itself as the provider of work, food, and medical care.

As time has progressed and the country has grown and become more diverse, so have family structures. Economic circumstances have required many families to extend themselves—by adding other members (grandparents, aunts, uncles, cousins, etc.). Stay-at-home mothers have gone out to the workplace, and often fathers and extended-family members have shared the nurturing roles.

Families have been separated, some through choice and some through economic situations. Death, illness, and war have affected the family unit.

In this century, the family can be defined as a "range from two parents, one male and one female, living together with one or more children (the nuclear family) to any number of people of any age or sex who choose to live together and nurture one another" (Rudman, 1995, p. 74). Thus, the family unit qualifies as diverse in nature. The challenge of every teacher is the acknowledgment of the diverse family structures and the feelings of the children within these families.

This chapter describes the infusion of children's literature that is multicultural in ways that lead each student toward the following goals:

1. Identifying one's own family structure
2. Recognizing different family structures
3. Identifying roles and stereotypes of individuals in a family

A great deal of controversy has resulted from the discussion of alternative family structures. Political campaigns have focused on the issue of family and the need to return to the "normal" family of two parents and several children, some pets, a home, and two cars in the garage. However, no matter how much political discussion takes place, the families that exist will remain, and the children of these families, having had no input into their structures, must feel accepted and welcome in the elementary classroom. So many times, teachers have neglected the diversity of families and have made the typical assignment to "draw a picture of your family" for primary children. This assignment can and does have relevance only if children understand that not all families will look alike and that, should their drawing be atypical, they will not be excluded or rejected by the teacher or their peers.

The implication of including in the elementary classroom activities that deal with diverse families is a powerful affirmation of acceptance of individual difference due to circumstance. Positive models that can be shared through real life as well as through children's literature are encouraged. Likewise, the success and survival of individuals in spite of family structure and economic status should be shared through story. Awareness of the need for respect and consideration of others results from inclusive representation of varied lifestyles and family configurations.

The activities included in this chapter reflect different individuals who have unique personalities that flourish within their particular family structures. Within the context of family, each student should be able to do the following:

1. Identify one's family structure and family members
2. Recognize different family structures
3. Identify the different roles in one's family
4. Identify and recognize stereotypes of individuals in a family
5. Understand the various definitions that people around the world have for the term *family*
6. Identify personal "roots" or develop a family tree

❖ Lesson Plans

Lessons presented in this chapter will include the following elements:

> *Rationale,* a statement that describes the purpose of the lesson (why and how it applies to multicultural integration within the curriculum)
>
> *Subject/content area* that will be covered with the lesson
>
> *Age level* for which the lesson would be most appropriate (The concepts and ideas could be upscaled or downscaled depending

upon the group of children and the level of expertise and comfort of the instructor; age levels were chosen instead of grade levels because many educational settings have moved toward multiage groupings.)

Goals that the teacher would set in regard to curricular infusion

Objectives for student competencies that could be demonstrated, observed, and measured

Materials that would be best used in the lesson

Terms/vocabulary that would be introduced, reviewed, or integrated within the lesson

Readiness/motivation, which involves setting the stage for the lesson and creating an atmosphere for learning for all students whatever their schemata (past experiences and prior knowledge)

Procedures/instructions, which delineate all the directions for carrying on the lesson (Within each step, the instructor can evaluate success or further document student progress as he or she sees fit.)

Student evaluation, which includes methods of assessing student performance of competencies and objectives

LESSON 1—"YOUR" MEMORIES HELP ME UNDERSTAND YOU BETTER

Rationale

The purpose of this lesson is to recognize the importance of accepting the contributions of the elderly/aged to our society and to encourage the sharing of memories that build cultures.

Subject/Content Area

Language arts

Age Level

7- to 10-year-olds

Goals

To have students begin or continue to accept others as members of different cultural, religious, ethnic, or gender groups—recognizing differences and similarities among people

To help students identify the common stereotypes that are held about groups or people

To have students increase their self-esteem as they begin to understand, recognize and appreciate their own heritages

To encourage students to share information with the group

To have students identify and recognize stereotypes of individuals in a family

To have students identify personal "roots" or develop a family tree

Objectives

1. Students will share memories of their lives orally.
2. Students will construct a Big Book of memories.

Materials

Wilfred Gordon McDonald Partridge by Mem Fox

Objects mentioned in the story

Blank Big Book

Markers

FIGURE 9–1 Big Book sharing of memories

Motivation/Readiness

Ask children to tell if they know any people whom they consider "old." Ask the children to explain what it means to them when we say that someone is old. Ask, "Do you have any grandparents or great-grandparents? What do they like to talk about, and what do they like to do?" Explain that many grandparents like to tell their grandchildren about their lives and the experiences they had when they were young. The story that they are about to hear is about a little boy and his friendship with an old woman.

Procedures/Instructions

1. Read *Wilfred Gordon McDonald Partridge.* After completion of the reading, ask the children to tell what a *memory* was to all the different characters in the story. If at all possible, have on hand examples of some of the objects mentioned in the story to share with the children.

2. Ask each child to write down and draw a picture of something that he or she can remember even now about life as a child. Put this collection of memories in a Big Book entitled "I Remember." When the book is complete, have children read the memories to one another during sharing time.

Resource: Fox, Mem, *Wilfred Gordon McDonald Partridge.* Brooklyn, NY: Kane/Miller, 1985.

LESSON PLAN 2—WHAT A GREAT HAT!!

Rationale

The purpose of this lesson is to allow students to share with one another about their families and special events in their families and cultures that can be symbolized through hats.

Subject/Content Area

Language arts

Age Level

7- to 12-year-olds

Goals

> To have the students accept themselves both as individuals and as members of unique racial or cultural groups
>
> To have the students work cooperatively, developing interpersonal skills
>
> To have the students perform tasks as individuals
>
> To have the students share information with the group

To have each student express him- or herself as "one of a kind"

To have the students describe favorite customs and traditions

To have the students associate objects, events, and artifacts with particular cultures

To have the students recognize different family structures

To have the students identify their own family structures and members

Objectives

1. Students will begin to recall specific personal events and occasions that have been important in their lives.

2. Students will recall the family members who were involved in these important events.

3. Students will share these special personal events and occasions with their classmates.

4. Students will participate in a "Hat Day," when each one will tell about at least one special event in his or her life and try to wear a hat that will help tell this story to the others.

5. Optional for older students: Students will create postage-stamp renditions of the story or representations of their favorite types of hats and family members.

Materials

Aunt Flossie's Hats (and Crab Cakes Later) by Elizabeth Fitzgerald Howard

Hats of all kinds

Readiness/Motivation

Before beginning the lesson, find a special hat that you as teacher can wear to introduce this lesson. Choose a hat to which you can relate a special event or story. Wearing the hat, gather all the students together for story sharing. Ask the students if they notice anything different about you. When they remark on and ask about the hat, tell them that a special story goes along with it. Share your story. Then tell the students that you will be reading them a story about a little girl and her great-aunt who has special hats.

Procedures/Instructions

1. Ask the students if they understand what it means to have a great-aunt. Ask if any of the children can name great-aunts in their families. Encourage sharing at this time.

2. Read the story. Be sure to point out the paintings by James Ransome that illustrate the book.

3. After the reading is completed, tell the children that in two more days, the group will be celebrating a special "Hat Day," when they can all wear hats of their choice to share with the other children.

4. Encourage each child to select a hat that has a special story behind it. They may also borrow special hats from family members and share the stories behind those particular hats.

5. Children are to share their stories while wearing their hats and modeling them for their classmates. You may even plan to have children parade around the school to show their individuality and their special hats to others in the school.

6. A parent letter (optional) is included in figure 9-2 should you find the need to use it.

FIGURE 9–2 Parent letter

Dear Parents and Guardians,

On _____ (day and date), our class will be having a "Hat Day." We hope that each student will be able to bring in a hat from home to wear and share with the class on that day.

The purpose of this activity is to help the children recall special events and activities in their lives and the lives of their family members and to connect these memories with hats that may have been worn when the events occurred. Your child may choose to share about events that involved only him or herself. Or the child may borrow a family member's hat and share about a special event that he or she has heard about. This technique helps in passing down family stories, traditions, and cultures.

If neither your child nor a family member has a hat to share, please feel free to construct a hat that could help tell about a special time in your child's life. We are happy to supply you with paper to make a hat.

Please send the hat in a special bag or package so that it will not be damaged on the way to school.

Thank you in advance for your help. We are sure that this event will be fun and valuable for all!

Sincerely yours,

_____ (teacher's signature)

FIGURE 9-3 *"Postage stamp"* student artwork by Melissa

7. Students can construct postage-stamp renditions of the story. Have them look at the designs of several different postage stamps. Using a pair of pinking shears or a one-hole paper punch, outline pieces of drawing paper. Then have students use colored pencils, markers, and other materials to create their own stamps that would retell the story or show various hats that their family members would wear. After the stamps are constructed, gather students together so they can share and explain their drawings.

Resource: Howard, Elizabeth Fitzgerald, *Aunt Flossie's Hats (and Crab Cakes Later)*. New York: Clarion Books, 1991.

LESSON PLAN 3—MY FAMILY TREE AND ME

Rationale

The purpose of this lesson is to allow students to share with one another about their families through the creation of family trees.

Subject/Content Area

Language arts and social studies

Age Level

9- to 12-year-olds

Goals

To have the students accept themselves both as individuals and as members of unique racial or cultural groups

To have the students perform tasks as individuals

To have the students share information with the group

To have each student express him- or herself as "one of a kind"

To have students recognize different family structures

To have the students identify their own family structures and members

Objectives

1. Students will interview current family members about past family members and the birth and death dates of these people.
2. Students will recall by name family members who are living or dead.
3. Students will create family trees and will share them with the rest of the class.

Materials

Cousins by Virginia Hamilton

Stone Fox by John Reynolds Gardiner (optional)

Poster board or large rolled paper

Markers and pencils

Rulers/yardsticks

Personal journals (notebooks/binders)

Readiness/Motivation

Set the stage for the story by sharing about the author Virginia Hamilton, born in 1936 in Yellow Springs, Ohio. The author's relatives were fugitive slaves, and from there came her interest in writing stories about African-Americans and her roots. As Hamilton wrote this particular story, she remembered her own extended family and their closeness to her when she was a child. Ask the students what you mean by "extended family." Tell them about any extended family members who have particularly influenced your life.

Procedures/Instructions

1. Ask the students if they have ever lost close family members. Being sensitive to their feelings, encourage the students to share about the feelings that they had during that very difficult time. If none are willing to share, you may have to tell about a former student who experienced the trauma of a family member's death or tell a personal story of your own. Be sure to stress that what the students share in the classroom should be kept in confidence and that you also will maintain that confidence.

2. Explain that the story the group will read and discuss concerns a young girl, Cammy, who lives in a rural midwestern town. Cammy has a grandmother who is close to dying, and the young girl must face this. Ask the students to think about their grandparents. Perhaps they would be willing to write in their personal journals about some experiences they have shared with their grandparents—good or bad.

3. Read the story orally. If you are able to secure multiple copies of the book, also ask the students to read it on their own. At the end of each chapter, ask the students to write in their journals answers to questions much like these:

   What did this chapter remind me of in my own life?

   What can I predict will happen in the next chapter?

   What did I particularly like or dislike about what the author said today?

   As the story progresses, create, as a group, a family tree for Cammy. Display it as a model for the next portion of the lesson.

4. After the story is completed, tell the students that they will be creating family trees of their own to share with the class. Assign each student the job of interviewing family members for accurate information about family members' birth dates, anniversaries, and deaths. Allow time for students to work in class on their family trees. Ask members of the local historical society to come into the classroom to discuss genealogy.

5. Share and display the family trees.

6. Option: Repeat the same activity, but use the book *Stone Fox.* (See the story map, figure 9-4), that reflects this book. You may have students create their own versions of both books using this model.

Resources: Gardiner, John Reynolds, *Stone Fox,* New York: HarperCollins Children's Books, 1983. Hamilton, Virginia, *Cousins.* New York: Scholastic, 1993.

LESSON PLAN 4—THIS IS HOW I FEEL . . .

Rationale

The purpose of this lesson is to allow students to recognize that different family structures can be imposed on young people and that survival is important.

FIGURE 9–4 *Stone Fox* student artwork elements by Mark

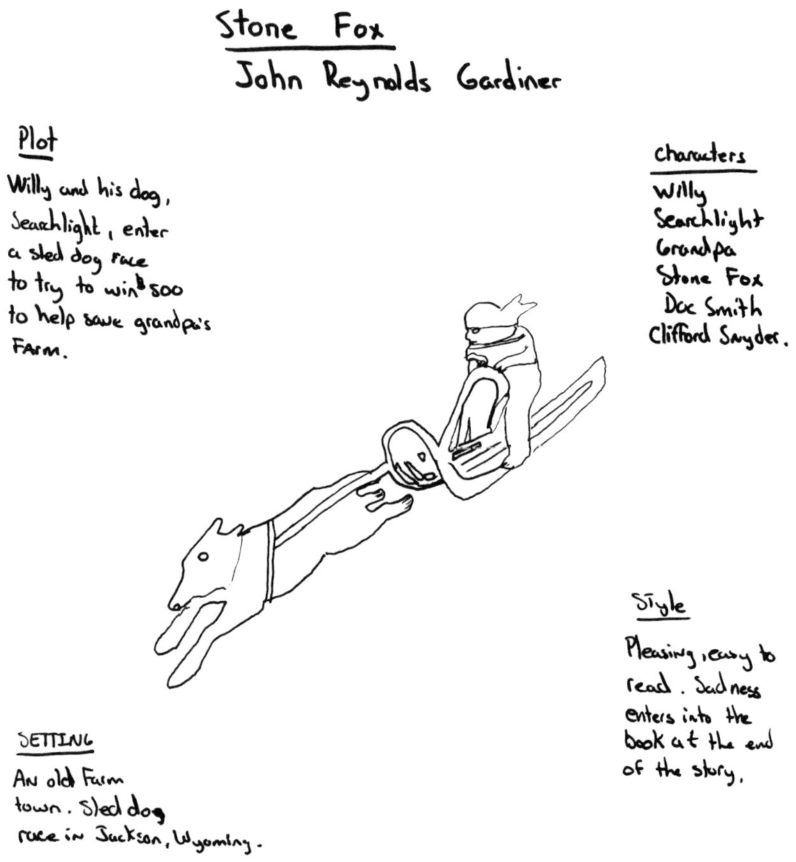

Stone Fox
John Reynolds Gardiner

Plot

Willy and his dog,
Searchlight, enter
a sled dog race
to try to win $500
to help save grandpa's
Farm.

Characters

Willy
Searchlight
Grandpa
Stone Fox
Doc Smith
Clifford Snyder.

Style

Pleasing, easy to
read. Sadness
enters into the
book at the end
of the story.

SETTING

An old Farm
town. Sled dog
race in Jackson, Wyoming.

Subject/Content Area

Language arts and social studies

Age Level

9- to 12-year-olds

Goals

To have the students perform tasks as individuals

To have the students share information with the group

To have each student express him- or herself as "one of a kind"

To have the students recognize different family structures

To have the students identify their own family structures and members

Objectives

1. Students will create "feelings webs" for the main character in the book.

2. Students will use the web as a basis for retelling the most exciting part of the book by acting it out without words for the group.

Materials

Hatchet by Gary Paulsen

12-inch by 18-inch paper

Markers and pencils

Readiness/Motivation

Ask the students if they have ever flown in an airplane. Ask them to describe the feelings they experienced during flight. (If they are unwilling to share aloud, then have them write down a few sentences that would describe those feelings.) Ask the students to brainstorm with one another about what *survival* means to them. Write the responses on chart paper, and hang it in the room for later reference.

Procedures/Instructions

1. Gather the students together and show them the book *Hatchet*. Ask them why they think the book has this title. Refer to the brainstorming about survival, and see if that provides a hint.

2. Explain that the story the group will read and discuss concerns a young boy whose parents have decided to separate. Because this story may be very sensitive for those who have experienced similar situations, let the students know that reading about others with similar problems sometimes helps us better to deal with our own circumstances and to realize that we are not alone.

3. Read the story orally. If you are able to secure multiple copies of the book, also ask the students to read it on their own. At the end of each chapter, ask the students to reflect on the feelings that Brian experienced. Have each student create a "feelings web" for Brian as he progresses through the story.

FIGURE 9–5 Feeling web for Brian

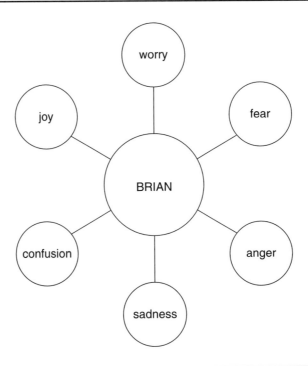

4. Encourage students to write down events in the book that they find particularly exciting or intriguing. Explain that each student will need to share an
event with the class in such a way that the audience will understand without
words. Set up an area in the classroom where students can make these presentations to the group. (You may or may not encourage the use of props or
materials.) Discuss the presentations. Have the students share what they
liked especially about their classmates' presentations.

Resource: Paulsen, Gary, (1987) *Hatchet.* New York: Bradbury, 1987.

LESSON PLAN 5—DEATH IN THE FAMILY

Rationale

The purpose of this lesson is to allow students to recognize that death can be
imposed on young people and their families and that they are not alone in the
process.

Subject/Content Area

Language arts and social studies

Age level

9- to 12-year-olds

Goals

To have the students perform tasks as individuals

To have the students share information with the group

To have each student express him- or herself as "one of a kind"

To have the students recognize different family structures

To have the students identify their own family structures and members

Objectives

1. Students will create a sequence map about a book.
2. Students will use the map as a basis for retelling the most exciting part of the book by acting it out without words for the group.

Materials

Missing May by Cynthia Rylant

12-inch by 18-inch paper

Markers and pencils

Readiness/Motivation

Tell students about the death of a friend or relative that you can recall. Share with them your feelings of loss and sorrow. Encourage them to tell about anyone close to them whom they may have lost to death.

Procedures/Instructions

1. Gather the students together and show them the book *Missing May.* Ask them why they think the book has this title. Refer to the discussion about losses and see if that might provide a hint.
2. Explain that the story the group will read and discuss deals with a death in the family. Because this story may be very sensitive for those who have experienced similar situations, let them know that reading about others with similar problems sometimes helps us better to deal with our own circumstances and to realize that we are not alone.
3. Introduce the story orally. If you are able to secure multiple copies of the book, also encourage the students to read it on their own. At the end of each

FIGURE 9–6 *Missing May* student artwork sequence

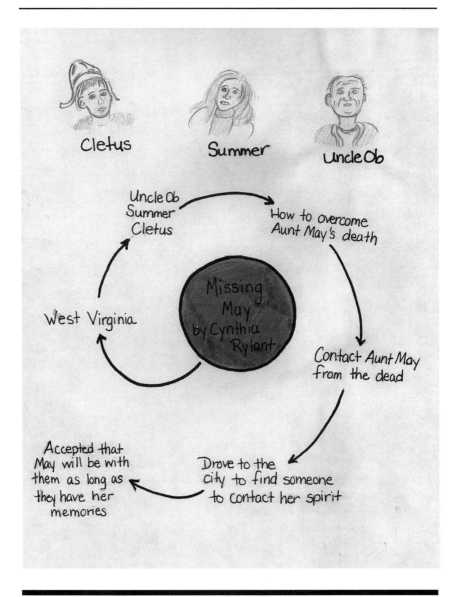

chapter, ask the students to reflect on the feelings that family members expressed in the story. Have each of the students create a sequence map of the story as they move through the book. Share and display the maps.

Resource: Rylant, Cynthia, *Missing May.* New York: Dell, 1992.

LESSON PLAN 6—WHEN SOMEONE YOU LOVE DIES . . .

Rationale

The purpose of this lesson is to allow students to recognize that young people face losses, too, and that personal survival is still important.

Subject/Content Area

Language arts and social studies

Age Level

9- to 12-year-olds

Goals

To have the students perform tasks as individuals

To have the students share information with the group

To have each student express him- or herself as "one of a kind"

To have students recognize different family structures

Objectives

1. Students will create a visual sequence of the story.
2. Students will use the visual aid as a basis for retelling the story for the group.

Materials

Sounder by William H. Armstrong

12-inch by 18-inch paper

Markers and pencils

Readiness/Motivation

Brainstorm with students about different family structures—single-parent, two-parent, extended, and foster families. Talk with the students about what is meant by *class* and *status*—what do they think of when they hear the word *poor* or *disadvantaged?* Remark to the students about the sensitivity of this discussion and stress that they should respect one another's privacy and feelings in these matters.

Procedures/Instructions

1. Gather the students together and show them the book *Sounder*. Explain that the book concerns a young boy whose family members work as *sharecroppers*. Ask students to define that term. Use reference materials if necessary.

2. Explain that the story the group will read and discuss deals with a young boy who lives through some very hard losses. Because this story may be very sensitive for those who have experienced similar situations, let the students know that reading about others with similar problems sometimes helps us better to deal with our own circumstances and to realize that we are not alone.

3. Read part of the story orally. If you are able to secure multiple copies of the book, also ask the students to read it on their own. At the end of each chapter, ask the students to reflect on the feelings that the boy had in the book. Have each student create a visual aid that will help to explain the sequence of events in the story. Share the visual aids in the large group.

4. Encourage the students to respond to the following questions:

   Who was your favorite character in the story and why?

   What questions came to your mind as you were reading the story?

   How did you feel about the ending of the story? Did you agree with the author's choice of ending? Why or why not? How might you have changed it?

5. Hold a group discussion in which students can share their responses with one another.

Resource: Armstrong, William H., *Sounder*. New York: HarperCollins Children's Books, 1969.

❖ Related Bibliography

Armstrong, W. H. (1969). *Sounder*. New York: HarperCollins Children's Books.

Fox, M. (1985). *Wilfred Gordon McDonald Partridge*. Brooklyn, NY: Kane/Miller.

Gardiner, J. R. (1983). *Stone Fox*. New York: HarperCollins Children's Books.

Hamilton, V. (1993). *Cousins*. New York: Scholastic.

Hildebrand, V., Phenice, L. A., Gray, M. M., & Hines, R. P. (1996). *Knowing and serving diverse families*. Englewood Cliffs, NJ: Merrill.

Howard, E. F. (1991). *Aunt Flossie's hats (and crab cakes later)*. New York: Clarion Books.

Paulsen, G. (1987). *Hatchet*. New York: Bradbury.

Rylant, C. (1992). *Missing May*. New York: Dell.

Rudman, M. K. (1995). Children's literature: An issues approach. White Plains, NY: Longman.

CHAPTER 10

Developing Values

Leading multiculturalists Bennett (1995), Nieto (1992), Sleeter and Grant (1995), and Banks and Banks (1995) write of the ethics of including multiculturalism in our educational systems. They are encouraging teachers to become critical thinkers and evaluators of their curricula and to become empowered with what they teach and how they teach it.

In other words, noted experts in the field of multicultural education are expecting teachers to identify their personal values and to help their students do the same. Geneva Gay (1995) has expanded on the contributions of these theories in an article entitled "Bridging Multicultural Theory and Practice":

> When theorists propose that the K-12 educational process be **transformed** by cultural diversity, they mean the most fundamental and deeply ingrained values, beliefs, and assumptions which determine all educational policies, content, procedures, and structures schooling will be **revolutionalized** by being culturally pluralized (p. 6).

When the values of curricula are discussed, then values and beliefs of the educated become part of the discussion. This chapter deals with the controversy of whether or not to teach values. It is this author's contention that empowering teachers to integrate multiculturalism into the regular curriculum means that they will address ethics, social justice, right and wrong decisions, critical thinking, and values.

Children's literature is a very viable vehicle for sharing the many diverging and similar values that one can see in our country and in others. The activities and approaches described in this chapter, though dealing with sensitive issues, are appropriate in today's elementary settings.

❖ Definition and Implications

One of the greatest challenges facing educators today is deciding whether or not to teach values to their students. Daily we are faced with this dilemma, and those of us who have been in the business of sharing our lives and our knowledge with children know that we teach values every time we walk into a classroom. By our mere examples and our attitudes about learning and regarding others, we share and impart our own value systems.

This chapter deals most specifically with bias, prejudice, and racism as they relate to children and their learning. Again, it is important to define terms. The following definitions have been taken from *Guidelines for Selecting Bias-Free Textbooks and Storybooks* issued in 1980 by the Council on Interracial Books for Children (cited in Derman-Sparks, 1989, p. 3):

> Bias: Any attitude, belief, or feeling that results in, and helps to justify, unfair treatment of an individual because of his/her identity;
>
> Prejudice: An attitude, opinion, or feeling formed without adequate prior knowledge, thought, or reason. Prejudice can be prejudgment for or against any person, group, or sex;
>
> Racism: Any attitude, action, or institutional practice backed up by institutional power that subordinates people because of their color. This includes the imposition of one ethnic group's culture in such a way as to withhold respect for, to demean, or to destroy the cultures of other races.

Most teachers are unaware of outright bias or prejudice that they may display in their own classrooms. However, studies show that bias is found regularly in teachers' classroom dealings with females and males—that in fact girls are not trained for independent activity but instead receive dosages of treatment that encourages "learned helplessness" (Froschl & Sprung, 1983, p. 21).

Similar behavior on the part of teachers occurs when they deal with minority groups of children. Research by Cross (1985) indicates that students can best resist racism when they can readily see their group membership represented in stories and curricula. In other words, all students benefit when all groups are better represented within the educational system. The purpose of this chapter is to help teachers infuse activities within the regular curriculum in such a way that values are addressed as students

1. recognize racism in society,
2. learn the value of not making prejudgments, and
3. identify key individuals from many cultures and their contributions to the world.

Today's educators have the responsibility to assess the existing curriculum for stereotypical approaches to learning. Active intervention is the remedy for cognitive, social-emotional, and physical deficits brought about by constraining gender and ethnic stereotypes, states Greenberg (1980). The clear implication is that if our children are to mature into adults with attitudes, knowledge, and skills that will change and influence the world in a positive way, the educational system must see that bias, prejudice, and racism are eliminated (Derman-Sparks, 1989).

Throughout the activities outlined in this chapter, students will have the opportunity to progress toward the following goals:

1. Recognize and develop appreciation of many cultures
2. Learn the value of not making prejudgments
3. Identify the contributions of various cultures to our society
4. Treat others fairly and justly
5. Recognize and identify prejudice concerning individuals
6. Recognize and identify discrimination against individuals
7. Recognize and identify racial inequity
8. Recognize and identify sexual inequity

❖ Lesson Plans

Lessons presented in this chapter will include the following elements:

Rationale, a statement that describes the purpose of the lesson (why and how it applies to multicultural integration within the curriculum)

Subject/content area that would be covered with the lesson

Age level for which the lesson would be most appropriate (The concepts and ideas could be upscaled or downscaled depending upon the group of children and the level of expertise and comfort of the instructor; age levels were chosen instead of grade levels because many educational settings have moved toward multiage groupings.)

Goals that the teacher would set in regard to curricular infusion

Objectives for student competencies that could be demonstrated, observed, and measured

Terms/vocabulary that would be introduced, reviewed, or integrated within the lesson

Materials that would be best used for the lesson

Readiness/Motivation, which involves setting the stage for the lesson and creating an atmosphere for learning for all students whatever their schemata (past experiences and prior knowledge)

Procedures/instructions, which delineate all the directions for carrying on the lesson (Within each step the instructor can evaluate success or further document student progress as he or she sees fit.)

Student evaluation, which includes methods of assessing student performance of competencies and objectives

LESSON PLAN 1—HOW THE BLUEBONNET GOT ITS NAME

Rationale

The purpose of this lesson is to give students an understanding of the origin of an old tale of the United States that is based on the customs and way of life of the Comanche people.

Subject/Content Area

Language arts and mathematics

Age Level

7- to 9-year-olds

Goals

To encourage students readily to share information about diverse cultures with one another and with others outside the classroom

To help students to discover the origins of games

To have students recognize the influence of various cultures on our everyday living

To have students recognize and develop appreciation of many cultures

To have the students identify the contributions of various cultures to our society

Objectives

1. Students will identify the state or national flower of the region where they live and compare it to the Texas lupine or bluebonnet.
2. Students will play a version of an Indian counting game.

Materials

Dried plum pits or small circles cut out of cardboard (5 in number)

The Legend of Blue Bonnet by Tomie dePaola

Readiness/Motivation

Show the picture on the back cover of *The Legend of Blue Bonnet.* Ask the children to describe what they see—the blue flower. Ask them to give the flower a name. Then introduce the book by showing the front cover and then reading the title. Explain that in some cultures stories are passed down from person to person, generation to generation to explain how things have happened in nature and how things got their names. This is how the Comanche Native American people gave a name to the flower of the state of Texas. Find Texas on a map or globe.

Procedures/Instructions

1. Read the selection. Pause to help define unknown or difficult vocabulary words such as *shaman, tipi, drought, and famine.* You may want to write these words on large paper or sentence strips so that students will feel free to use them later in their writings.
2. At the end of the reading, ask the students if they know what might be the state or national flower of the region where they live. Use a resource book (encyclopedia) to help students identify the flower of their region. (If none has been positively identified, then choose a flower that is common to the area.)
3. Allow the students to draw pictures of their state or national flower. Compare the drawings by color, size, and description with the lupine in the story.
4. Proceed with the Native American counting game to show the students that we have gained from this cultural group not only names of things but also different games and skills.

Game: Indian Counting Game

Country/Culture: American Indian, Native American

Directions

1. Assemble the plum pits or cardboard circles.

2. On four pits or circles, paint a half-moon shape on one side. On the fifth, paint a star shape on one side.

3. Place the pits in a shallow basket or wooden bowl.

4. Let one child at a time hold the basket and give it a shake. Then have the child count the number of shapes that turn up, alloting one point for each moon and two points for the star.

5. The child who has the highest number of points at the end of the game wins.

Resource: dePaola, Tomie, *The Legend of Blue Bonnet.* Boston MA: G. P. Putnam's Sons, 1983.

LESSON PLAN 2—UNDERSTANDING OUR ESKIMO FRIENDS

Rationale

The purpose of this lesson is to show students the importance of personal independence and decision making as evidenced by a young girl of a Canadian Inuit village in a multicultural story. It also affords students an opportunity to engage in typical games of a culture very different from their own.

Subject/Content Area

Language arts and physical education

Age Level

7- to 9-year-olds

Goals

To have students begin or continue to accept others as members of different cultural, religious, ethnic, or gender groups—recognizing differences and similarities among people

To have students work cooperatively, developing interpersonal skills

To ask students to perform tasks as individuals

To have students demonstrate self-control

To encourage students to show willingness to try new activities

To teach students how to treat others fairly and justly

To have the students recognize and identify sexual inequity

To have the students communicate verbally and nonverbally with other class members

Objectives

1. Students will list the characteristics of a very brave young Inuit girl after hearing a story about her.

2. Students will engage in a game (or two) that is typical of the Inuit culture to understand better how children from other cultures play.

Materials

Very Last First Time by Jan Andrews

Outdoor play area

Sturdy blanket (10 to 12 feet wide) or parachute

Ball or doll

Readiness/Motivation

Gather all the students together for story reading. Ask the students to share about some events in their lives when they had to do something very brave or make very hard or scary decisions. You might want to tell about an incident when you, the teacher, were very young and had to do something on your own that took a great deal of courage. Talk about what it takes to make good decisions and how young people often look to adults (especially parents) for help and guidance in making these decisions. Tell the students that the story to be read today deals with a young girl who does a very brave thing all alone for the very first time.

Procedures/Instructions

1. Read the story. Share the pictures. Remark on the watercolor illustrations by Ian Wallace throughout the book.

2. On completion of the reading, ask the children to help you make a list of words that describe the way Eva acted (encourage the children to describe her as brave, courageous, etc.). Write these words on a large piece of paper so that children can refer to the words later when writing in their journals.

3. Tell the children that the Inuit children play games just as they do. Explain that the group may play one of these games now.

Game: Muk

Country/Culture: Inuit Eskimo

Objectives

1. Students will use comical expressions and gestures to try to "break the muk" or silence.

Directions

1. Players sit in a circle.

2. One player enters the center and chooses a player from the outside, who must say "Muk."

3. This person must keep a straight face while the person in the center uses comical expressions and gestures to "break the muk."

4. When the muk is broken, that student replaces the one in the middle.

Game: Blanket Toss

Country/Culture: Eskimo, Native American

Objectives

1. Students will work cooperatively to keep an object from falling off a blanket as it is bounced in the air.

Directions

1. Have players distribute themselves evenly around the edge of the blanket, holding it firmly.

2. Holding the edges of the blanket, students should work as a team to gently toss the ball or doll into the air so that when it drops it falls back into the center of the blanket.

Resource: Andrews, Jan, *Very Last First Time.* New York: Margaret K. McEldemy Books, 1986.

LESSON PLAN 3—I LIKE YOU FOR WHO YOU ARE . . .

Rationale

The purpose of this lesson is to show students the importance of friendship and understanding of others; it also affords students an opportunity to engage in the making of a rag blanket to share with nursing home residents.

Subject/Content Area

Language arts and creative arts

Age Level

7- to 12-year-olds

Goals

To have students begin or continue to accept others as members of different cultural, religious, ethnic, or gender groups—recognizing differences and similarities among people

To have students work cooperatively, developing interpersonal skills

To ask students to perform tasks as individuals

To encourage students to show willingness to try new activities

To teach students how to treat others fairly and justly

To have students recognize and identify prejudice concerning individuals

To have students recognize and identify discrimination against individuals

Objectives

1. Students will retell how a young girl was discriminated against after hearing a story about this situation.

2. Students will engage in the creation of rag lap blankets in a cooperative fashion.

Materials

The Rag Coat by Lauren Mills

Paper for writing

Needles

Thread

Fabric Scraps (rags)

Bias tape or ribbon 2½ inches wide

Yardstick/tape measure/rulers

Fabric scissors

Readiness/Motivation

Gather all the students together for story reading. Ask the students to share about some events in their lives when they felt out of place or alone in certain situations—situations when they wished they were like all the other children in a group. You might want to tell about an incident when you, the teacher, were young and had to deal with that type of situation. Tell the students that the story to be read today deals with a young girl living in Appalachia who does not have a proper coat to wear to school and how she deals with this dilemma. You might show the front cover of the book and ask the children to predict the outcome of the story.

Procedures/Instructions

1. Read the story. Share the pictures. Remark on the watercolor illustrations by Lauren Mills throughout the book.

2. At the completion of the reading, send the children back to their work areas in groups of three or four. Instruct them to rewrite the story as a group and to be prepared to retell it to the class by the next reading time. At the set time,

gather all groups together, and ask one spokesperson from each group to read the "retelling" of the story to the class. Compare the groups' results as a class.

3. Tell the children that they will have an opportunity to use fabric scraps or rags from home to create a lap quilt that will be given to senior citizens at the local nursing home (or to a children's hospital, if you prefer). Send a note to the students' parents asking for fabric scraps or old clean clothing that may be cut into 3-inch by 3-inch squares. Ask for parent volunteers who are willing to help supervise the hand sewing of the quilts at a designated time.

4. Cut all fabric into 3-inch by 3-inch squares, and sew the squares together to create a rectangular quilt. After each group has sewn a quilt to measure 15 inches by 18 inches, edge the quilt, using bias tape or ribbon folded in half.

5. Arrange first to display the quilts at the school and then to deliver them to the local nursing home (or children's hospital).

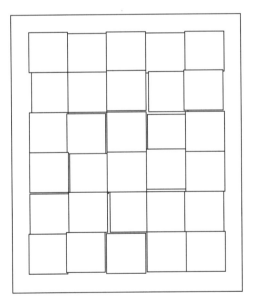

Resource: Mills, Lauren, *The Rag Coat.* Boston: Little, Brown, 1991.

LESSON PLAN 4—I WANT TO BE FIRST!!

Rationale

The purpose of this lesson is to show students the importance of sharing and cooperation.

Subject/Content Area

Language arts and creative arts

Age Level

4- to 6-year-olds

Goals

To have students work cooperatively, developing interpersonal skills

To teach students how to treat others fairly and justly

To have students demonstrate sharing within their classroom

Objectives

1. Students will participate in a shared reading about a very selfish pig.

2. Students will illustrate and rewrite a similar story about sharing, using other animals and characters.

Materials

Me First by Helen Lester

12-inch by 18-inch paper/experience paper

Crayons or markers

Readiness/Motivation

Gather all the students together for story reading. Ask the students to describe what it means to be selfish. Write their ideas on the board or on chart paper. Tell the students that the story to be read today deals with a little pig who always wants to be first. Remind the students that at the end of the reading they will be able to write a similar story about different animals and characters who are selfish.

Procedures/Instructions

1. Read the story. Share the pictures. Remark on the drawings by Lynn Munsinger that illustrate the book. Encourage students to participate in the reading by having them say, "Me first!" as Pinkerton does.

2. On completion of the reading, tell the children that the group will be writing its own version of a similar story about a different character or animal that is selfish. Brainstorm with the children about appropriate characters and their names. List actions that would be selfish ones that they would like included in the story. Encourage the students to select a character that would teach the selfish one a lesson. Have all students participate in dictating a story to you. Write the story on chart paper or 12-inch by 18-inch sheets. Distribute

the sheets to individuals or small groups to illustrate. Bind the book with yarn or the like, and then gather the group together to read the story aloud. Have the children take the book home to share with their parents and families. Establish a schedule where students can take turns taking the book home for sharing.

3. Finally, ask the students to make a set of classroom rules that reflect sharing at its best. Recognize in a positive fashion those students who remember to share with others.

Resource: Lester, Helen, *Me First.* Boston: Houghton Mifflin, 1992.

LESSON PLAN 5—A PYRAMID OF IDEAS

Rationale

The purpose of this lesson is to allow students to recognize prejudice and racism in their society; it also allows students to create a story pyramid about a particular story.

Subject/Content Area

Language arts

Age Level

9- to 12-year-olds

Goals

To have students begin or continue to accept others as members of different cultural, religious, ethnic, or gender groups—recognizing differences and similarities among people

To have students work cooperatively, developing interpersonal skills

To ask students to perform tasks as individuals

To encourage students to show willingness to try new activities

To teach students how to treat others fairly and justly

To have students recognize and identify prejudice concerning individuals

To have students recognize and identify discrimination against individuals

Objectives

1. Students will retell how a young man dealt with discrimination after hearing a story about him.

2. Students will engage in the creation of story pyramids about the characters, setting, and events.

3. Students will discuss how to deal with racism as young people in our society.

Materials

Maniac Magee by Jerry Spinelli

Paper for writing

Readiness/Motivation

Gather all the students together for discussion. Ask them to share about some events in their lives where they witnessed unfairness or prejudiced behavior. Ask students to define *prejudice*—prejudgment without cause. You might show the front cover of the book and ask the students to make predictions about the outcome of the story.

Procedures/Instructions

1. Read the story. If you have multiple copies of the book, encourage students to read the book on their own, and assign certain chapters for each reading session.

2. Throughout the book, engage the students in discussion with open-ended questions. Focus on the characters, setting, and action of the story. Ask the students if they would respond in similar fashion if they were the characters in the book.

3. On completion of the reading, have each of the students create a story pyramid that reflects the characters, setting, and events of the book. Give directions as follows:

   1. Write a word that names a character.
   2. Write 2 words that describe the character.
   3. Write 3 words that describe feelings of the character.
   4. Write 4 words in a sentence that explain action of the character.
   5. Write 5 words in a sentence that show the character in a different setting.

   (Adapt this format to reflect action, characters, and setting specifically.)

   ```
                              1. _____

                        2. _____   _____

                  3. _____   _____   _____

            4. _____   _____   _____   _____

      5. _____   _____   _____   _____   _____
   ```

4. Share and display student works

Resource: Spinelli, Jerry, *Maniac Magee.* New York: Scholastic, 1990.

LESSON PLAN 6—WHEN WAR HITS

Rationale

The purpose of this lesson is to allow students to recognize the effects of war in their world; it also allows students to create character maps or K-W-L charts about a particular book.

Subject/Content Area

Language arts, social studies

Age Level

9- to 12-year-olds

Goals

To have students begin or continue to accept others as members of different cultural, religious, ethnic, or gender groups—recognizing differences and similarities among people

To have students work cooperatively, developing interpersonal skills

To ask students to perform tasks as individuals

To encourage students to show willingness to try new activities

To teach students how to treat others fairly and justly

To have students recognize and identify prejudice concerning individuals

To have students recognize and identify discrimination against individuals

Objectives

1. Students will retell how a young girl dealt with war after hearing a story about her.
2. Students will engage in the creation of character webs.
3. Students will discuss how to deal with war as young people in our society.
4. Students will create a K-W-L chart about a particular event in history.

Materials

Number the Stars by Lois Lowry

The Boys' War by Jim Murphy (optional)

Paper for writing

Readiness/Motivation

Gather all the students together for discussion. Ask the students to share about wars that they know of. Write their responses so that all can see the names of the wars, the participants, and the outcomes.

Procedures/Instructions

1. Have the students relate what they know about World War II and the effect of the war on Jewish people. Introduce the story *Number the Stars.* Read the first chapter. Ask students to make predictions on the basis of what they have heard so far.

2. Throughout the book, engage the students in discussion with open-ended questions. Focus on the characters, setting, and action of the story. Ask the students if they would respond in similar fashion if they were the characters in the book.

3. On completion of the reading, have each of the students create a character map/web that describes the feelings, attitudes, and actions of one of the main characters.

4. Option: As a follow-up, extension, or optional activity, have the students complete a K-W-L chart on the story *The Boys' War.*

FIGURE 10–1 *Number the Stars* student character map by Shawna

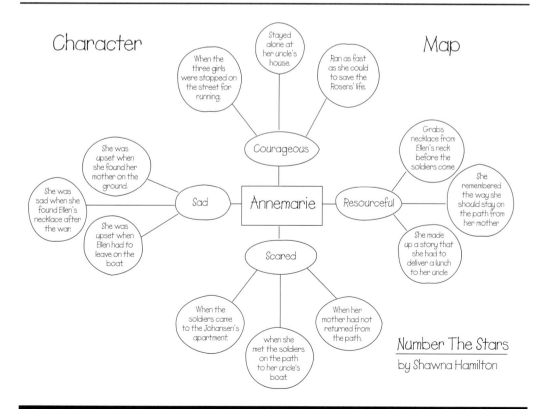

FIGURE 10–2 K-W-L strategy chart by David

K-W-L Strategy Chart

K What I KNOW about the Civil War	W What I WANT to Learn about the Civil War	L What I LEARNED about the Civil War
• More Americans died in this war than in all the others combined. • It started in 1861. It ended in 1865. • The slaves were freed. • R. E. Lee was the leader of the Confederate army. • U. S. Grant was the leader of the Union army. • It was fought mainly in the South. • Drums were used to send messages. • Many boys were needed to play the drums.	• What did they eat? • How did they train? • Did they have target practice? • What did boys do when they were not drumming? • What did they do when they had free time?	• Soldiers' rations consisted of salt pork, dried beef, beans, potatoes, turnips, and corn. • They got very little training except in marching, and many had to learn to shoot during a battle. • In camp they would carry water, gather wood, and cook. After a battle, they would carry the wounded off the field and help bury the dead. • Soldiers gambled, sang both popular songs and hymns, played practical jokes, wrote letters, and even visited the enemy.

Resources: Lowry, Lois, *Number the Stars.* New York: Dell, 1989.
Murphy, Jim, *The Boys' War.* New York: Scholastic, 1990.

❖ Related Bibliography

Andrews, J. (1986). *Very last first time.* New York: Margaret K. McEldemy Books.

Banks, J. A., & Banks, C. A. M. (Eds.). (1995). *Handbook of research on multicultural education.* New York: Macmillan

Bennett, C. I. (1995). *Comprehensive multicultural education:* Theory and practice (3rd ed.). Boston, MA: Allyn & Bacon.

Cross, W. E. (1985). Black identity: Rediscovering the distinctions between personal identity and reference group orientations. In M. B. Spencer, G. K. Brookins, & W. R. Allen (Eds.), *Beginnings: The social and affective development of black children* (155–171). Hillsdale, NJ: Erlbaum.

dePaola, T. (1983). *The Legend of Blue Bonnet.* Boston, MA: G. P. Putnam's Sons.

Derman-Sparks, L., and the A.B.C. Task Force. (1989). *Anti-bias curriculum: Tools for empowering young children*. Washington, DC: National Association for the Education of Young Children.

Froschl, M., & Sprung, B. (1983). Providing an anti-handicappist early childhood environment. *Interracial Books for Children Bulletin,* 14(7–8), 21–23.

Gay, G. (1995). Bridging multicultural theory and practice. *Multicultural Education,* 3(1), 4–9.

Greenberg, P. (1980). *The devil has slippery shoes: A biased biography of the Child Development Group of Mississippi.* London: Macmillan.

Lester, H. (1992). *Me first.* Boston: Houghton Mifflin.

Lowry, L. (1989). *Number the stars.* New York: Dell.

Mills, L. (1991). *The rag coat.* Boston: Little, Brown.

Murphy, J. (1990). *The boys' war.* New York: Scholastic.

Nieto, S. (1992). *Affirming diversity: The sociopolitical context of multicultural education.* New York: Longman.

Sleeter, C. E., & Grant, C. A. (1995), *Making choices for multicultural education: Five approaches to race, class, and gender* (2nd ed.). Columbus, OH: Merrill.

Spinelli, J. (1990). *Maniac Magee.* New York: Scholastic.

CHAPTER 11

Communicating
and Problem Solving

Earlier in this text, various terms related to multiculturalism were defined. In chapter 4, the reader encountered the notion that different communication systems exist in our country and in the world. These communication systems determine our ability to understand one another visually, auditorily, and kinesthetically.

The ways in which we speak (language and dialect), write (written communication/print), and view one another (non-verbal communication) express our understanding and respect for one another's differences and similarities. As Dag McLeod (1995) has stated, "It is the diversity of different groups that makes them the same; just as they can join together by respecting those things that set them apart" (p. 11).

This chapter on communication and problem solving recognizes the fact that in a community of learners, there may be many different ways to send the same message. The sending may be different from culture to culture. Misunderstanding results from a lack of knowledge of others' ways of communicating.

The activities and definitions presented in this chapter will offer a brief glance at ways for students to explore different communication systems and thus gain the knowledge needed to understand and respect others. For further treatment of this topic, it is important that the reader refer to chapter 4 of this text.

❖ Definition and Implications

Communication is a very broad area of curriculum. It includes both verbal and nonverbal communication—the interchange of information between people in various fashions. According to Richmond and McCroskey (1993), "The study of communication between people with differing cultural backgrounds is the most rapidly growing area in the field of communication" (p. 169). As teachers of elementary students face diverse classrooms that include students with cultural and language differences, they must recognize the difficulty of communicating the curriculum in the "normal" fashion.

Research on the degree of *homophyly* (similarity) that a teacher has with his or her students has indicated that the more culturally similar or more culturally sensitive the teacher is to the students, the more effective the teaching that takes place. The principle of homophyly is that "the more two people are alike, the more effectively they will communicate, and the more similar they will become" (McCroskey & Richmond, 1993, p. 235). With that principle in mind yet respecting and celebrating the differences that students bring to each learning situation, the author wrote this chapter to help students and teachers work toward the following goals:

Describing objects, places, and events verbally

Participating in class discussions

Speaking in front of small or large groups

Recognizing the importance of nonverbal communication

Role-playing

Thinking critically

Engaging in creative problem solving

Brainstorming

Identifying diverse communication systems

Attempting communication in a second language

As future teachers prepare for the classroom and as current educators begin to realize the impending population developments, they may be apprehensive about preparing for such diverse groups. However motivated we are as teachers, we need to explore new methods of communication (including technologies) that will meet the needs of our future students. The first step will be identifying our audience—our students—and enriching their environment with examples of our national culture as well as examples of their cultures and others of the nation and world. Print-rich and communication-rich environments promote learning through the integration of listening, speaking, reading, and writing—all communication driven.

The lessons that follow will address these issues in a real sense by having the students do the following:

1. Communicate verbally with other class members
2. Communicate nonverbally with other class members
3. Use words to describe objects, places, and events
4. Participate in verbal sharing
5. Participate in class discussions
6. Prepare speeches and deliver them to small groups
7. Prepare speeches and deliver them to large groups
8. Engage in role-playing
9. Demonstrate nonverbal communication
10. Demonstrate critical thinking
11. Engage in creative problem solving
12. Brainstorm
13. Identify diverse communication systems
14. Communicate in a second language (through writing or speaking)
15. Listen and respond to music of diverse cultures
16. Read and develop appreciation of multicultural literature
17. Read current reports in newspapers and periodicals, looking for cultural contributions
18. Report current events (e.g., in a television news/radio format)
19. Use various genres to express feelings about diverse cultures in writing
20. Compare and contrast various communication forms

❖ Lesson Plans

Lessons presented in this chapter will include the following elements:

Rationale, a statement that describes the purpose of the lesson (why and how it applies to multicultural integration within the curriculum)

Subject/content area that would be covered with the lesson

Age level for which the lesson would be most appropriate (The concepts and ideas could be upscaled or downscaled depending upon the group of children and the level of expertise and comfort of the instructor; age levels were chosen instead of grade levels because many educational settings have moved toward multiage groupings.)

Goals that the teacher would set in regard to curricular infusion

Objectives for student competencies that could be demonstrated, observed, and measured

Terms/vocabulary that would be introduced, reviewed, or integrated within the lesson

Materials that would be best used for the lesson

Readiness/motivation, which involves setting the stage for the lesson and creating an atmosphere for learning for all students whatever their schemata (past experiences and prior knowledge)

Procedures/instructions, which delineate all the directions for carrying on the lesson (within each step the instructor can evaluate success or further document student progress as he or she sees fit.)

Student evaluation, which includes methods of assessing student performance of competencies and objectives

LESSON 1—JAPANESE CULTURE

Rationale

The purpose of this lesson is to have students communicate and problem solve in a way that reflects another culture.

Subject/Content Area

Language arts, mathematics, and fine arts

Age Level

8- to 11-year-olds

Goals

To have students work cooperatively, developing interpersonal skills

To have students recognize the influence of various cultures on our everyday living

Objectives

1. The students will follow simple, yet specific directions in order to construct a boat origami style.

2. The students will recognize Japanese culture in the paper-folding activity.

3. The students will engage in creative problem solving and critical thinking.

4. The students will describe the customs and traditions of the Japanese culture.

Terms/Vocabulary

Origami

Materials

Origami paper or lightweight duplicating paper

The Funny Little Woman by Arlene Mosel

Readiness/Motivation

Show the children the book *The Funny Little Woman,* and ask them to predict what the story may be about. Ask them if they have ever heard about the country Japan. Show them something that may have been made in Japan. Explain that many of the things we do we have learned from other cultures. One of these is the art of paper folding, or *origami.* Tell students that after the story is read and shared, they will be trying some paper folding.

Procedures/Instructions

1. Read and share the story. Ask the children to tell about the customs and traditions that they heard about in this story.

2. Show a sample of Japanese origami. Explain in detail, step by step, how to construct the boat (see figure 11-1).

FIGURE 11–1 Japanese origami

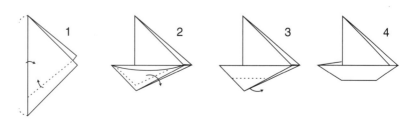

FIGURE 11–2 *The Funny Little Woman* student artwork maze by Lynette

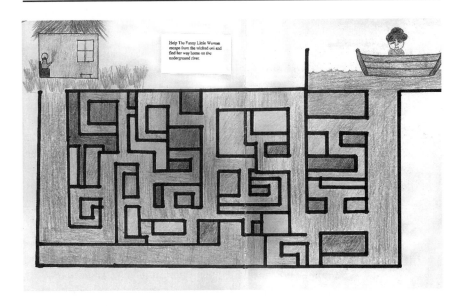

3. Distribute one piece of paper per student. Ask students to work slowly, carefully, and cooperatively in making the fish and the boat.

4. Punch holes in the finished products, and hang them for classroom display.

5. Optional: Create a maze that the funny little woman would follow. You may even have the students create their own and exchange them (see figure 11-2).

Resource: Mosel, Arlene, *The Funny Little Woman.* New York: E. P. Dutton, 1986.

LESSON 2—SIGNING

Rationale

The purpose of this lesson is to become more aware of different types of communication other than verbal communication (i.e., signing and symbols).

Subject/Content Area

Language arts

Age Level

All elementary; 5- to 12-year-olds

Goals

> To have students work cooperatively, developing interpersonal skills

> To have students begin to recognize the common bond of humanity among people of all cultures in a global society

> To have students communicate nonverbally with other class members

> To have students identify diverse communication systems

> To ask students to compare and contrast various communication forms

Objectives

1. Students will learn and demonstrate simple "signs" that deaf people use to communicate.

2. Students will learn and demonstrate simple "signs" used by Native American groups.

3. Students will compare and contrast the different signs that they have learned.

Materials

> Signing chart (deaf)

> *I Have a Sister—My Sister is Deaf* by Jeanne W. Peterson

> *Handsigns: A Sign Language Alphabet* by Kathleen Fain

> Native American tribe signs

Motivation/Readiness

Ask children to explain how they learned to talk and communicate with others. Now ask them to put their hands over their ears, and move your lips to give them a simple direction such as "Sit down." Ask the group if they understood what you had said. Using very simple sign language, motion, "I love you" (see directions in next paragraph). Ask the children to guess what you have signed. Explain that for many people who cannot hear, signing and lip reading are ways to communicate. Tell them that they will have the opportunity to learn various simple signs for letters and words.

Directions for "I love you": (1) Point to yourself; (2) raise your right hand and hold your ring finger and third finger down; (3) point to the other person.

Procedures/Instructions

1. Read the selection *I Have a Sister—My Sister is Deaf.* Engage in discussion about the story, asking such questions as these:

   What does it mean to be deaf?

FIGURE 11-3 Creating handsigns

Does it hurt to be deaf?

How do deaf people learn to talk to other people?

Can deaf people "hear" anything?

How does the girl in this story feel about her deaf sister?

Do you know anyone who is deaf?

2. Tell the children that there are signs that people who cannot hear or speak use to make words in communicating with others. This method is called "sign language." Display and demonstrate different symbols used in signing. Practice as a group. Try to spell names to one another. Students may refer to the book by Kathleen Fain entitled *Handsigns: A Sign Language Alphabet.*

3. Explain that, because Native American tribes were numerous, they needed sign language and pictures to communicate with members of different groups. Research, display, and demonstrate some of these signs. Encourage the students to try to duplicate these signs in their journals as they write and tell stories.

Resources: Fain, Kathleen, *Handsigns: A Sign Language Alphabet.* New York: Scholastic, 1993.

Peterson, Jeanne Whitehouse, *I Have a Sister—My Sister is Deaf.* New York: HarperCollins, 1977.

LESSON PLAN 3—COUNTING AND ALPHABETS IN ANOTHER CULTURE

Rationale

The purpose of this lesson is to give students an opportunity to recognize and discover different counting languages and symbols of the people of different cultures.

Subject/Content Area

Language arts and mathematics

Age Level

All ages; 6- to 12-year-olds

Goals

To have the students begin or continue to accept others as members of different cultural, religious, ethnic, or gender groups—recognizing differences and similarities among people

To help students recognize the common bond of humanity among people of all cultures in a global society

To help students readily share information about diverse cultures with one another and with people outside the classroom

To have students communicate verbally with other class members

To help students identify diverse communication systems

To have students communicate in a second language (through writing and speaking)

To have the students compare and contrast various communication forms

To have the students recognize and identify objects in a set

To have students note likenesses and differences

To have students identify activities that are common to all people

To help students locate various cultural groups in the world

Objectives

1. Students will identify different ways to count to 10 in different languages and symbols.
2. Students will construct a counting book (1 to 10) that will use their common language and at least one other language from a different culture.
3. Students will construct an alphabet chart using a language from a different culture.
4. Students will construct a puzzle showing the various tribes of the African culture.

Materials

Moja Means One: Swahili Counting Book by Muriel Feelings

Ashanti to Zulu by Margaret Musgrove

Index cards (10 per child)

Ring

Paper punch

Markers or crayons

Blank puzzle

African map

Readiness/Motivation

Ask the students to count to 10 aloud as a group. Tell them that children in other cultures or groups may say their numbers in different ways. Repeat the process with the alphabet. Explain that today the students will have an opportunity to see how people from another group count to 10 and how the alphabet stands for different things to a different cultural group—the Africans, representative of many different groups (tribes).

Procedures/Instructions

1. Share the book *Moja Means One: Swahili Counting Book.* As you read, encourage the students to repeat the new counting words aloud after you.

2. You may want to read the book twice so that the children can recall the counting words again.

3. In your room display the counting systems used in China and Saudi Arabia. Explain their sounds as well.

4. Instruct the students in the process of making a counting book. Give each child 10 index cards. On each card the child is to write the number word and symbol and draw something to show that number of objects.

5. Just for fun, have the children choose words from one of the other counting systems to write and illustrate on the backs of the cards.

6. Punch a hole in each card, and use rings to fasten the cards together in sets. (See illustration below.)

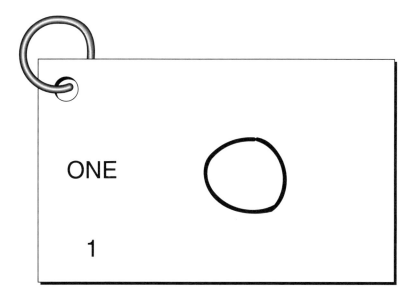

7. Share the book *Ashanti to Zulu.* Ask the students to describe what they see in this book (the alphabet). Point out that, within the book, there are 26 tribes described. Give the students the option to create a puzzle (from the blank puzzle form) that shows the various tribes described in the book or to design their own alphabet cards (see Figure 11-4) for each of the letters. Share and display the student products.

FIGURE 11-4 Puzzle

FIGURE 11–5 Alphabet cards by Brenda

Resources: Feelings, Muriel, *Moja Means One: Swahili Counting Book.* New York: Dial Books for Young Readers, 1971.
Musgrove, Margaret, *Ashanti to Zulu.* New York: Puffin Pied Piper, 1978.

LESSON PLAN 4—COMMUNICATING IN A DIFFERENT LANGUAGE

Rationale

The purpose of this lesson is to give students an opportunity to recognize and discover different counting languages and symbols of the people of different cultures.

Subject/Content Area

Language arts and social studies

Age Level

All ages; 5- to 12-year-olds

Goals

To have the students begin or continue to accept others as members of different cultural, religious, ethnic, or gender groups—recognizing differences and similarities among people

To help students recognize the common bond of humanity among people of all cultures in a global society

To help students readily share information about diverse cultures with one another and with others outside the classroom

To have students communicate verbally with other class members

To help students identify diverse communication systems

To have students communicate in a second language (through writing and speaking)

To have the students compare and contrast various communication forms

To have the students recognize and identify objects in a set

To have students note likenesses and differences

To have students identify activities that are common to all people

To help students locate various cultural groups in the world

Objectives

1. Students will identify different ways to count and write using different languages and symbols.
2. With a picture book as a model, students will construct a story book using the Russian language.

Materials

Here Comes the Cat! by Vladimir Vagin and Frank Asch

The First Thousand Words In Russian by Heather Amery and Katrina Kirilenko

Experience paper

Paper punch and yarn

Markers or crayons

Readiness/Motivation

Ask the students to repeat "Here comes the cat!" aloud as a group. Tell them that children in other cultures or groups may say that phrase in a different way. Explain that today the students will have an opportunity to see how another group says the phrase and then make their own repetitive story using a different language.

Procedures/Instructions

1. Share the book *Here Comes the Cat!* As you read, encourage the students to repeat the phrase aloud with you.

2. You may want to read the book twice so that the children can read it using the Russian pronunciation of the phrase.

3. Share the book *The First Thousand Words in Russian.*

4. Ask the students to identify common objects that they recognize in the Russian language book. For fun, encourage them to create their own "pictionary" of Russian words in a notebook or on paper.

5. Explain to the children that they will have the opportunity to write their own versions of *Here Comes the Cat!* using different Russian words and referring to *The First Thousand Words in Russian.*

6. Allow students to work independently or in groups to create their predictable books. Have them share the books with classmates and other classes when they are finished.

Resources: Vagin, Vladimir, and Asch, Frank, *Here Comes the Cat!* New York: Scholastic, 1989. Amery, Heather, and Kirilenko, Katrina, *The First Thousand Words In Russian.* London, England: Usborne, 1989.

LESSON PLAN 5—WRITING IN CHINESE

Rationale

The purpose of this lesson is to give students an opportunity to recognize and discover languages and symbols of the people of different cultures.

Subject/Content Area

Language arts and social studies

Age Level

7- to 12-year-olds

Goals

To have the students begin or continue to accept others as members of different cultural, religious, ethnic, or gender groups—recognizing differences and similarities among people

To help students recognize the common bond of humanity among people of all cultures in a global society

To help students readily share information about diverse cultures with one another and with others outside the classroom

To have students communicate verbally with other class members

To help students identify diverse communication systems

To have students communicate in a second language (through writing and speaking)

To have the students compare and contrast various communication forms

To have the students recognize and identify objects in a set

To have students note likenesses and differences

To have students identify activities that are common to all people

To help students locate various cultural groups in the world

Objectives

1. Students will identify different ways to write using different languages and symbols.

2. Students will recreate Chinese symbols, using paints and brushes to share a message.

Materials

The Chinese Word for Horse and Other Stories by John Lewis

Paintbrushes

Red and black paint

Paper for painting

8½-inch by 12-inch hard stock cards with selected Chinese writing—letters and words (calligraphy)—on them

Readiness/Motivation

Ask a student to write the word *horse* on the board. Tell the students that children in other cultures or groups may write that word in a different way. Explain that today the students will have an opportunity to see how another group writes the word and then create their own messages, using a different language and a new method of writing.

Procedures/Instructions

1. Share the book *The Chinese Word for Horse and Other Stories.* As you read the first story, which explains the word *horse,* encourage the students to look closely at the Chinese writing (better known as *calligraphy*).

2. As you share the story, have selected students hold up the large cards on which you have painted Chinese symbols.

3. Encourage the students to look closely at the Chinese words on the cards and those that appear in the book.

4. Explain to the students that they will have a try at calligraphy at their seats, using brushes, black and red paint, and paper.

5. Encourage the students to use the following symbols to create messages that others will have to decipher. Hang the finished products in the classroom or hallway.

man   cart   forest   rain cloud

gentleman   horse   stream

sword   growing field

Resource: Lewis, John, *The Chinese Word for Horse and Other Stories*. New York: Schocken Books, 1978.

❖ Related Bibliography

Amery, H., & Kirilenko, K. (1989). *The first thousand words in Russian*. London, England: Usborne.

Fain, K. (1993). *Handsigns: A sign language alphabet*. New York: Scholastic.

Feelings, M. (1971). *Moja means One: Swahili counting book*. New York: Dial Books for Young Readers.

Lewis, J. (1978). *The Chinese word for horse and other stories*. New York: Schocken Books.

McCroskey, J., & Richmond, V. P. (1993). Communication: Implications and reflections. In M. J. O'Hair & S. J. Odell (Eds.), *Diversity and teaching: Teacher education yearbook I* (235). Reston, VA: Association of Teacher Educators.

McLeod, D. (1995). Self-identification, pan-ethnicity, and the boundaries of group identity. *Multicultural Education, 3*(2), 8–11.

Mosel, A. (1986). *The funny little woman*. New York: E. P. Dutton.

Musgrove, M. (1978). *Ashanti to Zulu*. New York: Puffin Pied Piper.

Peterson, J. W. (1977). *I have a sister—my sister is deaf*. New York: HarperCollins.

Richmond, V. P., & McCroskey, J. (1993). Communication: Overview and framework. In J. D. Marshall & J. T. Sears (Eds.), *Diversity and teaching: Teacher education yearbook I* (p. 169). Harcourt Brace Jovanovich.

Vagin, V., & Asch, F. (1989). *Here comes the cat!* New York: Scholastic.

CHAPTER 12

Determining Group and Set Membership

The American educational system now includes a variety of constituencies. Many, many different groups are represented in our schools and on our staffs. As Allport (1979) states, "Americans have long divided people into ethnic categories. . . . As humans, people naturally generalize about others that are not part of their group. . . . Group membership provides a sense of personal security, and solidarity can be strengthened with hostility and alienation toward out-groups" (cited in Young & Pang, 1995, p. 4).

What impact does this information have on the implementation of curriculum in our elementary schools? Today's teachers need to be aware of stereotypes that can be applied to various groups of people. Generally, fear or lack of knowledge causes our students to regard others in a stereotypical fashion.

This chapter corresponds with chapter 4, in which various groups are discussed. Like previous chapters that deal with definitions, this chapter seeks to define group and set membership so we can help young people see how groups are formed and how group membership often is not a matter of choice for individuals. The purpose of this chapter is to engage the learner actively in lessons that reflect particular issues or concepts in multiculturalism. In these lessons, students will be able to investigate many different groups or sets of individuals as they are represented in children's literature.

This chapter does not attempt to generalize about various groups. In fact, it is important to continue investigating the makeup of many groups without evaluating the contributions or abilities of their members.

❖ Definition and Implications

When multicultural education is integrated within the regular curriculum, one of the easiest ways for teachers to start is by having elementary students determine how people and things belong to groups or sets. Teachers can begin by asking simple questions like these: "Where do you go to school?" "Who belongs to your family?" "What clubs or organizations do you belong to?" "What teams do you belong to?" These questions can then be extended beyond the individual to groups: "What are the different classes in this building?" "What different teams play basketball?" "What are some names of fruits or vegetables?" After this exercise, students can determine what constitutes belonging to a group or set. They should also be encouraged to recognize what groups are chosen by their members (e.g., social affiliations) and which ones do not involve choice (e.g., culture, race, gender).

When children begin to recognize their memberships in various groups, they will begin to understand more about themselves and ultimately will understand more about others. The common elements of group membership should be noted; recognition of these likenesses (similarities) can initiate greater understanding among classmates. The different elements within each group fortify its uniqueness. It is necessary to celebrate both the similarities and the differences that we notice.

The activities that follow will expose children to groups and sets so they can work toward the following goals:

1. Recognize and identify objects in a set
2. Recognize the following set designations for people: race, religion, age, sex, education, culture, and physical ability
3. Describe favorite customs and traditions
4. Associate objects, events, and artifacts with particular cultures

❖ Lesson Plans

Lessons presented in this chapter will include the following elements:

Rationale, a statement that describes the purpose of the lesson (why and how it applies to multicultural integration within the curriculum)

Subject/content area that will be covered with this lesson

Age level for which the lesson would be most appropriate (The concepts and ideas could be upscaled or downscaled depending upon the group of children and the level of expertise and comfort of the intructor; age levels were chosen instead of grade levels because many educational settings have moved toward multiage groupings.)

Goals that the teacher would set in regard to curricular infusion

Objectives for student competencies that could be demonstrated, observed, and measured

Terms/vocabulary that would be introduced, reviewed, or integrated within the lesson

Materials that would be best used for the lesson

Readiness/motivation, which involves setting the stage for the lesson and creating an atmosphere for learning for all students whatever their schemata (past experiences and prior knowledge)

Procedures/instructions, which delineate all the directions for carrying on the lesson (Within each step the instructor can evaluate success or further document student progress as he or she sees fit.)

Student evaluation, which includes methods of assessing student performance of competencies and objectives

LESSON PLAN 1—RHYTHM IN STORY

Rationale

The purpose of this lesson is to allow the students to experiment with multicultural literature that is predictable and rhythmic in nature while giving students insight and an opportunity to see how people of other cultures perceive their lands and people.

Subject/Content Area

Language arts

Age Level

6- to 8-year-olds

Goals

> To encourage students readily to share information about diverse cultures with one author and with others outside the classroom
>
> To help students to recognize the common bond of humanity among people of all cultures in a global society
>
> To help students to recognize the influence of various cultures on our everyday living
>
> To have students discover the origins of stories

Objectives

1. Students will participate in a game in which they make guesses as to where an object is hidden.
2. Students will join in the shared reading of a predictable, rhythmic African tale.

Readiness/Motivation

Refresh the students' memories of the old familiar story "The House That Jack Built." Tell them that other cultures have stories or tales that follow the pattern of this predictable story. Locate Africa on the globe. Find Kenya. Tell the students that this story takes place in Kenya and is about a very dry time in this country.

Procedures/Instructions

1. Read *Bringing the Rain to Kapiti Plain* to the group. While reading, encourage the students to read along aloud with the rhythmic, predictable portions. Point to the words while reading.
2. It may be advisable to read the story once with the group listening quietly and then read it a second time with the group joining in.
3. Upon completion of the reading and oral sharing, give instructions for playing a traditional African game.

Game: African Ring Game

Country/Culture: African-American

Objectives

1. Students will participate in a game in which they guess where an object is hidden.

Materials

Styrofoam cups/paper cups
Small plastic ring

Directions

1. Much as in a game that is played in Africa in celebration of Kwanzaa, have several paper cups, and assign one child to hide a small plastic ring under one of the cups.

2. Other children have one guess each to find the ring.

3. The one to find the ring gets to hide it next.

Resource: Aardema, Verna, *Bringing the Rain to Kapiti Plain.* New York: Scholastic, 1981.

LESSON PLAN 2—A VISIT TO ANOTHER COUNTRY AND CONTINENT

Rationale

The purpose of this lesson is to let the students see and hear multicultural literature written by a child who has visited a foreign country, giving students insight and an opportunity to see how people of their own country have viewed another culture, its lands and people.

Subject/Content Area

Language arts and social studies

Age Level

8- to 10-year-olds

Goals

To encourage students readily to share information about diverse cultures with one another and with others outside the classroom

To help students to recognize the common bond of humanity among people of all cultures in a global society

To help students to recognize the influence of various cultures on our everyday living

To help students identify certain artifacts and events with certain cultures

To help students recognize that race is only one set designation for people

Materials

  I am Eyes: Ni Macho by Leila Ward

  Learning to Swim in Swaziland by Nila K. Leigh

  Construction paper

  Unlined paper for drawing and writing

  Stapler

Objectives

1. Students will listen to a young person's viewpoint of a foreign country.
2. Students will create personal passports for fictitious visits to countries of their choice.
3. Students will write stories as if they had visited particular countries, following the model of a book shared. Encourage students to read another book about this part of the world entitled *I Am Eyes: Ni Macho* by Leila Ward.
4. Students will play a native game from the Congo River Basin.

Readiness/Motivation

Ask the students if they have traveled out of the country. If so, where did they visit and how long did they stay? What did they have to do to get ready for their journeys? Inform the students that they will be reading a story written by a young girl as she traveled and lived in Swaziland. Locate Swaziland on the map or globe.

Procedures/Instructions

1. Read *Learning to Swim in Swaziland.* Be sure to share the pictures and photos that are in the book.
2. Ask the students what makes this particular book different from other books from the library. What types of books do they prefer? Why is it important to hear a story from a young person's point of view? What kinds of groups and sets could they identify from the book? How are these groups similar to groups found in our country?
3. Upon completion of the reading and oral sharing, instruct the students to select countries of their choice to visit. They must construct passports out of construction paper. They must go to the library and find out as much as they can about their countries so that eventually each student can write a small book (or a letter to a friend or family member) that describes the experiences he or she had while traveling to the chosen place.
4. Assist students as they do their research. Encourage them to call people they know who may have visited their favorite places. Students should include illustrations and pictures of the countries and their people.

5. Display and share finished products.

6. Explain that the game that follows is traditionally played in the Congo River Basin.

Game: Antelope in the Net

Country/Culture: Congo

Objectives

1. Students will work cooperatively to keep an "antelope" in a "net."

Materials:

Outdoor play area

Directions

1. Choose one child to be the "antelope."

2. Others form a "net" (circle) around the child.

3. Students hold hands and chant: "Kasha Mu Bukandi! Kasha Mu Bukandi!"

4. The antelope tries to break out of the net by crawling under, climbing over, or running against the tightly joined hands.

5. When escaping, the antelope is pursued by the others.

6. The player who catches the antelope is the new antelope, and the game begins again.

Resource: Leigh, Nila K., *Learning to Swim in Swaziland*. New York: Scholastic, 1993.
Ward, Leila, *I Am Eyes: Ni Macho*. New York: Scholastic, 1988.

LESSON PLAN 3—STELLALUNA IS REALLY A BAT!

Rationale

The purpose of this lesson is to allow the students to see how belonging and acceptance are important for success and happiness.

Subject/Content Area

Language arts and science

Age Level

7- to 12-year-olds

Goals

To help students recognize the common bonds that group members have

To help students recognize the influence of group membership on creatures' everyday living

Materials

Stellaluna by Janell Cannon

Construction paper

Straws or rods

Objectives

1. Students will read a story about the confused identity of a bat.
2. Students will act out the story, using handmade puppets.

Readiness/Motivation

Ask the students if they have ever seen a bat. Do they have any unusual bat stories that they can share? Inform the students that they will be reading a story about a bat named Stellaluna.

Procedures/Instructions

1. Read *Stellaluna.* Be sure to share the pictures that are in the book.
2. Ask the students to describe Stellaluna and her actions in the book. If they were to act out the story, what would they want to do?
3. Upon completion of the reading, instruct the students to construct puppets out of construction paper (see figure 12-1). Each student may choose to be a bat or a bird.
4. When the students have made their puppets, have them form small groups and retell the story by acting out the parts while one person tells or reads the story.
5. Discuss in small groups the differences between Stellaluna's life mimicking that of a bird and that of a person trying to belong to a new group or club. What experiences have the students had in trying to belong to different groups? What can they do to help others feel accepted and welcome?

Resource: Cannon, Janell, *Stellaluna.* San Diego: Harcourt Brace Jovanovich, 1993.

LESSON PLAN 4—THE GREAT WALL OF CHINA

Rationale

The purpose of this lesson is to expose students to the Chinese culture while giving them opportunity to interact with one another through various reading techniques.

FIGURE 12-1 *Stellaluna* props

Subject/Content Area

Language arts and social studies

Age Level

9- to 12-year-olds

Goals

To encourage students readily to share information about diverse cultures with one another and with others outside the classroom

To help students recognize the common bond of humanity among people of all cultures in a global society

To help students recognize the influence of various cultures on our everyday living

To help students identify certain artifacts and events with certain cultures

To help students recognize that race is only one set designation for people

Materials

The Great Wall of China by Leonard E. Fisher

Construction paper

Soft wood (cut to size for printing)

Pencil

Mirror

Ink pad/tempera paint

Objectives

1. Students will gain knowledge about the Great Wall of China.
2. Students will recognize "namechops" as represented in the story.
3. Students will create their own namechops by writing their names backward on pieces of soft wood and printing with them.
4. Students will play a native game from China.

Readiness/Motivation

As students are introduced to this lesson, reference is made to things that they may know or think of when they think of the Chinese culture and its people. Leading questions activating the students' prior knowledge of China and its people prompt a brainstorming activity in which the students identify things that they think of as "typically Chinese." Likewise, the use of the book *The Great Wall of China* prepares students for the lesson and the activities to follow.

Procedures/Instructions

1. Gather all students together and ask the students to brainstorm all the things they think of as "typically Chinese." Discuss the danger of stereotyping people by their membership in groups. If students do not understand what stereotyping is, use the dictionary as a reference. Define *brainstorming* by having the students break apart the word and give meaning to its two parts. Students will then brainstorm to list the many things they think of when they think of China. Make particular note of things that deal with artistic contributions of the Chinese.

2. Ask the students to identify American folktales that they can remember—helping to set the stage. Ask questions like these:

   When we talk about folktales, what American folktales can you think of?

   What is common in most folktales?

   Why do people tell folktales?

   What types of messages do people get from folktales?

3. Explain that we will read *The Great Wall of China,* a book told in folktale fashion. Note the map of China, and compare and contrast its size with that of the United States. Remark on the Chinese population (one out of every five people in the world is Chinese). Read the book, particularly noting the use of "namechops" and calligraphy on each page.

4. At the completion of the reading, explain to the students that they will have the opportunity to create their own namechops as the author did in the book.

5. Explain the procedure. Students are to write their names backwards, first on pieces of paper. They check the writing by looking into a mirror (reversals, fine motor display, eye-hand coordination) to see if the image will be correct when printed. Students are then to transfer this writing to the wood piece, first in pencil, getting approval from the teacher before the final "carving." In the final stage, students are to rewrite their names, using pens on the soft wood, leaving lasting impressions for stamping. When the carving is completed, test with ink and print.

6. Explain that the game that follows is traditionally played in China.

Game: Dragon's Tail

Country/Culture: China

Objectives

1. Students will work cooperatively to add parts to the dragon's tail in a Chinese game.

Materials

> *Eyes of the Dragon* by Margaret Leaf
>
> Outdoor play area
>
> Ropes to mark boundaries or chalk to draw lines on the playgound

Directions

1. Establish boundaries within which children must stay.
2. Select one student to be the "dragon," whose goal is to catch another child and add to the dragon's length.
3. As each additional child is added to the "dragon," he or she must hold hands with the "dragon" and use the free hand to catch another classmate.
4. The "dragon" may split into smaller dragons to snare runners, but a unit must always be composed of no fewer than two players.
5. When only one runner is left, that child becomes the new "dragon."
6. After playing the game, encourage students to read another book featuring the Chinese dragon in *Eyes of the Dragon* by Margaret Leaf.

References: Fisher, Leonard, *The Great Wall of China*. New York: Macmillan, 1986.
Leaf, Margaret, *Eyes of the Dragon*. New York: Lothrup, Lee, & Shepard, 1987.

LESSON PLAN 5—A HOUSE IS MORE THAN JUST A HOUSE

Rationale

The purpose of this lesson is to encourage students to see not only the value of belonging but also the value of being an individual.

Subject/Content Area

Language arts and social studies

Age Level

8- to 9-year-olds

Goals

> To help students recognize the common bond of humanity among people of all cultures in a global society
>
> To help students recognize the influence of various group memberships on our everyday living
>
> To help students recognize that race is only one set designation for people

Materials

The Big Orange Splot by Daniel M. Pinkwater
Construction/drawing paper
Markers, crayons, pencils

Objectives

1. Students will retell the story of *The Big Orange Splot.*
2. Students will recognize the repetitiveness in the story.
3. Students will create their ideal houses that reflect themselves.

Readiness/Motivation

Gather students together and ask them to describe what they think they would see in a "neighborhood." Suggest that they describe what the houses and people look like in the area and what the children enjoy doing there.

FIGURE 12–2 Illustrating "my dream house"

Procedures/Instructions

1. Tell the students that they will be listening to a story about a man who lives in a neighborhood where everything is just about the same. How would you feel in such a neighborhood?

2. Read the story aloud, making sure that all students can see the illustrations. When students begin to predict portions of the book that follow, encourage them to respond in choral fashion.

3. At the conclusion of the story, ask the students to reflect on the statements "My house is me and I am it" and "Our street is us and we are it. Our street is where we like to be and it looks like all our dreams."

4. Give each student the opportunity to visualize and then create his or her own "dream house" on paper using markers, crayons, and pencils.

5. When students have completed their illustrations, have them put their dream houses on display as if they were part of a real neighborhood.

Resource: Pinkwater, Daniel M., *The Big Orange Splot.* Mamaroneck, NY: Hastings House, 1977.

❖ Related Bibliography

Aquino-Mackles, A., King, D. C., & Branson, M. S. (1979). *Myself and Others.* New York: Global Perspectives in Education.

Aardema, V. (1981). *Bringing the rain to Kapiti Plain.* New York: Scholastic.

Cannon, J. (1993). *Stellaluna.* San Diego: Harcourt Brace Jovanovich.

Dancy, E. (1983). *Multicultural early childhood resource guide.* Albany, NY: New York State Education Department. (ERIC Document Reproduction Service No. ED 238 512)

Fisher, L. E. (1986). *The Great Wall of China.* New York: Macmillan.

Hatcher, B., Pape, D., & Nicosia, R. T. (1988). Group games for global awareness. *Childhood Education, 65*(1), 8–12.

Leaf, M. (1987). *Eyes of the dragon.* New York: Lee Lothrop, & Shepard.

Leigh, N. K. (1993). *Learning to swim in Swaziland.* New York: Scholastic.

McNaught, H. (1982). *500 palabras nuevas para ti (500 words to grow on).* New York: Random House.

McWhirter, M. E. (Ed.) (1970). *Games enjoyed by children around the world.* Philadelphia: American Friends Service Committee.

Orlick, T. (1982) *The second cooperative sports and games book.* New York: Pantheon Books.

Pinkwater, D. M. (1977). *The big orange splot.* Mamaroneck, NY: Hastings House.

Ward, L. (1988). *I am eyes: Ni Macho.* New York: Scholastic.

Warren, J., & McKinnon, E. (1988). *Small world celebrations.* Everett, WA: Warren.

Young, R., & Pang, V. O. (1995). Asian Pacific American students: A rainbow of dreams. *Multicultural Education, 3*(2), 4–7.

Afterthoughts: Celebrating Diversity through Children's Literature

Throughout the writing of this text, many, many children's books have come into my hands. I have purchased most of them and have treasured them all. Within my college classes when I thought that this adventure of writing a college textbook was too difficult and awesome a task, I was continually reminded of the need to share my passion for cultural diversity and a pluralistic society. My colleagues at Edinboro University of Pennsylvania, my fellow teachers in Erie County, my friends, and my family members continually asked, "How is the book coming?" Their prodding and my prayers kept me going.

Drawing the writing to a close was difficult. Every time that I thought that I could end the text, another book would present itself. Finally, I decided that the last books would be added to affirm the theme of the book—one that serves all the children and celebrates similarities and differences in us all.

One of my personal favorites as a child was the story of Cinderella. My battered copy of the story has traveled with me from class to class and been shared with young and old readers. It was then fitting that I would most recently come across a collection of multicultural Cinderella stories. Shirley Climo wrote two multicultural tales entitled *The Egyptian Cinderella* (1989) and *The Korean Cinderella* (1993), both illustrated by Ruth Heller. Rhodopis is the Greek slave who is given a pair of red slippers by her master. Alone in Egypt without family and friends, she is dismayed when one of her slippers is taken away by a falcon. Little does she know that she will become the queen of Egypt when the Pharoah finds the matching red slipper that belongs to her. In contrast, Pear Blossom is a Korean beauty who must perform unrealistic tasks for her mean stepmother. Togkabis are magical creatures that enable Pear Blossom to overcome the hardships and become the bride of the magistrate. Brightly colored illustrations by Heller move the reader through both of these stories. Penny Pollock (1996) has retold the Zuni Cinderella story of *The Turkey Girl* and Ed Young has used pastel and oil crayon drawings to share the Native American tale of the Southwestern people. The Zuni tale is about a young girl who cares for turkeys, who in turn grant her the favor of creating a beautiful dress for her to wear to a dance. However, she must remember to return before the sun has set or they will abandon her forever. Lingering a bit too long, the girl comes home to find herself again in rags and her turkey companions gone. Russian culture is the basis of the tale told by Marianna Mayer (1994) in *Baba Yaga and Vasilisa the Brave*. Attaining a light from the evil witch of Baba Yaga was her job, but Vasilisa and her tiny doll were able to accomplish that for her stepmother and sisters. K. Y. Kraft's framed illustrations and introductory letters resembling tapestry move the reader from the tragedy of Vasilisa to the happy ending of marriage to the tzar. Finally, Shirley Climo retells the story of *The Irish Cinderlad* (1996). Locating a big boot instead of lost slippers is the desire of the Irish princess. The boot belongs to Becan who eventually overcomes a giant and a dragon and even saves the princess in the process. Different cultures have retold the Cinderella story in wonderful, rich new ways.

The Great Wall of China story has a special meaning for me in that Chinese folklore was the first I investigated. Doreen Rappaport (1991) shares *The Journey of Meng*, which is the tale of a young woman who waits for a year for the return of her husband Wan from his labor at the Great Wall. When he does not return, she courageously attempts to find him and bring him warm clothes, only to confront the Emperor himself. The tragic story is depicted with Yang Ming-Yi's delicate watercolors and Rappaport's lyrical words.

Reviewers' comments about this text included requests for more examples of authentic African tales, stories from Indian and Pakistani cultures, and examples of multicultural poetry. The following children's books are excellent selections that answer these needs.

Photographs of Niger and chants from Africa make Ann Grifalconi's *Flyaway Girl* (1992) so different and captivating. Nsia must help her mother gather reeds for the Ceremony of Beginnings. This story of the rite of passage for an African girl is authentic with *National Geographic* photos and an African ancestor chant.

Jewels of India can be found in Kristina Rodanas' retelling of *The Story of Wali Dâd* (1988). A teacher of elementary art, Rodanas has developed the progressive tale of the simple, yet generous Wali Dad who finally acts as matchmaker for the Prince of Nekabad and the Princess of Khaistan.

Poetry and other languages combine in Lydia Dabcovich's *The Keys to My Kingdom* (1992). The book jacket reads, "The Kingdom of the Imagination is both limitless and diverse," and so the poem progresses. A little girl moves the reader through the book/poem with her paints and brushes, creating a city, a town, a street, a lane, a yard, a house, a room, a bed, a basket, and flowers, all in French, Spanish, and English, and finally back to her keys of the kingdom—her brushes and paints.

Lastly, it is important that I reflect on the importance of angels in my writing. In the past couple of years, "angels" have been a trendy thing in contemporary American homes. My new home is no exception. I have a grand collection of angels, of all sizes, colors, shapes, and cultures. They have arrived from as far away as Mexico and appear in plaster, papier-mâché, fabric, yam, glass, and wood. Two are in paper: the most treasured books by Walter Dean Myers. His first attempt at depicting the angelic poses of children came in *Brown Angels: An Album of Pictures and Verse* (1993). The antique pictures of the African-American youngsters are matched with poems that were inspired simply by the photos or author's own memories. This tender collection was the inspiration for a second book entitled *Glorious Angels* (1995), which celebrates many cultures and many children. The words of Myers affirm the purpose of my book:

> "Let us celebrate the children
> Let us spin mysteries
> for their minds
> and wonders for their hearts" (Myers, 1995, p. 21).

The children in the collection are diverse, yet they carry similar smiles and searching, wanting eyes. Their faces and their clothing may be different but they are "all the children" to me.

The book *All for the Children* was written for and personally driven by the many children who have been a part of my life and who will appear in the future. All that I have done in my teaching career I have done for children, be they my own two sons or the many young people that I have met and taught. The books that are included in this text have been written about and thus chosen to be shared with *all* the children. They reflect the many diverse groups of children, their families, their lives, and their situations. The lessons have been designed to meet the varied needs of children in elementary classrooms. They can be incorporated into all classrooms for all children.

The other thing that I have noticed in the process of writing and researching this book is that we, the community of adult learners, are still children at heart. We continue to treasure the stories of old and enjoy immensely the contemporary children's genre as well. Perhaps we need to remind ourselves more often that if we could look at issues and situations with the enthusiasm and sincerity that children do, we would have so much more to celebrate.

And so, the message of the afterthoughts of this book is to celebrate the diversity. For in our celebration, we will see the childhood promises of love, community, and peace. *Celebrate the diversity! Celebrate all the children . . . and for all the children's sake.*

❖ Children's books cited:

Climo, S. (1989). *The Egyptian Cinderella*. New York: HarperCollins Publishers.

Climo, S. (1996). *The Irish Cinderlad*. New York: HarperCollins Publishers.

Climo, S. (1993). *The Korean Cinderella*. New York: HarperCollins Publishers.

Dabcovich, L. (1992). *The keys to my kingdom: A poem in three languages*. New York: Lothrop, Lee & Shepard Books.

Grifalconi, A. (1992). *Flyaway girl*. Boston: Little, Brown and Company.

Mayer, M. (1994). *Baba Yaga and Vasilisa the brave*. New York: Morrow Junior Books.

Myers, W. D. (1995). *Glorious angels*. New York: HarperCollins Publishers.

Myers, W. D. (1993). *Brown angels: An album of pictures and verse*. New York: HarperCollins Publishers.

Pollock, P. (1996). *The turkey girl: A Zuni Cinderella story*. New York: Little, Brown and Company.

Rappaport, D. (1991). *The journey of Meng*. New York: Dial Books for Young Readers.

Rodanas, K. (1988). *The story of Wali Dâd*. New York: Lothrop, Lee & Shepard Books.

Award-Winning Books for Children

APPENDIX A

❖ Randolph Caldecott Medal

The Caldecott Award is given annually to the illustrator of the most distinguished picture book for children published during the preceding year. The award is sponsored by the Association for Library Service to Children, a division of the American Library Association. Note: The illustrator is listed first and the author second (in parentheses).

1938

Animals of the Bible by Dorothy P. Lathrop (Helen Dean Fish)

Honor Books

Seven Simeons by Boris Artzybasheff

Four and Twenty Blackbirds by Robert Lawson (Helen Dean Fish)

1939

Mei Li by Thomas Handforth

Honor Books

Forest Pool by Laura Adams Armer

Wee Gillis by Robert Lawson (Munro Leaf)

Snow White and the Seven Dwarfs by Wanda Gag

Barkis by Clare Newberry

Andy and the Lion by James Daugherty

1940

Abraham Lincoln by Ingri and Edgar Parin d'Aulaire

Honor Books

Cock-a-Doodle Doo . . . by Berta and Elmer Hader

Madeline by Ludwig Bemelmans

The Ageless Story by Lauren Ford

1941

They Were Strong and Good by Robert Lawson

Honor Books

April's Kittens by Clare Newberry

1942

Make Way for Ducklings by Robert McCloskey

Honor Books

An American ABC by Maud and Miska Petersham

In My Mother's House by Velino Herrera (Ann Nolan Clark)

Paddle-to-the-Sea by Holling C. Holling

Nothing at All by Wanda Gag

1943

The Little House by Virginia Lee Burton

Honor Books

Dash and Dart by Mary and Conrad Buff

Marshmallow by Clare Newberry

1944

Many Moons by Louis Slobodkin (James Thurber)

Honor Books

Small Rain: Verses from the Bible by Elizabeth Orton Jones (selected by Jessie Orton Jones)

Pierre Pigeon by Arnold E. Bare (Lee Kingman)

A Child's Good Night Book by Jean Charlot (Margret Wise Brown)

Good Luck Horse by Plao Chan (Chin-Yi Chan)

1945

Prayer for a Child by Elizabeth Orton Jones (Rachel Field)

Honor Books

Mother Goose by Tasha Tudor

In the Forest by Marie Hall Ets

Yonie Wondernose by Marguerite de Angeli

The Christmas Anna Angel by Kate Seredy (Ruth Sawyer)

1946

The Rooster Crows . . . (traditional Mother Goose) by Maud and Miska Petersham

Honor Books

Little Lost Lamb by Leonard Weisgard (Golden MacDonald)

Sing Mother Goose by Marjorie Torrey (Opal Wheeler)

My Mother Is the Most Beautiful Woman in the World by Ruth Gannett (Becky Reyher)

You Can Write Chinese by Kurt Wiese

1947

The Little Island by Leonard Weisgard (Golden MacDonald)

Honor Books

Rain Drop Splash by Leonard Weisgard (Alvin Tresselt)

Boats on the River by Jay Hyde Barnum (Marjorie Flack)

Timothy Turtle by Tony Palazzo (Al Graham)

Pedro, the Angel of Olvera Street by Leo Politi

Sing in Praise: A Collection of the Best Loved Hymns by Marjorie Torrey (Opal Wheeler)

1948

White Snow, Bright Snow by Roger Duvoisin (Alvin Tresselt)

Honor Books

Stone Soup by Marcia Brown

McElligot's Pool by Dr. Seuss

Bambino the Clown by George Schreiber

Roger and the Fox by Hildegard Woodward (Lavinia Davis)

Song of Robin Hood by Virginia Lee Burton (edited by Anne Malcolmson)

1949

The Big Snow by Berta and Elmer Hader

Honor Books

Blueberries for Sal by Robert McCloskey

All around the Town by Helen Stone (Phyllis McGinley)

Juanita by Leo Politi

Fish in the Air by Kurt Wiese

1950

Song of the Swallows by Leo Politi

Honor Books

America's Ethan Allen by Lynd Ward (Stewart Holbrook)

The Wild Birthday Cake by Hildegard Woodward (Lavinia Davis)

The Happy Day by Marc Simont (Ruth Krauss)

Bartholomew and the Oobleck by Dr. Seuss

Henry Fisherman by Marcia Brown

1951

The Egg Tree by Katherine Milhous

Honor Books

Dick Whittington and His Cat by Marcia Brown

The Two Reds by Nicholas Mordvinoff (William Lipkind)

If I Ran the Zoo by Dr. Seuss

The Most Wonderful Doll in the World by Helen Stone (Phyllis McGinley)

T-Bone, the Baby Sitter by Clare Newberry

1952

Finders Keepers by Nicholas Mordvinoff (William Lipkind)

Honor Books

Mr. T. W. Anthony Woo by Marie Hall Ets

Skipper John's Cook by Marcia Brown

All Falling Down by Margaret Bloy Graham (Gene Zion)

Bear Party by William Pene du Bois

Feather Mountain by Elizabeth Olds

1953

The Biggest Bear by Lynd Ward

Honor Books

Puss in Boots, retold and illustrated by Marcia Brown (Charles Perrault)

One Morning in Maine by Robert McCloskey

Ape in a Cape by Fritz Eichenberg

The Storm Book by Margaret Bloy Graham (Charlotte Zolotow)

Five Little Monkeys by Juliet Kepes

1954

Madeline's Rescue by Ludwig Bemelmans

Honor Books

Journey Cake, Ho! by Robert McCloskey (Ruth Sawyer)

When Will the World Be Mine? by Jean Charlot (Miriam Schlein)

The Steadfast Tin Soldier by Marcia Brown (Hans Christian Andersen)

A Very Special House by Maurice Sendak (Ruth Krauss)

Green Eyes by A. Birnbaum

1955

Cinderella, or the Little Glass Slipper retold and illustrated by Marcia Brown (Charles Perrault)

Honor Books

Book of Nursery and Mother Goose Rhymes by Marguerite de Angeli

Wheel on the Chimney by Tibor Gergely (Margaret Wise Brown)

The Thanksgiving Story by Helen Sewell (Alice Dalgliesh)

1956

Frog Went A-Courtin' by Feodor Rojankovsky (John Langstaff)

Honor Books

Play with Me by Marie Hall Ets

Crow Boy by Taro Yashima

1957

A Tree Is Nice by Marc Simont (Janice May Udry)

Honor Books

Mr. Penny's Race Horse by Marie Hall Ets

1 is One by Tasha Tudor

Anatole by Paul Galdone (Eve Titus)

Gillespie and the Guards by James Daugherty (Benjamin Elkin)

Lion by William Pene du Bois

1958

Time of Wonder by Robert McCloskey

Honor Books

Fly High, Fly Low by Don Freeman

Anatole and the Cat by Paul Galdone (Eve Titus)

1959

Chanticleer and the Fox adapted and illustrated by Barbara Cooney

Honor Books

The House That Jack Built by Antonio Frasconi

What Do You Say, Dear? by Maurice Sendak (Sesyle Joslin)

Umbrella by Taro Yashima

1960

Nine Days to Christmas by Marie Hall Ets (Aurora Labastida, Marie Hall Ets)

Honor Books

Houses from the Sea by Adrienne Adams (Alice E. Goudey)

The Moon Jumpers by Maurice Sendak (Janice May Udry)

1961

Baboushka and the Three Kings by Nicholas Sidjakov (Ruth Robbins)

Honor Book

Inch by Inch by Leo Lionni

1962

Once a Mouse . . . by Marcia Brown

Honor Books

Fox Went Out on a Chilly Night by Peter Spier

Little Bear's Visit by Maurice Sendak (Else Holmelund Minarik)

The Day We Saw the Sun Come Up by Adrienne Adams (Alice Goudey)

1963

The Snowy Day by Ezra Jack Keats

Honor Books

The Sun Is a Golden Earring by Bernarda Bryson (Natalia M. Belting)

Mr. Rabbit and the Lovely Present by Maurice Sendak (Charlotte Zolotow)

1964

Where the Wild Things Are by Maurice Sendak

Honor Books

Swimmy by Leo Lionni

All in the Morning Early by Evaline Ness (Sorche Nic Leodhas)

Mother Goose and Nursery Rhymes by Philip Reed

1965

May I Bring a Friend? by Beni Montresor (Beatrice Schenk de Regniers)

Honor Books

Rain Makes Applesauce by Marvin Bileck (Julian Scheer)

The Wave by Blair Lent (Margaret Hodges)

A Pocketful of Cricket by Evaline Ness (Rebecca Caudill)

1966

Always Room for One More by Nonny Hogrogian (Sorche Nic Leodhas)

Honor Books

Hide and Seek Fog by Roger Duvoisin (Alvin Tresselt)

Just Me by Marie Hall Ets

Tom Tit Tot by Evaline Ness

1967

Sam, Bangs and Moonshine by Evaline Ness

Honor Book

One Wide River to Cross by Ed Emberley (Barbara Emberley)

1968

Drummer Hoff by Ed Emberley (Barbara Emberley)

Honor Books
> *Frederick* by Leo Lionni
>
> *Seashore Story* by Taro Yashima
>
> *The Emperor and the Kite* by Ed Young

1969

> *The Fool of the World and the Flying Ship* by Uri Shulevitz (Arthur Ransome)

Honor Book
> *Why the Sun and the Moon Live in the Sky* by Blair Lent (Elphinstone Dayrell)

1970

> *Sylvester and the Magic Pebble* by William Steig

Honor Books
> *Goggles!* by Ezra Jack Keats
>
> *Alexander and the Wind-Up Mouse* by Leo Lionni
>
> *Pop Corn and Ma Goodness* by Robert Andrew Parker (Edna Mitchell Preston)
>
> *Thy Friend, Obadiah* by Brinton Turkle
>
> *The Judge* by Margot Zemach (Harve Zemach)

1971

> *A Story—A Story* by Gail E. Haley

Honor Books
> *The Angry Moon* by Blair Lent (William Sleator)
>
> *Frog and Toad Are Friends* by Arnold Lobel
>
> *In the Night Kitchen* by Maurice Sendak

1972

> *One Fine Day* by Nonny Hogrogian

Honor Books
> *If All the Seas Were One Sea* by Janina Domanska
>
> *Moja Means One: Swahili Counting Book* by Tom Feelings (Muriel Feelings)
>
> *Hildilid's Night* by Arnold Lobel (Cheli Duran Ryan)

1973

The Funny Little Woman by Blair Lent (retold by Arlene Mosel)

Honor Books

Anansi the Spider, adapted and illustrated by Gerald McDermott

Hosie's Alphabet by Leonard Baskin (Hosea, Tobias, and Lisa Baskin)

Snow White and the Seven Dwarfs by Nancy Ekholm Burkert (transated by Randall Jarrell)

When Clay Sings by Tom Bahti (Byrd Baylor)

1974

Duffy and the Devil by Margot Zemach (Harve Zemach)

Honor Books

Three Jovial Huntsmen by Susan Jeffers

Cathedral: The Story of Its Construction by David Macaulay

1975

Arrow to the Sun retold and illustrated by Gerald McDermott

Honor Book

Jambo Means Hello by Tom Feelings (Muriel Feelings)

1976

Why Mosquitoes Buzz in People's Ears by Leo and Diane Dillon

Honor Books

The Desert Is Theirs by Peter Parnall (Byrd Baylor)

Strega Nona, retold and illustrated by Tomie dePaola

1977

Ashanti to Zulu: African Traditions by Leo and Diane Dillon (Margaret Musgrove)

Honor Books

The Amazing Bone by William Steig

The Contest, retold and illustrated by Nonny Hogrogian

Fish for Supper by M. B. Goffstein

The Golem: A Jewish Legend by Beverly Brodsky McDermott

Hawk, I'm Your Brother by Peter Parnall (Byrd Baylor)

1978

Noah's Ark by Peter Spier

Honor Books
Castle by David Macaulay
It Could Always Be Worse by Margot Zemach

1979

The Girl Who Loved Wild Horses by Paul Goble

Honor Books
Freight Train by Donald Crews
The Way to Start a Day by Peter Parnall (Byrd Baylor)

1980

Ox-Cart Man by Barbara Conney (Donald Hall)

Honor Books
Ben's Trumpet by Rachel Isadora
The Treasure by Uri Shulevitz
The Garden of Abdul Gasazi by Chris Van Allsburg

1981

Fables by Arnold Lobel

Honor Books
The Bremen-Town Musicians by Ilse Plume
The Grey Land and the Strawberry Snatcher by Molly Bang
Mice Twice by Joseph Low
Truck by Donald Crews

1982

Jumanji by Chris Van Allsburg

Honor Books
On Market Street by Anita Lobel (Arnold Lobel)
Outside over There by Maurice Sendak
A Visit to William Blake's Inn: Poems for Innocent and Experienced Travelers by Alice and Martin Provensen (Nancy Willard)
Where the Buffaloes Begin by Stephan Gammell (Olaf Baker)

1983

Shadow by Marcia Brown (Blaise Cendrars)

Honor Books

A Chair for My Mother by Vera B. Williams

When I Was Young in the Mountains by Diane Goode (Cynthia Rylant)

1984

The Glorious Flight: Across the Channel with Louis Bleriot by Alice and Martin Provensen

Honor Books

Little Red Riding Hood, retold and illustrated by Trina Schart Hyman

Ten, Nine, Eight by Molly Bang

1985

Saint George and the Dragon by Trina Schart Hyman (retold by Margaret Hodges)

Honor Books

Hansel and Gretel by Paul O. Zelinsky (retold by Rika Lesser)

Have You Seen My Duckling? by Nancy Tafuri

The Story of Jumping Mouse, retold and illustrated by John Steptoe

1986

The Polar Express by Chris Van Allsburg

Honor Books

The Relatives Came by Stephen Gammell (Cynthia Rylant)

King Bidgood's in the Bathtub by Don Wood (Audrey Wood)

1987

Hey, Al by Richard Egielski

Honor Books

The Village of Round and Square Houses by Ann Grigalconi

Alphabatics by Suse MacDonald

Rumpelstiltskin by Paul O. Zelinsky

1988

Owl Moon by John Schoenherr (Jane Yolen)

Honor Book
Mufaro's Beautiful Daughters by John Steptoe

1989

Song and Dance Man by Stephen Gammell (Karen Ackerman)

Honor Books
The Boy of the Three-Year Nap by Allen Say (Dianne Snyder)
Free Fall by David Wiesner
Goldilocks and the Three Bears by James Marshall
Mirandy and Brother Wind by Jerry Pinkney (Patricia McKissack)

1990

Lon Po Po: A Red Riding Hood Story from China by Ed Young

Honor Books
Bill Peet: An Autobiography by Bill Peet
Color Zoo by Lois Ehlert
Hershel and the Hanukkah Goblins by Trina Schart Hyman (Eric Kimmel)
The Talking Eggs by Jerry Pinkney (Robert San Souci)

1991

Black and White by David Macaulay

Honor Books
"More More More" Said the Baby: Three Love Stories by Vera B. Williams
Puss in Boots by Fred Marcellino (Charles Perrault, translated by Malcolm Arthur)

1992

Mirette on the High Wire by Emily Arnold McCully

Honor Books
The Stinky Cheese Man by Lane Smith (Jon Scieszka)
Working Cotton by Carole Byard (Sherley Anne Williams)
Seven Blind Mice by Ed Young

1993

Grandfather's Journey by Allen Say

1994

Tuesday by David Wiesner

Honor Book
Tar Beach by Faith Ringgold

1995

Smoky Night by Eve Bunting

Honor Books
Swamp Angel by Anne Isaacs

John Henry by Julius Lester

Time Flies by Eric Rohmann

1996

Officer Buckle and Gloria by Peggy Rathman

Honor Books
The Alphabet City by Stephen Johnson

Zin, Zin, Zin the Violin by Lloyd Moss

APPENDIX B

❖ John Newbery Medal

The Newbery Award is given annually to the author of the most distinguished contribution to children's literature published during the preceding year. The award is sponsored by the Association for Library Service to Children, a division of the American Library Association.

1922

The Story of Mankind by Hendrik Willem van Loon

Honor Books
The Great Quest by Charles Hawes

Cedric the Forester by Bernard Marshall

The Old Tobacco Shop by William Bowen

The Golden Fleece and the Heroes Who Lived before Achilles by Padraic Colum

Windy Hill by Cornelia Meigs

1923

The Voyages of Doctor Doolittle by Hugh Lofting

1924

The Dark Frigate by Charles Hawes

1925

Tales from Silver Lands by Charles Finger

Honor Books
Nicholas by Anne Carroll Moore

Dream Coach by Anne Parrish

1926

Shen of the Sea by Arthur Bowie Chrisman

Honor Book
Voyagers by Padraic Colum

1927

Smoky, the Cowhorse by Will James

1928

Gayneck, the Story of a Pigeon by Dhan Gopal Mukerji

Honor Books

The Wonder Smith and His Son by Ella Young

Downright Dencey by Caroline Snedeker

1929

The Trumpeter of Krakow by Eric P. Kelly

Honor Books

Pigtail of Ah Lee Ben Loo by John Bennett

Millions of Cats by Wanda Gag

The Boy Who Was by Grace Hallock

Clearing Weather by Cornelia Meigs

Runaway Papoose by Grace Moon

Todd of the Fens by Elinor Whitney

1930

Hitty, Her First Hundred Years by Rachel Field

Honor Books

Daughter of the Seine by Jeanette Eaton

Pran of Albania by Elizabeth Miller

Jumping-Off Place by Marian Hurd McNeely

Tangle-Coated Horse and Other Tales by Ella Young

Vaino by Julia Davis Adams

Little Blacknose by Hildegard Swift

1931

The Cat Who Went to Heaven by Elizabeth Coatsworth

Honor Books

Floating Island by Anne Parrish

The Dark Star of Itza by Alida Malkus

Queer Person by Ralph Hubbard

Mountains Are Free by Julia Davis Adams

Spice and the Devil's Cave by Agnes Hewes

Meggy Macintosh by Elizabeth Janet Gray

Garram the Hunter by Herbert Best

Ood-Le-Uk the Wanderer by Alice Lide and Margaret Johansen

1932

Waterless Mountain by Laura Adams Armer

Honor Books

The Fairy Circus by Dorthy P. Lathrop

Calico Bush by Rachel Field

Boy of the South Seas by Eunice Tietjens

Out of the Flame by Eloise Lownsbery

Jane's Island by Marjorie Allee

Truce of the Wolf and Other Tales of Old Italy by Mary Gould Davis

1933

Young Fu of the Upper Yangtze by Elizabeth Foreman Lewis

Honor Books

Swift Rivers by Cornelia Meigs

The Railroad to Freedom by Hildegarde Swift

Children of the Soil by Nora Burglon

1934

Invincible Louisa by Cornelia Meigs

Honor Books

The Forgotten Daughter by Caroline Snedeker

Swords of Steel by Elsie Singmaster

ABC Bunny by Wanda Gag

Winged Girl of Knossos by Erik Berry

New Land by Sarah Schmidt

Big Tree of Bunlahy by Padraic Colum

Glory of the Seas by Agnes Hewes

Apprentice of Florence by Ann Kyle

1935

Dorby by Monica Shannon

Honor Books

Pageant of Chinese History by Elizabeth Seeger

Davy Crockett by Constance Rourke

Day on Skates by Hilda Van Stockum

1936

Caddie Woodlawn by Carol Ryrie Brink

Honor Books

Honk, the Moose by Phil Strong

The Good Master by Kate Seredy

Young Walter Scott by Elizabeth Janet Gray

All Sail Set by Armstrong Sperry

1937

Roller Skates by Ruth Sawyer

Honor Books

Phoebe Fairchild: Her Book by Lois Lenski

Whistler's Van by Idwal Jones

Golden Basket by Ludwig Bemelmans

Winterbound by Margery Blanco

Audubon by Constance Rourke

The Codfish Musket by Agnes Hewes

1938

The White Stag by Kate Seredy

Honor Books

Pecos Bill by James Cloyd Bowman

Bright Island by Mabel Robinson

On the Banks of Plum Creek by Laura Ingalls Wilder

1939

Thimble Summer by Elizabeth Enright

Honor Books

Nino by Valenti Angelo

Mr. Popper's Penguins by Richard and Florence Atwater

Hello the Boat! by Phyllis Crawford

Leader by Destiny: George Washington, Man and Patriot by Jeanette Eaton

Penn by Elizabeth Janet Gray

1940

Daniel Boone by James Daugherty

Honor Books

The Singing Tree by Kate Seredy

Runner of the Mountain Tops by Mabel Robinson

By the Shores of Silver Lake by Laura Ingalls Wilder

Boy with a Pack by Stephen W. Meader

1941

Call It Courage by Armstrong Sperry

Honor Books

Blue Willow by Doris Gates

Young Mac of Fort Vancouver by Mary Jane Carr

The Long Winter by Laura Ingalls Wilder

Nansen by Anna Gertrude Hall

1942

The Matchlock Gun by Walter D. Edmunds

Honor Books

Little Town on the Prairie by Laura Ingalls Wilder

George Washington's World by Genevieve Foster

Indian Captive: The Story of Mary Jemison by Lois Lenski

Down Ryton Water by Eva Roe Gaggin

1943

Adam of the Road by Elizabeth Janet Gray

Honor Books

The Middle Moffat by Eleanor Estes

Have You Seen Tom Thumb? by Mabel Leigh Hunt

1944

Johnny Tremain by Esther Forbes

Honor Books

These Happy Golden Years by Laura Ingalls Wilder

Fog Magic by Julia Sauer

Rufus M. by Eleanor Estes

Mountain Born by Elizabeth Yates

1945

Rabbit Hill by Robert Lawson

Honor Books

The Hundred Dresses by Eleanor Estes

The Silver Pencil by Alice Dalgliesh

Abraham Lincoln's World by Genevieve Foster

Lone Journey: The Life of Roger Williams by Jeanette Eaton

1946

Strawberry Girl by Lois Lenski

Honor Books

Justin Morgan Had a Horse by Marguerite Henry

The Moved-Outers by Florence Crannel Means

Bhimsa, the Dancing Bear by Christine Weston

New Found World by Katherine Shippen

1947

Miss Hickory by Carolyn Sherwin Bailey

Honor Books

Wonderful Year by Nancy Barnes

Big Tree by Mary and Conrad Buff

The Heavenly Tenants by William Maxwell

The Avion My Uncle Flew by Cyrus Fisher

The Hidden Treasure of Glaston by Eleanore Jewett

1948

The Twenty-One Balloons by William Pene du Bois

Honor Books

Pancakes-Paris by Claire Huchet Bishop

Li Lun, Lad of Courage by Carolyn Treffeinger

The Quaint and Curious Quest of Johnny Longfoot by Catherine Besterman

The Cow-Tail Switch, and Other West African Stories by Harold Courlander

Misty of Chincoteague by Marguerite Henry

1949

King of the Wind by Marguerite Henry

Honor Books

Seabird by Holling C. Holling

Daughter of the Mountains by Louise Rankin

My Father's Dragon by Ruth S. Gannett

Story of the Negro by Arma Bontemps

1950

The Door in the Wall by Marguerite de Angeli

Honor Books

Tree of Freedom by Rebecca Caudill

The Blue Cat of Castle Town by Catherine Coblentz

Kildee House by Rutherford Montgomery

George Washington by Genevieve Foster

Song of the Pines by Walter and Marion Havinghurst

1951

Amos Fortune, Free Man by Elizabeth Yates

Honor Books

Better Known as Johnny Appleseed by Mabel Leigh Hunt

Gandhi: Fighter without a Sword by Jeanette Eaton

Abraham Lincoln, Friend of the People by Clara Ingram Judson

The Story of Appleby Capple by Anne Parrish

1952

Ginger Pye by Eleanor Estes

Honor Books

Americans before Columbus by Elizabeth Baity

Minn of the Mississippi by Holling C. Holling

The Defender by Nicholas Kakashnikoff

The Light at Tern Rock by Julia Sauer

The Apple and the Arrow by Mary and Conrad Buff

1953

Secret of the Andes by Ann Nolan Clark

Honor Books

Charlotte's Web by E. B. White

Moccasin Trail by Eloise McGraw

The Bears on Hemlock Mountain by Alice Dalgliesh

Birthdays of Freedom, Vol. 1 by Genevieve Foster

1954

. . . And Now Miguel by Joseph Krumgold

Honor Books

All Alone by Claire Huchet Bishop

Shadrach by Meindert DeJong

Hurry Home, Candy by Meindert DeJong

Theodore Roosevelt, Fighting Patriot by Clara Ingram Judson

Magic Maize by Mary and Conrad Buff

1955

The Wheel on the School by Meindert DeJong

Honor Books

The Courage of Sarah Nobel by Alice Dalgliesh

Banner in the Sky by James Ullman

1956

Carry on, Mr. Bowditch by Jean Lee Latham

Honor Books

The Secret River by Marjorie Kinnan Rawlings

The Golden Name Day by Jennie Linquist

Men, Microscopes, and Living Things by Katherine Shippen

1957

Miracles on Maple Hill by Virginia Sorensen

Honor Books

> *Old Yeller* by Fred Gipson
>
> *The House of Sixty Fathers* by Meindert DeJong
>
> *Mr. Justice Holmes* by Clara Ingram Judson
>
> *The Corn Grows Ripe* by Dorothy Rhoads
>
> *Black Fox of Lorne* by Marguerite de Angeli

1958

> *Rifles for Watie* by Harold Keith

Honor Books

> *The Horsecatcher* by Mari Sandoz
>
> *Gone-Away Lake* by Elizabeth Enright
>
> *The Great Wheel* by Robert Lawson
>
> *Tom Paine, Freedom's Apostle* by Leo Gurko

1959

> *The Witch of Blackbird Pond* by Elizabeth George Speare

Honor Books

> *The Family under the Bridge* by Natalie Savage Carlson
>
> *Along Came a Dog* by Meindert DeJong
>
> *Chucaro: Wild Pony of the Pampa* by Francis Kalnay
>
> *The Perilous Road* by William O. Steele

1960

> *Onion John* by Joseph Krumgold

Honor Books

> *My Side of the Mountain* by Jean George
>
> *America Is Born* by Gerald W. Johnson
>
> *The Gammage Cup* by Carol Kendall

1961

> *Island of the Blue Dolphins* by Scott O'Dell

Honor Books

> *America Moves Forward* by Gerald W. Johnson
>
> *Old Ramon* by Jack Schaefer
>
> *The Cricket in Times Square* by George Selden

1962

The Bronze Bow by Elizabeth George Speare

Honor Books
Frontier Living by Edwin Tunis
The Golden Goblet by Eloise McGraw
Belling the Tiger by Mary Stolz

1963

A Wrinkle in Time by Madeleine L'Engle

Honor Books
Thistle and Thyme by Sorche Nic Leodhas
Men of Athens by Olivia Coolidge

1964

It's Like This, Cat by Emily Cheney Neville

Honor Books
Rascal by Sterling North
The Loner by Ester Wier

1965

Shadow of a Bull by Maia Wojciechowska

Honor Book
Across Five Aprils by Irene Hunt

1966

I, Juan de Pareja by Elizabeth Borten de Trevino

Honor Books
The Black Cauldron by Lloyd Alexander
The Animal Family by Randall Jarrell
The Noonday Friends by Mary Stolz

1967

Up a Road Slowly by Irene Hunt

Honor Books
The King's Fifth by Scott O'Dell

Zlateh the Goat and Other Stories by Isaac Bashevis Singer

The Jazz Man by Mary S. Weik

1968

From the Mixed-Up Files of Mrs. Basil E. Frankweiler by E. L. Konigsburg

Honor Books

Jennifer, Hecate, Macbeth, William McKinley, and Me, Elizabeth by E. L. Konigsburg

The Black Pearl by Scott O'Dell

The Fearsome Inn by Isaac Bashevis Singer

The Egypt Game by Zilpha Keatley Snyder

1969

The High King by Lloyd Alexander

Honor Books

To Be a Slave by Julius Lester

When Shlemiel Went to Warsaw and Other Stories by Isaac Bashevis Singer

1970

Sounder by William H. Armstrong

Honor Books

Our Eddie by Sulamith Ish-Kishor

The Many Ways of Seeing: An Introduction to the Pleasures of Art by Janet Gaylord Moore

Journey Outside by Mary Q. Steele

1971

Summer of the Swans by Betsy Byars

Honor Books

Kneeknock Rise by Natalie Babbitt

Enchantress from the Stars by Sylvia Louise Engdahl

Sing Down the Moon by Scott O'Dell

1972

Mrs. Frisby and the Rats of NIMH by Robert C. O'Brien

Honor Books

Incident at Hawk's Hill by Allan W. Eckert

The Planet of Junior Brown by Virginia Hamilton

The Tombs of Atuan by Ursula K. Le Guin

Annie and the Old One by Miska Miles

The Headless Cupid by Zilpha Keatley Snyder

1973

Julie of the Wolves by Jean Craighead George

Honor Books

Frog and Toad Together by Arnold Lobel

The Upstairs Room by Johanna Reiss

The Witches of Worm by Zilpha Keatley Snyder

1974

The Slave Dancer by Paula Fox

Honor Book

The Dark Is Rising by Susan Cooper

1975

M. C. Higgins, the Great by Virginia Hamilton

Honor Books

Figgs & Phantoms by Ellen Raskin

My Brother Sam Is Dead by James Lincoln Collier and Christopher Collier

The Perilous Gard by Elizabeth Marie Pope

Philip Hall Likes Me. I Reckon Maybe by Bette Greene

1976

The Grey King by Susan Cooper

Honor Books

The Hundred Penny Box by Sharon Bell Mathis

Dragonwings by Laurence Yep

1977

Roll of Thunder, Hear My Cry by Mildred D. Taylor

Honor Books
Abel's Island by Willaim Steig
A String in the Harp by Nancy Bond

1978

Bridge to Terabithia by Katherine Paterson

Honor Books
Ramona and Her Father by Beverly Cleary
Anpao: An American Indian Odyssey by Jamake Highwater

1979

The Westing Game by Ellen Raskin

Honor Books
The Great Gilly Hopkins by Katherine Paterson

1980

A Gathering of Days: A New England Girl's Journal, 1830–32 by Joan Blos

Honor Book
The Road from Home: The Story of an Armenian Girl by David Kherdian

1981

Jacob Have I Loved by Katherine Paterson

Honor Books
The Fledgling by Jane Langton
A Ring of Endless Light by Madeleine L'Engle

1982

A Visit to William Blake's Inn: Poems for Innocent and Experienced Travelers by Nancy Willard

Honor Books
Ramona Quimby, Age 8 by Beverly Cleary
Upon the Head of the Goat: A Childhood in Hungary, 1939–1944 by Aranka Siegel

1983

Dicey's Song by Cynthia Voigt

Honor Books

The Blue Sword by Robin McKinley

Dr. De Soto by William Steig

Graven Images by Paul Fleischman

Homesick: My Own Story by Jean Fritz

Sweet Whispers, Brother Rush by Virginia Hamilton

1984

Dear Mr. Henshaw by Beverly Cleary

Honor Books

The Wish Giver: Three Tales of Coven Tree by Bill Brittain

A Solitary Blue by Cynthia Voigt

The Sign of the Beaver by Elizabeth George Speare

Sugaring Time by Kathryn Lasky

1985

The Hero and the Crown by Robin McKinley

Honor Books

The Moves Make the Man by Bruce Brooks

One-Eyed Cat by Paula Fox

Like Jake and Me by Mavis Jukes

1986

Sarah, Plain and Tall by Patricia MacLachlan

Honor Books

Commodore Perry in the Land of Shogun by Rhoda Blumberg

Dogson by Gary Paulsen

1987

The Whipping Boy by Sid Fleishman

Honor Books

On My Honor by Marion Dane Bauer

A Fine White Dust by Cynthia Rylant

Volcano by Patricia Lauber

1988

Lincoln: A Photobiography by Russell Freedman

Honor Books
> *Hatchet* by Gary Paulsen
>
> *After the Rain* by Norma Fox Mazer

1989

> *Joyful Noise: Poems for Two Voices* by Paul Fleischman

Honor Books
> *In the Beginning: Creation Stories from around the World* by Virginia Hamilton
>
> *Scorpions* by Walter Dean Myers

1990

> *Number the Stars* by Lois Lowry

Honor Books
> *Afternoon of the Elves* by Janet Taylor Lisle
>
> *Shabanu: Daughter of the Wind* by Suzanne Fisher Staples
>
> *The Winter Room* by Gary Paulsen

1991

> *Maniac Magee* by Jerry Spinelli

Honor Book
> *The True Confessions of Charlotte Doyle* by Avi

1992

> *Shiloh* by Phyllis Reynolds Naylor

Honor Books
> *Nothing but the Truth: A Documentary Novel* by Avi
>
> *The Wright Brothers: How They Invented the Airplane* by Russell Freedman

1993

> *Missing May* by Cynthia Rylant

Honor Books
> *What Hearts* by Bruce Brooks

The Dark Thirty: Southern Tales of the Supernatural by Patricia C. McKissack

Somewhere in the Darkness by Walter Dean Myers

1994

The Giver by Lois Lowry

1995

Walk Two Moons by Sharon Creech

Honor Books

Catherine, Called Birdy by Karen Cushman

The Ear, the Eye and the Arm by Nancy Farmer

1996

The Midwife's Apprentice by Karen Cushman

Honor Books

Yolanda's Genius by Carol Fenner

Watson Goes to Birmingham by Christopher Curtis

What Jamie Saw by Carolyn Curtis

APPENDIX C

❖ Coretta Scott King Awards

These awards are given in continued recognition of the contributions of Martin Luther King Jr. and his wife Coretta Scott King, who continues his work in peace and world brotherhood. Awards are given annually to a black author and a black illustrator for outstanding inspirational and educational contributions produced during the previous year.

1970

Author: Lillie Patterson, *Martin Luther King, Jr.: Man of Peace*
Illustrator: no award

1971

Author: Charlemae Rollins, *Black Troubador: Langston Hughes*
Illustrator: no award

1972

Author: Elston C. Fax, *17 Black Artists*
Illustrator: no award

1973

Author: Jackie Robinson (as told to Alfred Duckett), *I Never Had It Made: The Autobiography of Jackie Robinson*
Illustrator: no award

1974

Author: Sharon Bell Mathis, *Ray Charles*
Illustrator: George Ford, *Ray Charles* by Sharon Bell Mathis

1975

Author: Dorothy Robinson, *The Legend of Africana*
Illustrator: Herbert Temple, *The Legend of Africana* by Dorothy Robinson

1976

Author: Pearl Bailey, *Duey's Tale*
Illustrator: no award

1977

Author: James Haskins, *The Story of Stevie Wonder*

Illustrator: no award

1978

Author: Eloise Greenfield, *Africa Dream*

Illustrator: Carole Byard, *Africa Dream* by Eloise Greenfield

1979

Author: Ossie Davis, *Escape to Freedom*

Illustrator: Tom Feelings, *Something on My Mind* by Nikki Grimes

1980

Author: Walter Dean Myers, *The Young Landlords*

Illustrator: Carole Byard, *Cornrows* by Camille Yarbrough

1981

Author: Sidney Poiter, *This Life*

Illustrator: Ashley Bryan, *Beat the Story-Drum, Pum-Pum*, also written by Ashley Bryan

1982

Author: Mildred D. Taylor, *Let the Circle Be Unbroken*

Illustrator: John Steptoe, *Mother Crocodile: An Uncle Amadou Tale from Senegal*, adapted by Rosa Guy

1983

Author: Virginia Hamilton, *Sweet Whispers, Brother Rush*

Illustrator: Peter Mugabane, *Black Child*, also written by Peter Mugabane

1984

Author: Lucille Clifton, *Everett Anderson's Goodbye*

Illustrator: Pat Cummings, *My Mama Needs Me* by Mildred Pitts Walter

1985

Author: Walter Dean Myers, *Motown and Didi*

Illustrator: no award

1986

Author: Virginia Hamilton, *The People Could Fly: American Black Folk Tales*

Illustrator: Jerry Pinkney, *The Patchwork Quilt* by Valerie Flournoy

1987

Author: Mildred Pitts Walter, *Justin and the Best Biscuits in the World*

Illustrator: Jerry Pinkney, *Half a Moon and One Whole Star* by Crescent Dragonwagon

1988

Author: Mildred D. Taylor, *The Friendship*

Illustrator: John Steptoe, *Mufaro's Beautiful Daughters: An African Tale*, also written by John Steptoe

1989

Author: Walter Dean Myers, *Fallen Angels*

Illustrator: Jerry Pinkney, *Mirandy and Brother Wind* by Patricia McKissack

1990

Author: Patricia and Fredrick McKissack, *A Long Hard Journey: The Story of the Pullman Porter*

Illustrator: Jan Spivey Gilchrist, *Nathaniel Talking* by Eloise Greenfield

1991

Author: Mildred D. Taylor, *The Road to Memphis*

Illustrator: Leo and Diane Dillon, *Aida*, told by Leontyne Price

1992

Author: Walter Dean Myers, *Now Is Your Time! The African American Struggle for Freedom*

Illustrator: Faith Ringgold, *Tar Beach*, also written by Faith Ringgold

1993

Author: Patricia C. McKissack, *The Dark-Thirty: Southern Tales of the Supernatural*

Illustrator: Katherine Atkins Wilson, *The Origin of Life on Earth: An African Myth*, retold by David A. Anderson

1994

Author: Angela Johnson, *Toning the Sweep*

Illustrator: Tom Feelings, *Soul Looks Back in Wonder*, also written by Tom Feelings

1995

Author: Patricia and Fredrick McKissack, *Christmas in the Big House, Christmas in the Quarters*

Illustrator: James Ransome, *The Creation* by James Weldon Johnson

1996

Author: Virginia Hamilton, *Her Stories*

Illustrator: Tom Feelings, *The Middle Passage: White Ships/Black Cargo*, also written by Tom Feelings

Subject Index

Author–Title Index